9/2010

Hey PATTY,

I hope that this
will help with
your experimenting!
Enjoy!!!

Casie Bishop

DAISY

MORNING, NOON AND NIGHT

DAISY: MORNING, NOON AND NIGHT

Bringing Your Family Together
with Everyday Latin Dishes

DAISY MARTINEZ

WITH CHRIS STYLER

Photographs by Joseph De Leo

ATRIA BOOKS

NEW YORK   LONDON   TORONTO   SYDNEY

ATRIA BOOKS

A Division of Simon & Schuster, Inc.
1230 Avenue of the Americas
New York, NY 10020

First Atria Books hardcover edition March 2010

ATRIA BOOKS and colophon are trademarks of Simon & Schuster, Inc.

For information about special discounts for bulk purchases,
please contact Simon & Schuster Special Sales at
1-866-506-1949 or business@simonandschuster.com.

The Simon & Schuster Speakers Bureau can bring authors
to your live event. For more information or to book an event,
contact the Simon & Schuster Speakers Bureau at
1-866-248-3049 or visit our website at www.simonspeakers.com.

Designed by Dana Sloan

Manufactured in the United States of America

10   9   8   7   6   5   4   3   2   1

Library of Congress Cataloging-in-Publication Data

Martinez, Daisy.
    Daisy : morning, noon and night : bringing your family together with
everyday Latin dishes / Daisy Martinez with Chris Styler.
        p.   cm.
    1. Cookery, Latin American.   2. Cookery, Puerto Rican.
3. Cookery, Spanish.   I. Styler, Christopher.   II. Title.
TX716.A1M237   2010
641.598—dc22   2009027568

ISBN 978-1-4391-5753-4
ISBN 978-1-4391-6968-1 (ebook)

Frontispiece: Shrimp Tacos with Tomato-Avo Salsa (page 145),
            Mango and Black Bean Salad (page 160)

I dedicate this book to the memory of my grandmothers,

Valentina Martinez Perez
and
Clotilde Rodriguez Gonzalez

"¡Abuelita, tus refranes me hacen reir!"

—WILLIE COLÓN

Asparagus with Brown
Butter and Pecans
(page 231)

CONTENTS

INTRODUCTION

To say that I am a bit obsessed when it comes to Latin food would be the understatement of the year. I've been known to chase people down the street in pursuit of the perfect tamale or to engage the cashier at my corner supermarket in a conversation about healthier refried beans. (If you were behind me, sorry!) But even though I took every opportunity to ask, probe, research, and eat in New York's incredibly diverse Latino restaurants, I found that, with time, I had begun exhausting my resources. At least, I hope that that was the case and not that people ran the other way when they saw me coming!

A new source of inspiration and way to feed the fire of my curiosity occurred to me when my youngest child, Angela, turned eight and Santa Claus, coincidentally, stopped visiting our house. I sat my children down (all four of them!) and said that in previous years, my husband, Jerry, and I had spent a small fortune on gifts for Christmas that were all but forgotten within two weeks. From now on, Mom and Dad would be giving them memories as holiday gifts. You could have heard a pin drop in that room. Before they could shake off their shock and begin to protest, I explained that starting the following year, we would travel as a family to a different country each year during the week between Christmas and New Year's Day in order to experience that country through its food, historic sites, and culture. The whoops and hollers were exactly the response I had hoped for.

Since that conversation, I have been able to gift my family with visits to Barcelona and Madrid, Cuzco and Lima, Oaxaca and the Yucatán, Puerto Rico, and, most recently, the beautiful city of Buenos Aires. I am positive that my children can't remember what they received for the Christmas of 2003, but I can guarantee you that they can tell you exactly what we had for Christmas dinner in 2005 in the enticing city of Cuzco, Peru.

Of course, as time goes by, and the children grow up, go away to college, and move out on their own, it is more and more challenging for me to get my family to sit together and share meals and memories. But never let it be said that I'm not one to rise to the occasion and meet a challenge head-on!

During all those wonderful trips, I kept careful notes on the food we enjoyed, including what dishes were whose favorites. I'm not above making Erik's favorite chocolate dessert, *Tierrita Dulce* ("Sweet Earth," page 236), which he first tasted in Puerto Rico, to lure him back from Philadelphia, where he lives now. If David and Marc get distracted by school, work, and their social schedules, I let it leak that I'll be whipping up an *ají de gallina* (chicken in a yellow pepper puree—David's favorite, page 273) so we can reminisce about climbing the Sorcerer's Temple in Chichén Itzá, or a batch of *arroz con pollo* (page 270; pull up a chair, Markie!) so the boys can laugh about the ice-cold waterfall in El Yunque while we pass the plates around. Angela and Jerry are the two I can rely on to share dinner with me almost every night, so they are subjected to a constant flow of experiments and recipe testing, thereby reaping a lot of benefits. It's a tough gig, but they put themselves on the line and take one for the team!

Recapturing the flavors and dishes we shared when traveling as a family—and keeping those memories alive—was the inspiration for writing this book. I find that whenever I re-create dishes from the trips we have taken, my family not only enjoys the fruits of my labor, but also shares the memories, stories, and laughter from those trips. It occurred to me that with everybody's crazy schedule, these trips were really the only time when we were all together as a family—morning, noon, and night. Throughout the book, I share memories of our trips, the people we met, and the food we ate through a series of travelogues. What better way to organize the book than around the meals that we relished during those memorable holiday vacations?

You will find that the majority of these recipes are simple, nutritious, user friendly, and easy on the wallet, which in these chaotic times is a comfort. I am still on a mission to teach the world how to achieve the perfect pot of rice, and while I feel that I have made some progress on that front (you all know who you are!), I believe that there is still a way to go.

When I first embarked on this excursion into the Latin kitchen, I was so excited to learn about the similarities within the entire community. But when I stopped to think that Latin America is made up of thirty-eight countries, I realized that I had to be ready for some diversity as well. Today, I know that while some of us in the United States still think of Tex-Mex as "Latin food," many more people have come a long way in regard to their understanding of the diversity of the Latino kitchen. I even like to think that maybe in a very small way I have had something to do with that. I could even go so far as to compare it to the phenomenon that we witnessed with Italian food, where people's understanding evolved from "red sauce and cheese" to embracing the complexities of Italian cuisine and the specificities of all of its regional cooking. And that's just *one* country! Multiply that by thirty-eight, and then by the different regions within those thirty-eight countries, and you can see how that translates into a beautiful mosaic of color, flavors, and aromas!

While traveling with my family, I came upon something I'd never expected. I was surprised to find that contemporary cooking in Latin America mirrors the evolution that food has undergone here in the United States. In every country, I discovered many dishes that were part of the integral fiber of the cuisine but were actually adapted from those of immigrant populations that made that specific country their own. And so you find *kippe* in the Dominican Republic (which started out as kibbeh, a dish that is Arabic in origin) and *chaufa,* a Peruvian version of fried rice and a gift from that country's Chinese population. And on and on. Now, if I could only find time to study the population of Puerto Ricans who have made their way to Hawaii: I'd give an eyetooth to learn the way they have developed dishes involving pork. It makes for very delicious and interesting food, not to mention a whole lot of fun in the kitchen!

I have had the pleasure of enjoying a very different journey as well. I've had the pleasure of meeting many of you and hearing your food memories and stories, and the experiences that you have had as Latinos or just as someone with an interest in Latino cuisine. I am eternally grateful that you have invited me to be part of your experiences as I have invited you to share mine, and it is with utmost warmth and pleasure that I invite you to pull up a chair, alongside my family, and enjoy a little bit of the Daisy experience morning, noon, and night.

HOW TO USE THIS BOOK

Dig into the recipes in this book however you like. If you are new to Latin food or to cooking in general, start off with a simple side dish from the Weeknight Dinners section or start your day with a simple recipe from the Everyday Breakfasts section.

Some menus and prep schedules are included. So, if you're looking to plan a weeknight dinner for four or host a party for sixteen, make use of these menus and prep schedules on pages 294 through 302. I would, of course, love it if you ended up incorporating these recipes into your daily life and mixing and matching them in ways that suit you (and may never have occurred to me!).

Just because the Quinoa Polenta (which is delicious, BTW; page 229) ended up in the Side Dishes section of the Dinner Parties chapter doesn't mean it can't be a side dish for a weeknight meal. It is certainly fast and easy enough to qualify. And while the Banana and Dulce de Leche Strudel (page 242) does make an elegant finish for a dinner party, it would be equally at home at a weekend barbecue.

Almost all of the ingredients in these recipes can be found in any well-stocked grocery store. I have given Internet sources for those that may be a bit more difficult to track down. Ingredients that may be less familiar to some are highlighted in green, indicating that a description for each can be found in the Ingredients section (starting on page 310).

Churros (page 22) and Chile-Spiked Hot Chocolate (page 12)

Breakfast

"**Breakfast** is the most important meal of the day." We've all heard this a thousand or so times. How come no one ever adds, "And the easiest to skip"? Modern life doesn't include much room for a mom dressed in a frilly apron turning out round after round of made-from-scratch waffles on a weekday morning. Apart from keeping fruit, healthful cereals, and whole-grain breads for toast on hand, I have come to rely on this handful of trusty morning recipes. Some of them are ready in minutes, like Breakfast Polenta (page 8)—a holdover from my childhood that became part of my children's childhood, and beyond. (My oldest, Erik, still asks—at twenty-six!—for a bowl of "creamy *maíz*" on occasion.) The Mayan Omelet (page 2), another made-in-minutes marvel that I picked up in my travels, fits nicely into morning routines. Not only is it delicious, it gives you a leg up on the five-to-seven daily servings of fruits and veggies. If you can't coerce your kids (or yourself) into sitting still in the morning for the classic Latin-Caribbean breakfast of fried eggs, chorizo sausage, and sautéed sweet plantains (page 5), you may at least be able to hand them a toasty-warm breakfast sandwich (page 9) on their way out the door. That sandwich, by the way, like the Spanish French Toast on page 6, can be set up the night before and cooked lickety-split the next morning. So, no excuses—eat your breakfast!

MORNING

EVERYDAY BREAKFASTS

Mayan Omelet

Chaya—a plant that tastes like spinach with a little kick—was a part of the ancient Mayan diet. Chaya isn't readily available in the States, so I played around with the idea, using a mix of spinach and arugula. The intense flavor that is coaxed out of the mushrooms and greens with just a few minutes of cooking time is really pretty remarkable. Fairly high heat is the trick.

**MAKES 4 SERVINGS • PREP TIME: 5 MINUTES • COOK TIME: 5 MINUTES PER OMELET
(20 MINUTES TOTAL, OR 10 MINUTES WITH 2 PANS; SEE TIP)**

1 packed cup baby spinach leaves

1 packed cup baby arugula leaves

4 tablespoons unsalted butter

One 10-ounce package cremini mushrooms, cut into ½-inch slices

8 extra-large eggs

Kosher or fine sea salt and freshly ground pepper

1. Toss the spinach and arugula together in a bowl. Heat 3 tablespoons of the butter in a large (about 10-inch) nonstick pan over medium-high heat until foaming. Add the mushrooms and cook, stirring, just until they begin to brown, about 4 minutes. Remove from the heat, scoop out all but one-fourth of the mushrooms, and set them aside.

2. Beat 2 of the eggs in a bowl. Put the mushrooms remaining in the pan over medium-high heat and wait until they're sizzling. Add one-fourth of the greens and a small dab of the remaining butter and cook just until the greens are wilted. Pour in the beaten eggs and tilt the pan until the eggs coat the bottom. With a wooden spoon or heatproof spatula, lift the edges of the omelet so any uncooked egg from the top runs underneath the omelet, and cook just until the eggs are set, about 1 minute. Season with salt and pepper to taste. Roll out onto a plate by tilting the pan and freeing the edge of the omelet closest to you, then nudging it into a roll and onto the plate. Repeat with the remaining mushrooms, greens, and eggs, adding a little of the remaining butter and heating the mushrooms until sizzling before cooking each omelet.

TIP: Once you get the hang of omelet making, you may want to work two pans at once, cutting your time at the stove to a mere 10 minutes for 4 omelets.

Eggs with Chorizo and Ripe Plantain

Think of this as the Latino version of the classic American diner breakfast—two sunny-side-up eggs with home fries and bacon. Here chorizo stands in for the bacon, and ripe, sweet plantain takes the place of home fries. It is a very simple breakfast, and a very satisfying one, too.

MAKES 2 SERVINGS • PREP TIME: 5 MINUTES • COOK TIME: 10 MINUTES

1 ripe plantain (the skin should be mostly black with a few streaks of yellow; see photo, page 315)

2 links Spanish chorizo

Olive oil

4 extra-large eggs

1. Peel the plantain and cut it on a sharp diagonal into ½-inch slices. Slice the chorizo links the same way.
2. Pour just enough olive oil into a large skillet (nonstick is nice) to coat the bottom of the pan and heat over medium heat. Add the plantain and chorizo slices and cook, turning once, until they are well browned on both sides, about 5 minutes. Check the plantain slices often— depending on how much sugar the plantain contains, they may brown and/or stick fairly quickly. Drain both on paper towels.
3. Cook the eggs: Return the pan to medium-low heat and add a little more oil if necessary to coat the bottom. Crack the eggs into the pan and cook just until the tops of the whites are set, about 4 minutes; the yolks should still be runny.
4. To serve, lay 3 or 4 plantain slices side by side on one side of each plate. Top each with a slice of chorizo. If there are extra slices of chorizo, tuck them between the slices of plantain, nibble on them while you cook the eggs, or set them aside for another use. Set the eggs on the other side of the plate. To enjoy, make sure you get a little bit of chorizo, plantain, and egg (especially the runny yolk!) in each bite.

Spanish French Toast ✑ TORREJAS

Although this sounds like a breakfast dish with dual citizenship, it is really Spain's take on what we commonly think of as French toast. Of course, every country where there is leftover bread has some version of it. *Torrejas* is not a delicate dish—it should be made with thick slices of dense-textured country bread that is slightly stale. You will probably be surprised by how much of the orange-scented egg-and-milk bath a single slice will soak up. But that, along with slow, even cooking, is what gives *torrejas* its custardy texture. The other thing to note is that this isn't really a sweet dish, though a little sugar sprinkled over the warm toast right before digging in is nice.

MAKES 4 SERVINGS • PREP TIME: 10 MINUTES (PLUS 30 MINUTES OR UP TO OVERNIGHT UNATTENDED SOAKING TIME) • COOK TIME: 10 MINUTES

1 cup milk	Pinch of salt
Four 1-inch-wide strips orange zest, removed with a vegetable peeler	Four 1½-inch slices crusty country-style bread
8 extra-large eggs	Unsalted butter or vegetable oil cooking spray
1 teaspoon sugar	
½ teaspoon almond extract	Confectioners' sugar, for serving

1. Heat the milk in a small saucepan over low heat just until steaming. Drop in the orange zest, remove from the heat, and let stand for at least 15 minutes, or up to 2 hours, at room temperature. (The milk and zest can be refrigerated for up to 1 day.)

2. Strain the milk and discard the zest. Beat the milk, eggs, sugar, almond extract, and salt together in a baking dish large enough to hold the bread slices in a single layer. Lay the bread in the dish and let it soak until it is saturated and has absorbed nearly all the egg mixture. This will take at least 30 minutes. Turn the bread several times so it soaks evenly. (The bread can be soaked overnight in the refrigerator—handle it carefully in the morning.)

3. Heat a large griddle over low heat. A few drops of water flicked onto it should dance for 2 to 3 seconds before they evaporate. If they evaporate any faster than that, turn down the heat and wait a few minutes. The griddle can't be too hot, or the bread will overbrown before the egg mixture in the center of the slices has a chance to cook through. Grease the griddle lightly with butter or cooking spray.

4. Lay as many slices of soaked bread on the griddle as will fit comfortably. Cook until the undersides are deep golden brown, 4 to 5 minutes. If the bread browns before that, remove the griddle from the heat, lower the heat, and wait a few minutes before returning the griddle to the heat. Flip the bread and cook until the second side is deep golden brown and the centers of the slices feel firm when gently poked, about 4 minutes. Serve hot, sprinkling some confectioners' sugar over each slice.

TIP: If your bread is fresh, cut it into slices the night before to give it a chance to dry out a little.

Breakfast Polenta ✆ CREMA DE MAÍZ

This is my idea of the ultimate comfort food—perfect for a gray winter morning (or any morning *you're* feeling a little gray). When *Mami* made this for us as kids, she used to pour a little bit of milk around the edges of the plate. We'd pull some of the milk into the hot polenta with our spoons to cool it off a little before we ate it.

MAKES 2 SERVINGS • COOK TIME: 10 MINUTES

2 cups milk, plus more for drizzling if desired

1 extra-large egg

1½ tablespoons sugar

½ teaspoon vanilla extract

⅛ teaspoon ground nutmeg, preferably freshly grated

Heaping ½ cup coarse yellow cornmeal (see Note)

1. Whisk 2 cups milk, the egg, sugar, vanilla, and nutmeg together in a small saucepan. Put over medium-low heat and stir in the cornmeal. Cook, stirring constantly, until the milk starts to bubble and the mixture is thickened, about 10 minutes.

2. Spoon the cereal onto the center of flat plates and let it run slowly out the edges. If you like, drizzle a little milk around the edges of the cereal.

NOTE: You can also make this with fine cornmeal. Fine cornmeal makes very creamy and smooth *crema de maíz,* while coarse cornmeal gives you something with a little more texture. Try them both and see which one you prefer.

Pressed Turkey, Ham, and Cheese Breakfast Sandwich with Roasted Pepper Spread

This sandwich, called a *media luna* in Argentina, sounds more like lunch than breakfast—and it does make a great lunch—but I first had something like it as part of a memorable breakfast at a café in Argentina. The recipe makes a lot of the red pepper spread, but that is no accident: its sweet-and-tangy flavor make it perfect for serving as a dip with crudités or chips, tucking into an omelet, or using as a sauce for grilled fish.

MAKES 4 SERVINGS • PREP TIME: 10 MINUTES • COOK TIME: 5 TO 10 MINUTES

FOR THE SPREAD (MAKES 2 CUPS)

1 cup whole-milk ricotta

½ cup mayonnaise

1 red bell pepper, roasted, seeded, and peeled (see page 274) or 1 bottled roasted red pepper, well drained

FOR THE SANDWICHES

4 croissants, split

4 thin slices deli ham

4 thin slices turkey

4 thin slices cheddar cheese

1. Make the spread: Process the ricotta, mayonnaise, and bell pepper in the work bowl of a food processor until smooth. Scrape the spread into a bowl or storage container. (The spread can be refrigerated for up to 1 week.)
2. Brush one cut side of each croissant generously with the spread. Layer a slice of ham, turkey, and cheese over the spread, folding them as necessary to make a more or less even layer of each. Top off the sandwiches with the remaining croissant halves. (The sandwiches can be assembled the night before you plan to serve them. Wrap and refrigerate.)
3. Cook the sandwiches in a panini press until the centers are warmed through and the croissants are grill-marked, about 5 minutes. (See Tip on page 78 for grilling sandwiches without a press.) Serve warm.

VARIATION: For a heartier lunchtime sandwich, substitute firm crusty rolls for the croissants. (Portuguese rolls work well.) Double the amount of ham, turkey, and cheese, and proceed as above.

The Media Luna

Christmas morning 2007 found us starving after an evening of festivities with our friends, the Strada family. It was already about 11:30 by the time we'd woken up and ventured out from our apartment in Buenos Aires, hoping to find a restaurant that was serving breakfast. We didn't have to venture far: on a nearby corner was the busy Santa Fe Café. We found a table and settled in, ready to eat every single thing on the menu! I dove into a cup of coffee and the kids enjoyed a *submarino*—hot milk served with a little chocolate bar, the "submarine." Sink the submarine, stir, and you've got hot chocolate!

Sitting outside at a sidewalk table is not what immediately comes to the mind of a native New Yorker thinking "Christmas breakfast." But watching the locals greet each other with hugs and kisses and exclamations of "*¡Feliz Navidad!*" put us right in the spirit. Families on their way to church services in their holiday best smiled as they passed. I could make out a faint tango coming from a radio somewhere close by.

We did end up ordering practically everything on the menu: crisp empanadas filled with creamy corn and *picadillo* (pages 65 and 24), of course, and also paper-thin golden brown *milanesas* (page 142) served with wedges of lime, fluffy omelets fat with prosciutto and mozzarella cheese, and what turned out to be the highlight, a *media luna* sandwich. When we ordered our *media lunas* ("half-moons"), we were asked if we'd like them *crudo o cocido* (*crudo* is cured, uncooked ham, like prosciutto or serrano, while *cocido* is more like deli ham) and *plancha o sin plancha* (*plancha* means "grilled"). Order a *media luna plancha*, and the

sandwich is put in a press like a *cubano*. We opted for *crudo con plancha*, and what we were served was a little piece of heaven on a croissant (hence the "half-moon" moniker). The saltiness of the ham was balanced by the sweetness of the roll and the tang of the Argentinean Sardo cheese, which was melted to a gooey rapture on the crispy, buttery croissant. It was such a hit that we ordered another one, sharing and enjoying it as we watched the traffic go by on our balmy *Navidad* morning.

At home, I can re-create those little shivers of delight we shared on Christmas morning while breakfasting alfresco in Buenos Aires, because this quick but delicious breakfast sandwich fits in well with our crazy schedules here. I used to make them in a pan, but since my girlfriend Loni gave me a fancy Breville sandwich press as a gift, I can rock three or four of these babies in no time!

And if I close my eyes, I can almost make out a faint tango in the distance.

Angela, Marc, David, and Santa enjoy a submarino at Santa Fe Café.

Cinnamon-Scented Coffee ∽ CAFE DE OLLA

A distillery may seem like an odd place for a memorable meal, but Rancho Zapata restaurant, at the Mezcal Beneva distillery in Oaxaca, was the setting for one of the best meals we had in Mexico. The tour included a trip through the agave fields and the cellar of the distillery, where the hearts (or *piñas*) of the agave plant are ground by mule power between two millstones before they are fermented and distilled into *mezcal.* Lunch at Rancho Zapata featured *caldo de gato,* or "cat soup," which thankfully featured no cat, but rather ox spine (which looks similar to oxtail) that was roasted and made into a beautiful, rich broth finished with noodles and a squeeze of lime. There were tamales, as well, and *cochinita pibil*—the classic pit-roasted pork that is to the Yucatán what barbecued brisket is to Texas. All we could manage after the meal was a light fruit dessert and this delicious, fragrant coffee, which we asked for everywhere we went in Mexico. The cinnamon provides a lovely top note of flavor, and the chocolate adds richness and depth.

MAKES 8 SERVINGS • PREP TIME: 5 MINUTES • COOK TIME: 10 MINUTES

½ cup packed dark brown sugar

3 cinnamon sticks

4 whole cloves

1 tablespoon molasses

5 heaping tablespoons Latin-style coffee, such as Bustelo or El Pico, or ground espresso beans

2 cups milk

¼ cup finely chopped unsweetened chocolate (about 1½ ounces)

Dark brown and/or granulated sugar, for serving

1. Bring 6 cups water, the brown sugar, cinnamon sticks, and cloves to a boil in a large saucepan over medium-high heat, stirring until the sugar is dissolved. Stir in the molasses and return to a boil, skimming any foam from the top.

2. Remove the saucepan from the heat, stir in the coffee, and let steep for 6 to 7 minutes. Strain and set aside.

3. Heat the milk in a small saucepan until the edges begin to bubble. Discard any skin from the top of the milk and whisk in the chocolate until it is melted.

4. Divide the milk among 8 warm coffee cups. Fill the remainder of the cups with the hot coffee. Pass brown and/or white sugar at the table for people to adjust the sweetness as they like.

Chile-Spiked Hot Chocolate

It may seem that I love my chiles so much that I'm even sneaking them into hot chocolate—but that's only partly true. The pairing of chocolate and chiles goes back to pre-Columbian Mayan culture, so I am just the latest in a long line of chile-and-chocolate lovers. I wouldn't call this rich, cinnamon-scented drink spicy; it just gets a little extra warmth from the tiny bit of chile in it—enough to warm up even the chilliest morning.

MAKES 2 SERVINGS • PREP TIME: 10 MINUTES • COOK TIME: 10 MINUTES

1 smallish dried chile de árbol
   (see Note) or a pinch of cayenne
   pepper
1½ cups milk
2 cinnamon sticks

One 3-ounce round of Mexican chocolate
   (Nestlé's Abuelita, Ibarra, and Cortés
   are all good choices), grated on the
   coarse side of a grater
2 tablespoons dark brown sugar

1. Heat a small saucepan (the one you'll use to make the hot chocolate) over medium-low heat. Toast the chile, turning it once, just until it begins to change color and smell wonderful, less than a minute. Remove the chile and let cool, then grind it fine in a spice mill.

2. Warm the milk and cinnamon sticks in the saucepan over low heat until bubbles form around the edges. Let steep over low heat for at least 5 minutes, or up to 10 minutes for a stronger cinnamon flavor.

3. Remove the cinnamon sticks and set aside. Add the chocolate, sugar, and a large pinch of the ground chile to the milk. Whisk vigorously to melt the chocolate and foam the milk. Pour into warm mugs and slip a cinnamon stick into each one.

NOTE: Chiles de árbol are long, very thin dried chiles with a brick-red color and fair amount of heat. Usually the seeds from dried chiles are discarded before the chiles are toasted, but that is not the case with chiles de árbol. Toast and grind the chile, seeds and all. You will find chiles de árbol in all Latin markets and some well-stocked supermarkets. Often they are found among the other spices and labeled simply "dried chiles."

LEISURELY BREAKFASTS AND BRUNCHES

"Maybe This Will Shut You Up" Eggs
✑ HUEVOS A LA PALOMA

My son David has a particularly impish sense of humor. Never was it more evident than on the morning I had just finished enjoying this delicious dish. My family and I were on one of our holiday trips to Mexico, staying in a hotel. That day, the plan was to tour the nearby famous Monte Alban ruins in Oaxaca. But right after breakfast, I learned that the concierge had misplaced our reservations. He and I had a long "conversation," and eventually we cleared up the misunderstanding. By the time I got back to my room (which was next to the boys' room), the hotel had delivered a fruit basket with a note attached. I felt much better about the whole situation until I looked at the card on the basket, which read, "Maybe This Will Shut You Up." To put it mildly, I went ballistic. I was in the middle of telling Jerry that he had to go to the front desk and complain about this rudeness, when he noticed a banana peel in the trash and said, "Wow, they ate a banana from the basket!" I was ready to pass out from indignation.

While I was ranting at Jerry to get down to the front desk, Angela sauntered into the boys' room to let them know that Jerry was going to the manager to complain and that I was ready to blow a gasket! Upon hearing this, David jumped out of bed and ran into my room, yelling, "It was me! It was me! It's only a joke!" It took me a minute to comprehend, but eventually it sank in. I would have boxed his ears, but I was laughing too hard. Now, every time I serve these eggs, we all laugh, remembering how, once again, David got one over on me. Banana peels and rants aside, to say that I couldn't wait to make this dish at home would be an understatement. And from the first time I tried these eggs, they have been a staple at my table. They are too good, in fact, to serve just for breakfast—paired with a lovely green salad, they make a terrific light supper.

MAKES 6 SERVINGS • PREP TIME: 35 MINUTES (INCLUDES MAKING TOMATO SAUCE)
• COOK TIME: 15 MINUTES (INCLUDES FRYING EGGS)

FOR THE TOMATO SAUCE

1 tablespoon olive oil

2 tablespoons coarsely grated Spanish onion

1 clove garlic, minced

1¼ teaspoons chile powder

½ teaspoon ground cumin

½ teaspoon dried oregano

One 8-ounce can Spanish-style tomato sauce

Kosher or fine sea salt and freshly ground pepper

¼ cup vegetable broth or water

1½ cups Mexican chorizo (removed from casing and crumbled)

2 ripe Hass avocados

Juice of 1 lime

Kosher or fine sea salt and freshly ground pepper

Vegetable oil cooking spray

1 dozen extra-large eggs

1 cup shredded Oaxaca cheese or mozzarella cheese

½ cup crema Mexicana or sour cream

Minced fresh cilantro, for garnish

Layer the sliced avocados over the chorizo in each casserole.

Arrange the fried eggs over the avocado.

Top the casseroles with the tomato sauce and cheese.

1. Make the tomato sauce: Heat the olive oil in a small saucepan over medium heat. Add the onion and garlic and cook, stirring, until the onion is translucent, about 5 minutes. Stir in the chile powder, cumin, and oregano and cook, stirring, until fragrant, 1 to 2 minutes. Stir in the tomato sauce and broth and bring to a boil, then adjust the heat so the sauce is simmering. Cook, stirring occasionally, until the sauce is slightly thickened. Season with salt and pepper and remove from the heat.

2. Meanwhile, cook the chorizo in a medium skillet over medium heat, stirring to break up clumps, until cooked through and fragrant, 3 to 4 minutes. Drain on paper towels.

3. Cut the avocados in half, remove the pits, and peel the halves. Cut each half lengthwise into 6 thin slices. Toss together in a medium bowl with the lime juice.

4. Set the rack about 4 inches from the broiler and preheat the broiler. Divide the chorizo among 6 flameproof 5½-inch casseroles (see Note). Top the chorizo in each casserole with 4 slices of avocado.

5. Cook the eggs: Spray a large skillet or griddle with cooking spray and heat over medium heat. Add only as many eggs as will fit without touching and cook until the undersides of the eggs are set, about 1 minute. Season lightly with salt and pepper, reduce the heat to low, and cook until the whites are completely set, about 3 minutes. Place 2 eggs on top of the avocado in each casserole. Repeat with the remaining eggs.

6. Spoon the tomato sauce over the eggs, topping them with a thin, even layer of sauce. Sprinkle the cheese over the sauce, dividing it evenly. Put as many of the casseroles onto a baking sheet as will fit comfortably. Broil just until the cheese melts, 2 to 3 minutes. Repeat with the remaining casseroles if necessary. Drizzle a teaspoon of crema over each casserole and sprinkle with minced cilantro. Pass the remaining crema separately.

NOTE: Individual 5½ × 1-inch clay *cazuelas* from Spain or Mexico are ideal for this dish. You can find them in some Latin markets and specialty cookware stores or online at www.tienda.com.

Egg, Refried Bean, and Mushroom Casserole

⌒ HUEVOS BALAM

I love it when kitchen magic happens, as it does in this casserole. The sauce is super-simple and rich with flavor, thanks to the two types of mushrooms that steep in the mushroom broth (page 304). The magic happens when the sauce meets the beans and eggs—an unusual combination but a delicious one. The mushroom sauce would be equally at home with grilled skirt steak or short ribs (pages 90 and 88) or even plain white rice or pasta. This is nice when the beans are freshly made and still warm. If you make the mushroom broth in advance, the rest of the prep for the casseroles can be done while the beans cook. However, if you want to save even more time, make the beans a day or two ahead and rewarm them gently, loosening them up with a little mushroom broth or water.

MAKES 4 SERVINGS • PREP TIME: 1 HOUR (INCLUDES MAKING REFRIED
BEANS AND MUSHROOM SAUCE) • COOK TIME: 15 MINUTES

FOR THE MUSHROOM SAUCE

2 cups Mushroom Broth (page 304)

One 10-ounce package cremini mushrooms, thinly sliced

1 bay leaf

Kosher or fine sea salt and freshly ground pepper

3 tablespoons cornstarch

New-Style "Refried" Beans (page 162)

8 extra-large eggs

Unsalted butter or vegetable oil cooking spray

2 cups grated mozzarella or Monterey Jack cheese (7 to 8 ounces)

1. Make the mushroom sauce: Put the broth, sliced cremini mushrooms, and bay leaf in a small saucepan and bring to a simmer. Cover and simmer over low heat for 20 minutes. Discard the bay leaf. Season the broth with salt and pepper to taste. (The sauce can be made to this point up to 2 days in advance. Refrigerate right in the saucepan. Heat to a simmer before continuing.)

2. Stir the cornstarch and ¼ cup water together in a small bowl. Stir this slurry into the mushroom broth and simmer until the sauce is slightly thickened, a minute or two. Set the sauce aside.

3. Set the rack about 8 inches from the broiler and preheat the broiler. If necessary, rewarm the beans over very low heat. Spread one-fourth of the beans over the bottom of each of four 5½-inch flameproof casseroles (see Note, page 16)

(continued)

4. Cook the eggs: Butter a skillet or griddle or spray with cooking spray and heat over medium heat. Add only as many eggs as will fit without touching and cook until the undersides of the eggs are set, about 1 minute. Reduce the heat to low and cook until the whites are completely set, about 3 minutes. Place 2 eggs on top of the beans in each casserole. Repeat with the remaining eggs.

5. Ladle one-fourth of the mushroom sauce (about $\frac{1}{2}$ cup) over the eggs in each casserole. Scatter the cheese over the sauce, dividing it evenly. Broil the casseroles until the cheese is bubbly and lightly browned, about 3 minutes. Serve.

Soft-Scrambled Eggs with Shrimp

A double boiler (or improvised double boiler) is a must for this recipe, which I borrowed from Café Biela in Buenos Aires. The delicate heat cooks the shrimp to tenderness without any trace of rubberiness and gives the eggs a beautiful velvety texture that would be impossible to duplicate in a skillet, even over very low heat. The bonus is the sweet, subtle shrimp flavor that permeates the eggs.

This could easily make a weekday breakfast, even though it feels so special. It is very quick to make, and who doesn't need a little "special" on the occasional weekday morning? But it is in the "leisurely" section because, to enjoy this dish at its best, it should be made one serving at a time. Maybe your house is that serene during the week, but mine sure isn't! This could, of course, be lunch too, or dinner, with a salad.

MAKES 1 SERVING (REPEAT AS NEEDED) • PREP TIME: 5 MINUTES • COOK TIME: 5 MINUTES

1 tablespoon unsalted butter
$\frac{1}{4}$ pound medium shrimp (30 to 40 per pound), peeled and deveined
3 extra-large eggs, well beaten

2 tablespoons heavy cream
1 teaspoon chopped fresh chives
Kosher or fine sea salt and freshly ground pepper

1. Melt the butter in the top of a double boiler set over simmering water (or in a heatproof bowl set over a saucepan of simmering water). Pat the shrimp dry with paper towels, add them to the butter, and turn them with a rubber spatula until they start to turn pink, about 1 minute.

2. Add the eggs and continue stirring just until they begin to set, about 1 minute. Add the heavy cream and chives and continue stirring until the eggs are just barely set and very creamy, about 3 minutes. You may see a little liquid given off by the shrimp—that is fine. Scoop the eggs onto a warm plate, season with salt and pepper, and eat right away.

Plantain Fritters ("Little Spiders") ∽ ARAÑITAS

The nickname "little spiders" comes from the shape of the finished fritters. They resemble fat little spiders with spindly legs. (Maybe that's why kids love them.) *Arañitas* are made with a mix of green and ripe *(maduro)* plantains. The green plantains lend the starch needed to hold the fritters together and the *maduros* cut the starch and add sweetness. If your house is like mine, there are always plantains in varying stages of ripeness—this is a way to make use of the greenest and the ripest.

MAKES ABOUT 16 FRITTERS • PREP TIME: 15 MINUTES • COOK TIME: 15 TO 20 MINUTES

2 sweet (mostly-but-not-all-black) plantains
2 green plantains
2 cloves garlic, minced
1 teaspoon ground cumin
Kosher or fine sea salt and freshly ground pepper
Canola oil, for frying
Vinagre (page 308) or Cilantro Pesto (page 104)

1. Peel the sweet and green plantains (see page 315). Shred them both on the coarse side of a box grater into a large mixing bowl. Add the garlic, cumin, and salt and pepper to taste.

2. Heat about an inch of canola oil in a large heavy skillet until the tip of the handle of a wooden spoon dipped in the oil gives off a steady sizzle (about 350°F). Carefully slip the batter by heaping tablespoons into the oil, frying only as many fritters as will fit without crowding in each batch. Cook, turning once, until browned on both sides, about 4 minutes. Lift the little spiders out of the oil and drain them on paper towels. As you fry the rest of the fritters, adjust the heat so the little bits of batter that fall into the oil don't burn. Serve as hot as possible, with the *vinagre* or cilantro pesto for dipping.

Arepas ⅋ CORN CAKES

Arepas are gluten-free corn cakes that are popular in Colombia, Venezuela, and Ecuador. In Venezuela, they are served as a side dish with *huevos pericos* (scrambled eggs with tomato, bell pepper, and onion). They can also be split, some of the creamy filling scooped out (or not!), and filled with mozzarella cheese, any type of ham, or the above-mentioned scrambled eggs, among other things.

MAKES ABOUT TWENTY 3-INCH AREPAS • PREP TIME: 30 MINUTES (MOSTLY
UNATTENDED RESTING TIME) • COOK TIME: 35 MINUTES

1 cup precooked white cornmeal (The most
    common brand is Harina P.A.N.)
1 cup finely grated cotija cheese
1 tablespoon minced fresh chives
1 teaspoon salt

1. Stir the cornmeal, cotija, chives, salt, and 1¼ cups hot water together in a large mixing bowl. Stir to make a slightly sticky dough. Set aside to rest until the dough is softer and no longer sticky, at least 20 minutes, or up to 2 hours.
2. Preheat the oven to 350°F.
3. Form 3 tablespoons of the dough into a ball, then press it flat to make a 3-inch disk about ½ inch thick. Repeat with the remaining dough. Line the disks up on a baking sheet as you form them.
4. Heat a large well-seasoned cast-iron skillet or heavy nonstick skillet over medium heat. Add as many of the cakes as will fit without crowding and cook, turning once, until browned in spots on both sides, about 8 minutes. Transfer to a separate baking sheet and repeat with the remaining dough.
5. Bake until the cakes are crisp and feel light when picked up, about 25 minutes. Let stand for a few minutes before serving.

VARIATION:

AREPAS FILLED WITH HAM AND CHEESE: Form 4-inch arepas using about ¼ cup of the dough for each. (This recipe will yield about twelve 4-inch arepas.) Panfry and bake as above. Slice fresh mozzarella ¼ inch thick (you'll need 8 to 12 ounces) and cut into pieces more or less the size of the arepas. After the arepas have rested for a few minutes, split them into top and bottom halves and scoop out most of the creamy center, or leave it in if you like. (Careful, the centers will be quite warm.) Lay a slice of cheese and a thin slice of deli ham, folded as necessary, over the bottom of each arepa. Top them off and serve warm.

Churros ✑ MEXICAN CRULLERS (see photo, page 1)

You think people get out of bed fast when they smell coffee brewing or bacon cooking? Try frying up a pan of *churros* some morning and then, while they are piping hot, tossing them in a cinnamon-sugar coating. This dough is nothing more than the classic French *pâte à choux* used to make cream puffs, éclairs, and the cheese puffs laced with Gruyère cheese known as *gougères*. Fried, as it is here, the dough puffs up just as nicely but gets even crisper.

MAKES 12 TO 15 *CHURROS* • PREP TIME: 20 MINUTES • COOK TIME: 30 MINUTES

4 tablespoons unsalted butter

2 tablespoons light brown sugar

1 teaspoon vanilla extract

1/4 teaspoon salt

1 cup all-purpose flour

4 or 5 extra-large eggs

Canola oil, for frying

1/2 cup granulated sugar

1/2 teaspoon ground cinnamon

1. Combine 1 cup water, the butter, brown sugar, vanilla, and salt in a medium saucepan and heat over medium-high heat until the liquid starts to bubble around the edges. Add the flour all at once and stir briskly with a wooden spoon until well mixed and no lumps of flour remain.

2. Remove from the heat. Add 4 eggs one at a time, beating well with the wooden spoon after each addition, making sure to get into the corners and all along the sides and bottom of the pan. The dough should look soft and glossy and keep a "hook" shape when the spoon is pulled from the dough. If it does not, beat in the last egg.

3. Scrape the dough into a pastry bag fitted with a large star tip. Pour enough canola oil into a deep heavy skillet (cast iron is ideal) to come to 1 inch. Heat over medium heat until the tip of the handle of a wooden spoon dipped in the oil gives off a steady stream of tiny bubbles (about 350°F). Carefully pipe the dough into the oil, forming 6-inch-long crullers, and making only as many crullers as will fit comfortably. Overcrowding the pan will result in soggy crullers. Fry, turning once, until golden brown on each side, about 6 minutes. Drain on paper towels. Repeat with the remaining dough.

4. Put the granulated sugar and cinnamon in a paper bag, crimp the top, and shake well to mix. Drop a few crullers at a time into the bag and shake until coated. These are best served as soon as possible.

VARIATION

FRIED CINNAMON DOUGH: Steep a cinnamon stick in the water over low heat for 10 minutes. Remove the cinnamon stick and proceed as above, but drop the dough by rounded tablespoonfuls—carefully—into the oil. Makes about 30 puffs.

Scoop the dough into the pastry bag.

Carefully pipe the *churros* into the hot oil.

Remove the finished *churros* from the oil.

Weekend Tamales

Tamales for breakfast? You betcha. In Mexico, the porky version given below can very easily be a breakfast entrée. In Peru, the olive-and-raisin variation makes a morning meal, maybe with a little scrambled egg on the side. The olive-and-raisin version can just as easily be made with vegetable stock, keeping it completely vegan.

I'm all about options—and that's what you've got with this recipe. The pork picadillo makes enough for 24 tamales *and* either 10 or so empanadas (page 61) or a main course—with white rice, of course!—for four. My feeling is this: Aside from the time needed to shred the "extra" pork, which is all of 10 minutes, it takes no longer to make a healthy-size batch of pork picadillo, so why not do it? The picadillo will keep in the refrigerator, waiting to be turned into a weeknight dinner, for up to 3 days. Or, if you choose the bonus empanada route, they can be frozen before baking and then thawed and baked as need be. And in case you're thinking, "What am I going to do with 24 tamales?" I have the answer—freeze any you're not going to serve right away and then pop them, still frozen, into a steamer basket for a no-effort breakfast, lunch, or dinner. Just like with the pork picadillo, you're already in the kitchen, so what's a few extra minutes when it comes to that kind of payoff down the road?

MAKES 24 TAMALES, PLUS ENOUGH PICADILLO TO FILL 10 EMPANADAS OR TO SERVE 4 AS A MAIN COURSE
• PREP TIME: 5 HOURS (INCLUDES COOKING THE PORK FILLING, MOST OF IT UNATTENDED)
• COOK TIME: 1 HOUR (UNATTENDED)

FOR THE SHREDDED PORK

One 4½-pound bone-in pork butt, boned
   (by the butcher), bone reserved

1 large Spanish onion, unpeeled

1 big bunch cilantro

2 bay leaves

2 tablespoons kosher or fine sea salt

1 tablespoon black peppercorns

FOR THE PICADILLO

½ cup Achiote Oil (page 306)

1 cup Sofrito (page 305)

½ teaspoon ground cumin

⅛ teaspoon ground allspice

⅛ teaspoon ground cloves

Kosher or fine sea salt and freshly ground
   pepper

One 4-ounce package dried corn husks
   (see Note)

FOR THE MASA (MAKES 6 CUPS)

3 cups instant corn masa flour, such as
   Maseca

1 tablespoon ground cumin

1 tablespoon kosher or fine sea salt

1 tablespoon ancho or other chile powder

4 cups reserved pork broth (pork cooking
   liquid), warmed

1 cup vegetable oil

1. Preheat the oven to 400°F.

2. Put the pork bone in a small roasting pan and roast until mahogany brown, about 1 hour.

3. Meanwhile, put the pork butt, onion, cilantro, bay leaves, salt, and peppercorns in a pot large enough to hold them and the pork bone comfortably, pour in enough cold water to cover the pork completely, and bring to a boil over high heat. Adjust the heat so the liquid is simmering, and cook, skimming the foam and fat off the surface, until the pork is falling-apart tender, about 3 hours; add the bone when it comes out of the oven. (Skim often, especially at the beginning of the cooking—you'll be surprised how much stuff surfaces.) Discard the bone and cool the pork in the broth. (The broth and pork can be made up to 2 days in advance. Refrigerate the pork and broth right in the pot and rewarm as necessary over gentle heat before continuing.)

4. As soon as it is cool enough to handle (or rewarmed enough to make shredding easy), remove the pork—set the broth aside—and coarsely shred the meat, removing most but not all of the fat as you go. The fat will add a melting tenderness and flavor to the pork. Set aside.

5. Make the picadillo: Heat the achiote oil in a large deep skillet over medium heat. Add the sofrito and cook, stirring, until the liquid has evaporated and the sofrito is sizzling. Stir in the cumin, allspice, and cloves and stir for a minute or two. Add the shredded pork. Season lightly with salt and pepper and cook, stirring, until the pork is heated through and coated with the seasonings. Continue cooking and stirring until the pork begins to stick to the skillet. Pour in ½ cup of the pork broth and stir until almost all of it is evaporated. Set the picadillo aside. (The picadillo can be made up to 2 days in advance. Reheat over low heat, adding a little water if necessary, until warmed through.)

6. Take the corn husks out of the package and put them in a large bowl. Pour enough warm water over them to cover them completely. Weight the husks down with a plate or overturned bowl to keep them submerged and soak until pliable, about 1 hour. Set up a steamer (see Tips).

7. Make the masa: Stir the corn masa flour, cumin, salt, and chile powder together in a large bowl until well mixed. Add the warm broth and the vegetable oil and stir to make a smooth, moist, but not sticky dough. Set aside.

8. Form the tamales: The corn husks will be different sizes—start with those that are at least 7 inches across or so at the widest point and save the smaller husks for backup. Open up a husk on the work surface with the shorter end closest to you. Center ¼ cup of the corn masa on the husk. Make a little indentation down the center of the masa, spreading the masa out as you go but making sure to leave at least 1 inch free along the top and bottom edges and 2 inches along the sides so the tamale can be folded up easily. Spoon 2 tablespoons of the picadillo into the indentation. Fold the sides of the husk over to completely cover the filling,

then fold the end closest to you up and over the filling. Leave the other end open. Put the tamales seam side down on a baking sheet, and make 23 more tamales in the same manner, lining them up on the baking sheet.

9. Freeze as many of the tamales as you'd like to. Refrigerate or freeze any remaining picadillo (see headnote). Steam the remaining tamales until the dough is tender and moist—1 hour should do it. Check the level of the water every 15 minutes and replenish as necessary.

10. Serve the tamales hot on a platter. Let people help themselves and unwrap their own tamales. Careful, they stay hot for a while.

NOTE: Dried corn husks can be found in Mexican groceries and any supermarket with a well-stocked Latin food aisle. Because they vary in size within a package and are very inexpensive, you might want to pick up 2 packages to be on the safe side.

VARIATIONS

OLIVE-AND-RAISIN TAMALES: Toss a generous ¾ cup pitted small (such as Niçoise) olives and a generous ½ cup raisins together in a small bowl to mix them. Proceed from step 6, using a scant tablespoon of the olive-raisin mix to fill each tamale. If you run out of filling, simply toss together a little more of the olive-raisin mix.

If you prefer, make the filling substituting 4 pounds of boneless chicken thighs for the pork. The chicken thighs will need only about 30 minutes simmering time.

TIPS: To be honest, it's hard to make pork broth interesting—it just doesn't have that much oomph. Using the roasted bone is a big step toward giving it body and flavor.

Before making the masa and putting the tamales together, set up a steamer based on how many tamales you will be steaming. To cook a small amount—6 to 8 tamales or so—a circular cooling rack or collapsible metal steamer basket set into a deep skillet with a tight-fitting lid or a Dutch oven will do. To steam larger amounts, it is helpful to have a large bamboo steamer or a large pot with a steamer insert. Lay the tamales seam side down in a row across the bottom of a bamboo steamer. Stack them, if need be, no higher than 3 layers. Or, for a pot with a steamer insert, stand the tamales up side by side (open ends up, of course!). You can always divide larger amounts of tamales between 2 steamers if they don't all fit in 1. Pour enough water into the skillet or pot to come within ½ inch of the bottom of the steamer insert. Bring to a boil, then adjust the heat so the water is at a gentle boil.

Creamed Spinach Crepes with Mushroom-Tomato Sauce

This is one of the delicious recipes that we enjoyed on Christmas morning at the Santa Fe Café in Buenos Aires. The creamed spinach has a whisper of nutmeg, and the warmth from the spice balances nicely with the acidity of the tomato sauce and the earthiness of the mushrooms. This is another one of those recipes that can be enjoyed morning, noon, and night!

MAKES 6 SERVINGS • PREP TIME: 1 HOUR (MORE WITH HOMEMADE CREPES) • COOK TIME: 15 MINUTES

Twelve 7- to 8-inch Basic Crepes (recipe follows) or store-bought crepes

Creamed Spinach (page 279)

FOR THE TOMATO SAUCE

1 tablespoon olive oil

2 cloves garlic, minced

One 10-ounce package cremini mushrooms, cut into ¼-inch slices

One 29-ounce can tomato sauce

4 large fresh basil leaves, cut into thin ribbons

¼ teaspoon dried oregano

Kosher or fine sea salt and freshly ground pepper

3 tablespoons chopped fresh flat-leaf parsley, for garnish

2 cups shredded mozzarella

1. Make the crepes (if necessary) and the creamed spinach. (Both can be made up to a day in advance and refrigerated; rewarm the spinach in a saucepan over gentle heat before using.)

2. Make the tomato sauce: Heat the oil in a medium saucepan over medium heat. Add the garlic and cook until it is sizzling but not browned. Add the mushrooms and stir until they start to brown. If the mushrooms give off liquid, boil that off first, then start to brown them. Pour in the tomato sauce, add the basil and oregano, and season lightly with salt and pepper. Bring to a boil, then adjust the heat so the sauce is simmering and cook, stirring occasionally, until slightly thickened, about 20 minutes. Remove from the heat. (The sauce can be prepared up to a day in advance and refrigerated; bring to a simmer in a small saucepan before using.)

3. Preheat the oven to 400°F.

4. Spoon enough tomato sauce over the bottom of a 9 × 11-inch baking dish to coat the bottom. Spoon ¼ cup of the spinach filling down the center of a crepe, roll up the crepe, and put it seam side down into the baking dish (see Tip). Repeat with the remaining spinach and crepes. Spoon enough tomato sauce over the crepes to completely coat the tops. (Any remaining sauce can be

reheated and passed at the table.) Scatter the mozzarella evenly over the sauce. Bake until the cheese is melted and the sauce is bubbling, about 15 minutes. Garnish with the chopped parsley.

TIP: Depending on the size and shape of your baking dish, you may want to tuck the ends of the crepes in or make the filled crepes either a little stouter or thinner. The idea is to end up with an even layer of crepes that fit snugly in the baking dish.

VARIATION

CREAMED SPINACH–FILLED TORTILLAS: A very good version of the dish can be made by substituting 12 store-bought corn tortillas for the crepes. It's surprising how different the two versions "feel," considering the only difference is the wrapper. Spray a medium skillet with vegetable oil cooking spray and heat over medium heat. Lay a corn tortilla in the skillet and cook, turning once, until warmed through and softened, about 1 minute. Transfer to a plate and repeat with the remaining tortillas, respraying the pan as necessary. Then proceed from step 3, using the tortillas in place of the crepes.

Basic Crepes

These are good all-purpose crepes. You can add a little more sugar if you're using them for desserts, or leave it out altogether if you're making a savory crepe dish, but the bit of sugar does help make a nice lacy golden brown pattern and doesn't sweeten the crepes all that much. One thing to keep in mind when preparing crepes—and there is no way around it—is that the first few crepes will most likely turn out poorly. (Think of these as your offerings to the kitchen gods.) Once you get your rhythm down and the heat adjusted, you'll sail through the rest of them.

MAKES ABOUT 12 LARGE (7- TO 8-INCH) OR 18 MEDIUM (6-INCH) CREPES
PREP TIME: 10 MINUTES (PLUS RESTING TIME) • COOK TIME: 30 TO 45 MINUTES

1¼ cups milk

1 cup all-purpose flour

3 tablespoons unsalted butter, melted,
plus more for cooking the crepes

1 extra-large egg

1 tablespoon sugar

¼ teaspoon kosher or fine sea salt

1. Put all the ingredients in a blender jar and blend on low speed just until smooth. Pour into a bowl or storage container and refrigerate for at least 1 hour, or up to 1 day.

2. Spoon a small amount (about ¼ teaspoon) of melted butter into a 6- to 8-inch crepe pan set over medium heat. Alternatively, brush the bottom of the pan with the butter using a pastry brush. (A nonstick or well-seasoned crepe pan will help tremendously.) The temperature of the pan is important too. The butter should take a few seconds to begin to sizzle. If the butter sizzles and browns immediately after you add it to the pan, the pan is too hot. Remove it from the heat and give it a few minutes to cool off. Pour enough batter into the pan to coat the bottom after you tilt the pan, about a generous 2 tablespoons for a 6-inch pan or 3 tablespoons for an 8-inch pan. Immediately tilt the pan as necessary to get the batter to coat the entire bottom of the pan as quickly and evenly as you can. (Try this: Tilt the pan slowly from left to right while simultaneously pulling the pan toward you and pushing it away rather quickly. It's a bit like patting your head and rubbing your tummy—once you get the hang of it, it isn't all that hard.) The batter should sizzle a little when it hits the pan, and the underside of the crepe should brown in about 2 minutes; if not, increase the heat slightly. Cook until the bottom is a beautiful, lacy golden brown. Flip the crepe and cook until the second side is a golden brown in spots (the second sides will never be the same lacy brown as the first). Remove to a plate and repeat with the remaining batter, giving the pan a few seconds to heat up between crepes. The stacked crepes can be wrapped in plastic wrap and stored at room temperature for up to 3 hours, refrigerated for up to 2 days, or frozen for up to 3 months.

Ladle the batter into the pan.

Tilt the pan to coat the bottom evenly with batter.

Make sure to cover the entire surface of the pan with batter.

Egg-Stuffed Baked Tomatoes

This is my take on *huevos flamencos,* the traditional casserole that features eggs, chorizo, and tomato sauce. Here the "casserole" is a hollowed-out tomato shell and the chorizo is replaced with cured ham. A smattering of peas and asparagus in the sauce lightens things up a little and makes for a pretty plate.

MAKES 6 SERVINGS • PREP TIME: 30 MINUTES • COOK TIME: 40 MINUTES (SOME UNATTENDED)

6 large ripe tomatoes (about 8 ounces each)
2 tablespoons olive oil, plus more for
   brushing the tomatoes
1 clove garlic, finely chopped
1 fresh thyme sprig
12 very thin slices serrano ham or prosciutto
6 extra-large eggs

Tips from 1 bunch pencil-thin asparagus
   (about 2 cups)
1 cup frozen peas, defrosted
Six 1/2-inch slices crusty country-style
   bread, panfried in olive oil until golden
   brown

1. Cut 1/2 inch off the tops of the tomatoes. With a tablespoon, scoop out the pulp and seeds from the centers, leaving only the flesh that is attached to the skin. (This is important—the more pulp left behind, the greater the chances that the baked tomatoes will end up mushy.) Remove as many seeds from the pulp as you can easily; don't worry if there are some seeds left in the pulp. Coarsely chop all the pulp. Cut a very thin sliver from the bottom of each tomato—the idea is to make the slice as thin as possible while creating a small hole at the bottom of the tomato, so that during and after baking, any liquid given off by the tomato will drain out of the bottom. Set the tomatoes, with the bottom slices replaced, on a rack over a baking sheet. Brush them lightly with olive oil and set aside.

2. Preheat the oven to 400°F.

3. Meanwhile, heat the olive oil in a small skillet over medium heat. Add the chopped tomato pulp, the garlic, and thyme and bring to a boil, then adjust the heat so the sauce is simmering. Cook until most of the liquid the tomatoes give off is evaporated, about 15 minutes. Remove from the heat.

4. Line the inside of each tomato shell with 2 slices of the ham, overlapping and trimming the slices of ham as necessary so they cover the insides of the tomato entirely and the edges of the ham stick out of the tomato a little bit. (The edges will brown as the tomatoes bake and will look pretty.) Crack an egg into each tomato "basket." Bake on the rack, until the tomatoes are softened and the eggs are cooked but the yolks are still runny, about 20 minutes. Remove the tomatoes from the oven and set them aside to rest while finishing the sauce.

(continued)

5. Return the sauce to a simmer and stir in the asparagus and peas. Cook just until the asparagus is crisp-tender, about 3 minutes.

6. To serve, remove the sprig of thyme and spoon the sauce over the centers of 6 plates. Using a slotted spoon, carefully lift each tomato off the rack, leaving the bottom slice behind, and hold it for a few seconds to drain off any liquid, then center the tomato over the sauce on each plate. Serve hot, with a piece of toast off to the side of each tomato.

TIPS: If the tomatoes don't drain well during and after cooking, they will retain a lot of liquid that will mix with the egg as you eat it (and does not make a pretty picture). To make sure that you're removing as much of the liquid as possible:

- Scoop out as much of the pulp and seeds as possible when hollowing out the tomatoes.
- Cut just enough tomato off the bottom of each one to allow liquid to escape during baking. Cutting off too much could make the tomato collapse.
- Lift each tomato carefully after baking and give it a few seconds to drain completely before plating.

Caribbean Breeze ∽ BRISAS DEL CARIBE

On a trip to the Caribbean, we all felt a little beat after the flight and shlepping all our baggage to the hotel. But before we even checked in, we were served a chilled fruit juice cocktail similar to this one, which instantly changed our outlook. Everyone I have ever made this for has had the same reaction— it is a completely refreshing, uplifting drink. With a little spiking (rum comes to mind) and a spritz of club soda, it would make a nice adult beverage fit for any brunch, barbecue, or lazy evening outdoors.

MAKES 12 CUPS (ABOUT 12 SERVINGS; CAN BE EASILY CUT IN HALF) • PREP TIME: 25 MINUTES (5 MINUTES IF USING STORE-BOUGHT CUBED FRUIT)

One 2½-pound pineapple
1 small seedless watermelon (about 8
    pounds), cut into quarters, rind removed,
    and flesh cut into 1-inch cubes (about
    16 cups)

½ honeydew melon (about 2½ pounds),
    peeled, seeded, and cut into
    1-inch cubes (about 4 cups)
2 pint baskets strawberries, hulled
    and quartered
Juice of 1 lime

1. Cut the top off the pineapple and discard it. Cut a thin slice off the bottom of the pineapple so the pineapple stands steadily on the cutting board. With a big knife, cut the rind from the pineapple, with as little flesh attached as possible. Cut the pineapple lengthwise into quarters, then into 1-inch cubes.

2. Working in batches, pass the pineapple, melons, and strawberries through a juicer into a large measuring cup (see Note.) Pour each cupful of the juice through a fine strainer into a pitcher, to remove any froth. Stir in the lime juice. Chill thoroughly before serving. (The drink will keep for a day or two in the refrigerator.)

NOTE: The juice can also be prepared using a food processor. Process the fruits in batches as thoroughly as possible. Strain as above. The yield will be considerably less than juice made with a juicer.

TIP: Most supermarkets now sell pineapple and melon that have been peeled and cut into cubes.

Potato "Jelly Roll" with Tuna Salad Filling

✐ CAUSA LIMEÑA

Pairing two simple-to-make comfort foods—mashed potatoes and tuna salad—makes for a perfect brunch or even dinner party entrée: the "jelly roll" must be made ahead (no last-minute work), most people have never sampled anything like this, and, of course, it's absolutely delicious. Try to pick up some bottled *ají amarillo* paste for this if you can—not only will it make the dish authentically Peruvian, it will color the potatoes a vibrant yellow. If you can't find it, I've provided a nice substitution—see page 37.

MAKES 12 SERVINGS • PREP TIME: 1 HOUR • COOK TIME: 35 MINUTES (FOR THE POTATOES)

FOR THE MASHED POTATOES
4 large Idaho (baking) potatoes (about
    3 1/2 pounds), scrubbed
6 tablespoons *ají amarillo* paste or
    1/3 cup Improvised *Ají Amarillo* Puree
    (page 37)
Kosher or fine sea salt and freshly ground
    pepper

FOR THE TUNA FILLING
Two 12-ounce cans solid white albacore
    tuna in water, thoroughly drained
2/3 cup mayonnaise, homemade (page 54)
    or store-bought

1 stalk celery, cut into 1/4-inch dice (about
    1/2 cup)
2 tablespoons chopped fresh cilantro
1/2 jalapeño, with or without seeds, finely
    chopped
Grated zest and juice of 1 lime

———————————————

Vegetable oil cooking spray
1/2 Hass avocado, pitted, peeled, and cut
    lengthwise into 1/4-inch slices
Strips of roasted red bell pepper, homemade
    (see page 274) or bottled, and/or black
    olives, for decorating (optional)
Creamy Avocado Sauce (recipe follows)

1. Put the potatoes in a pot large enough to hold them comfortably and pour in enough cold water to cover them well. Salt the water to taste. Bring to a boil, adjust the heat so the water is simmering, and cook the potatoes until tender when poked with a paring knife, about 35 minutes; drain.

2. Meanwhile, make the tuna filling: Stir the tuna, mayonnaise, celery, cilantro, jalapeño, and lime zest and juice together in a mixing bowl, breaking up the tuna, until all the ingredients are evenly distributed and the filling is fairly smooth.

3. As soon as they are cool enough to handle, but still quite warm, peel the potatoes and pass them through a ricer or food mill fitted with the fine disk. (Or mash them as fine as you can,

then whisk until nearly smooth. Be advised—lumpy potatoes may make it difficult to roll up the jelly roll.) Stir in the *ají amarillo* paste and season with salt and pepper to taste.

4. Tear off a 30-inch length of 18-inch-wide heavy-duty aluminum foil. Spray it generously with cooking spray and lay the foil on the work surface with one of the long ends closest to you. Turn the potato mixture out onto the center of the foil and use a rolling pin to roll out the mixture to a rectangle about 18 × 12 inches and about ¼ inch thick, with a long side toward you. Don't worry if the rectangle isn't perfect. Spread the tuna salad evenly over the potatoes, leaving a 1-inch border along the short ends of the rectangle and a 2-inch border along the long sides. Top the tuna salad with the avocado slices, laying them parallel to one of the long sides and spacing them evenly over the tuna.

5. Set a platter large enough to hold the finished roll nearby. Grab hold of the edge of the foil closest to you and lift it gently so the tuna-topped potatoes start to roll up; nudge the potatoes gently to get the roll going if need be. Almost certainly, the roll will crack in a few places as it rolls. Don't worry at all about the "interior" cracks—they won't show. Surface cracks that show can be easily fixed later. Lift the roll, still on the foil, onto the platter and gently give it one last roll to transfer it onto the platter. Don't worry about ragged edges—just trim them off or ignore them. To patch rough spots or tears, simply smooth the potatoes over them with a rubber spatula dipped in warm water. Cover with plastic wrap and chill on the platter for at least 2 hours or up to 1 day.

6. Before serving, decorate the top of the roll with strips of red pepper and/or black olives if you like. Serve chilled, cut crosswise into 1-inch slices, with the avocado sauce.

VARIATION

INDIVIDUAL *CAUSA* TIMBALES: These make a very nice first course for a sit-down dinner or main course for brunch, lunch, or dinner. Prepare the tuna filling as above, but dice the avocado and stir it into the tuna filling. Prepare the potato mixture as above. Lightly oil eight 6-ounce custard cups or ramekins (for a first course) or six 8-ounce custard cups or ramekins (for a main course). Spread enough of the potato mixture over the bottom and up the sides of the cups to make an even layer about ⅓ inch thick. Spoon the tuna filling into the cups, dividing it evenly. Cover the filling with the remaining potato mixture. Chill until firm, then invert the timbales onto serving plates. Spoon some of the avocado sauce around each timbale and decorate the plates with a little dressed green salad.

Improvised *Ají Amarillo* Puree

The *ají amarillo* is a wonderful, bold yellow pepper that is used extensively in Peruvian cooking. It is sweet and tart, and packs a little bit of heat. The chiles are virtually impossible to find fresh in the States, but I have come up with a pretty close approximation by playing around in the kitchen. This recipe makes more than you will need for the *causa* recipe or the Chicken Braised in Peruvian Yellow Pepper Puree on page 273, but you won't mind. It makes a terrific accompaniment to grilled fish and chicken (marinate the fish or chicken in the puree before cooking, brush more on it while it's grilling, and pass still more at the table if you like) and a delicious sauce for everything from plain white rice to panfried pork chops.

MAKES ABOUT 1½ CUPS • PREP TIME: 30 TO 40 MINUTES

4 yellow bell peppers, roasted, seeded, and peeled (see page 274)
1 jalapeño, stemmed but seeds left intact
Juice of 1 lime
½ to 1 teaspoon turmeric

Process the roasted peppers, jalapeño, and lime juice in the work bowl of a food processor until very smooth. Add ½ teaspoon turmeric and process until blended, stopping once or twice to scrape down the sides of the work bowl. If that isn't enough to turn the puree a vibrant yellow, add the remaining ½ teaspoon turmeric and process again. The puree can be refrigerated for up to 4 days.

Creamy Avocado Sauce

In all of 5 minutes, you can have this cooling, tart sauce to accompany any chicken or fish off the grill or even a bowl of chips. Try it with Clam Fritters (page 195), or the shrimp skewers on page 95.

MAKES 2 CUPS • PREP TIME: 5 MINUTES

2 ripe Hass avocados, halved, pitted, peeled, and cut into large chunks
2 tablespoons fresh lime juice
2 teaspoons hot red pepper sauce or 2 tablespoons *Vinagre* (page 308)
½ cup sour cream
Kosher or fine sea salt

Process the avocado, lime juice, and hot red pepper sauce in the work bowl of a food processor until smooth. Scrape into a serving bowl and beat in the sour cream and salt to taste. Serve at room temperature. The sauce can be prepared up to a day in advance. Refrigerate with a piece of plastic wrap pressed directly onto the surface and bring to room temperature before serving.

Sweet Tomato "Conserva" with Salty Cheese

It may seem a little out of place to feature tomatoes in a dessert, but the tomato is, after all, a fruit. And you'll never look at this particular fruit the same way after trying this dessert. Steeping peeled tomato halves in a cinnamon-and-allspice syrup imbues them with a rich sweetness that doesn't mask the tomatoey-ness of the main ingredient. The real kicker is the pairing of sweet tomatoes and a crumbly, salty cheese in a friendly rivalry that brings out the best in both.

MAKES 6 SERVINGS • PREP TIME: 20 MINUTES • COOK TIME: 40 MINUTES (LARGELY UNATTENDED)

2 cups sugar

2 cinnamon sticks

6 whole allspice berries

2 pounds ripe plum tomatoes, peeled,
   halved, and seeded (see below)

8 to 12 ounces firm salty cheese, such as
   queso fresco, feta, or ricotta salata, cut
   into ¼-inch slices

1. Bring 3 cups water, the sugar, cinnamon, and allspice to a boil in a medium saucepan over high heat. Adjust the heat to the lowest setting and let steep for 20 minutes.
2. Add the tomatoes and adjust the heat so the syrup is simmering gently. Cook until the syrup has thickened, about another 20 minutes. Let cool, then chill.
3. Serve the tomatoes in a compote dish or small bowl with a drizzle of the syrup, accompanied by a plate of the sliced cheese.

To Peel and Seed Tomatoes

Bring a large pot of water to a boil. Have ready a bowl of ice water and a spider (see page 154) or slotted spoon. With a paring knife, cut the stems out of each tomato and cut an X in the opposite end. Slip the tomatoes into the boiling water and leave them until the skin around the X starts to loosen, 30 seconds to 1 minute. With the spider, scoop the tomatoes into the ice water. When they are cool enough to handle, slip the skins off the tomatoes. To seed them, cut plum tomatoes lengthwise in half and round tomatoes in half through the "equator." Scoop out and discard the seeds.

Puerto Rican Shortbread Cookies

✑ MANTECADAS

I can thank my cousin Janet for this version of a Puerto Rican staple. They are buttery, crumbly, not too sweet, and delicious. Guava jelly is nice (and traditional) but any kind of jelly you like will do.

MAKES ABOUT 30 COOKIES • PREP TIME: 20 MINUTES • COOK TIME: 25 MINUTES

2 cups all-purpose flour

1 cup almond flour

1/3 cup sugar

Pinch of salt

2 sticks (8 ounces) cold, unsalted butter, cut into 16 pieces

2 extra-large eggs, well beaten

About 2/3 cup guava (or other) jelly

1. Preheat the oven to 350°F. Line 2 baking sheets with parchment paper (or use nonstick baking sheets).

2. Stir the all-purpose and almond flours, the sugar, and salt together in a medium bowl. Add the butter and work it into the dry ingredients with your fingertips until there is almost no trace left of butter. The dough should be loose and crumbly. Add the eggs and stir until the dough is smooth and no longer crumbly.

3. Using 1 level tablespoon for each, roll the dough into balls and set them about 1½ inches apart on the prepared baking sheets. Press down firmly on the center of each dough ball with your thumb to flatten it out and create a deep well. Spoon about ½ teaspoon of the jelly into each well.

4. Bake until the cookies are very pale golden around the edges, about 25 minutes. Let cool completely before serving. The cookies can be stored in an airtight container at room temperature for up to 3 days—but handle them gently; they are very crumbly.

From bottom left: Puerto Rican Shortbread Cookies, Cafecito (page 42), and Coconut Kisses (page 169)

Cafecito (see photo, page 40)

Cafecitos, or little coffees, are sweet little endings to a meal. And they make a nice tableside show. Beating the sugar and the coffee together at the table one cupful at a time is a labor of love, but the sweet little cups of strong coffee with their foamy crowns are worth it.

MAKES 6 DEMITASSE-SIZE SERVINGS • PREP TIME: 5 MINUTES

3 rounded tablespoons Latin-style coffee,
　　such as Bustelo or El Pico
6 tablespoons sugar, plus more if you like

1. Put the coffee into the strainer of a moka-style coffeepot and fill the base with water. Brew the coffee according to the manufacturer's directions, and bring the pot to the table.

2. For each serving, spoon 1 tablespoon of the sugar into a demitasse cup. Add a few drops of the hot coffee and beat vigorously with an espresso spoon until the sugar absorbs the coffee and is evenly colored. Repeat a few more times, adding only a few drops of coffee and beating well each time, until the sugar mixture is creamy and tan. Pour the hot espresso into the cup and let the foam *(espumita)* rise to the top.

VARIATION

CUBAN COFFEE: While the coffee is brewing, heat some milk in a small saucepan over low heat until bubbles form around the edges. Pour the milk into a small pitcher and bring to the table. Pass the milk and let guests add it to taste to their *cafecitos*.

Grilled Vegetable Salad (page 114)

Maybe I'm lucky, but when the kids were growing up—even in the middle of SATs, drama rehearsals, Jerry's schedule, and the general mayhem of life—our family had a pretty good track record when it came to sharing meals around the dinner table. The real luxury as the kids got older was a family lunch. We could pretty much write off the midweek family lunch except for those rare days during school holidays or the occasional snowbound Tuesday that found everyone at home. But on weekends and summer vacations, lunch worked better than dinner in some ways to get the family together. I caught the kids after they rolled out of bed but before they got under way with their plans. They enjoyed it because they got to hang out together, which they love (told you I'm lucky!), before they went their separate ways for the rest of the day and night.

In Latin America, the midday meal is the big deal. Everything closes down, and then it's siesta time. I look at family lunches as a nice little once-in-a-while treat, a way to stop and smell the roses. Or, in my house, to smell the soup.

NOON

LUNCHES

SOUPS

Grilled-Tomato-and-Onion Soup

The next time you have the grill sparked up and an overflow of perfect summer tomatoes in hand, give this recipe a shot. Or, if it's the middle of winter and you're hankering for a little summer-fresh flavor, pick up some nice ripe plum tomatoes at the supermarket and cook them and the onion under the broiler (see Variation below). Grilling or broiling intensifies the flavor of the vegetables, and starting the soup with a roux (a mix of flour and fat, in this case butter) gives the soup an elegant texture while keeping its rustic flavors.

MAKES 6 CUPS (6 LUNCHTIME SERVINGS) • PREP TIME: 20 MINUTES • COOK TIME: 1 HOUR

12 ripe plum tomatoes (about 3 pounds, or 3 pounds of any ripe, juicy tomatoes), cored, halved, and seeds removed

1 Spanish onion, peeled and quartered through the root but root left intact

1½ tablespoons olive oil

2 large red bell peppers (about 1 pound), roasted, peeled, and seeded (see page 276)

3 cups vegetable broth

2 tablespoons unsalted butter

2 tablespoons all-purpose flour

3 cloves garlic, minced

1 teaspoon dried oregano

½ teaspoon ground cumin

Kosher or fine sea salt and freshly ground pepper

2 tablespoons chopped fresh cilantro

1. Preheat a gas grill to high or build a charcoal fire, and when the coals are glowing red, spread them out into an even layer.

2. Toss the tomato halves and onion quarters with the oil in a large bowl to coat. Place the tomatoes, skin side down, and onion quarters on the grill and lower the heat to medium (if you have a hinged grill basket, these tomatoes are a great reason to use it). Or, if using a charcoal

Grilled-Tomato-and-Onion Soup and Empanadas with Creamy Corn Filling (page 65)

grill, place the onion quarters around the edges of the grill, where the heat will be less intense. Grill the tomatoes until the skin blisters and splits, 2 to 3 minutes, then flip them over and grill until softened, another 2 minutes or so. Remove the tomatoes and continue cooking the onion quarters, turning occasionally, until softened and a bit charred, about 8 minutes total.

3. Remove and discard the skins from the tomatoes, and coarsely chop the tomatoes. Cut the root ends off the onion quarters. Put the onion, tomatoes, and roasted peppers in a blender or processor and puree until smooth. With the motor running, pour in about half the vegetable broth and puree until very smooth.

4. Heat the butter in a medium heavy saucepan over medium heat until foaming. Add the flour and garlic and cook, stirring, until smooth and bubbling, about 3 minutes. Add the tomato mixture and the remaining broth and stir well until boiling. Adjust the heat so the soup is simmering, add the oregano and cumin, and season lightly with salt and pepper. Cook, stirring occasionally, until slightly thickened, about 20 minutes. The soup can be prepared to this point up to 3 days in advance and refrigerated once cooled; it can also be frozen for up to 2 months.

5. Stir the chopped cilantro into the soup, taste, and season with salt and pepper if necessary. Serve hot, or let cool to room temperature and chill before serving.

VARIATION

BROILED-TOMATO-AND-ONION SOUP: Place the rack about 6 inches from the broiler and preheat the broiler. Spread out the oiled tomatoes, skin side up, and the onion quarters on the broiler pan and broil until the tomato skins are blackened, about 4 minutes. Flip the tomatoes over and broil until softened, about 3 minutes. Remove the tomatoes and continue broiling the onion, if necessary, until blackened in spots and softened. Remove the skins from the tomatoes and the root ends from the onion and proceed as above, adding any juices from the broiling pan to the blender.

A STITCH IN TIME: The recipe can easily be doubled and half the soup frozen—good to know when a well-meaning neighbor drops off half a bushel of tomatoes.

Cream of Zucchini Soup with Crabmeat

During our trip to Peru, my family and I enjoyed a dish called *zapallitos rellenos,* which was basically a zucchini cup filled with shellfish in a creamy tomato sauce. I decided to play with the elements of that dish and came up with this delightful soup that makes a terrific quick lunch, or even an elegant first course.

MAKES 6 CUPS (6 LUNCHTIME SERVINGS) • PREP TIME: 20 MINUTES (PLUS TIME FOR PREPARING CHICKEN BROTH) • COOK TIME: 35 MINUTES

¹/₄ cup olive oil

1 small yellow onion, finely diced (about 1¹/₄ cups)

1 leek, white part only, washed well and thinly sliced (about 1 cup)

4 cloves garlic, minced

4 small zucchini (about 1 pound), shredded (about 4 cups)

2 teaspoons chopped fresh thyme

¹/₄ cup all-purpose flour

3 cups Homemade Chicken Broth (page 303) or "Paging Doctored Broth!" (page 305)

1 bay leaf

¹/₂ cup heavy cream

Kosher or fine sea salt and freshly ground pepper (preferably white)

¹/₂ pound jumbo lump crabmeat, picked over for shells and cartilage

¹/₂ cup finely diced yellow bell pepper or peeled and seeded tomato (see page 38), for garnish

1. Heat the olive oil in a large saucepan over medium-low heat. Add the onion, leek, and garlic and cook, stirring, until fragrant and soft, but with no color, about 4 minutes. Add the zucchini and thyme and stir until the zucchini is softened, 2 to 3 minutes.

2. Sprinkle the flour over the vegetables, stirring to incorporate it, and cook for a few minutes so the flour will lose its raw flavor. Add the chicken broth and bring to a boil, stirring to get rid of any lumps. Adjust the heat so the broth is simmering, toss the bay leaf into the soup, and simmer for 15 minutes to blend the flavors.

3. Remove the bay leaf and, working in small batches, blend the soup until smooth. (Overloading the blender may cause the top to pop off and spatter hot soup; if you can, let the soup cool to tepid before blending.) The soup can be made to this point up to 3 days in advance and refrigerated.

4. Return the soup to the saucepan, stir in the cream, and season with salt and pepper to taste. Bring to a simmer over low heat, then stir in the crabmeat gently, to preserve the "lumps," and cook until just heated through. Recheck the seasonings, adding salt and pepper if necessary, and ladle into warm bowls, scattering some of the diced yellow pepper over each bowl.

The Marquis' Soup ❧ SOPA DEL MARQUÉS

I first tasted this soup on a trip to Mexico when our family was en route to Chichén Itzá. We stopped for lunch in a little colonial town called Valladolid. The restaurant where we ate was in a hotel that, in its past life, had been the grand home of an actual marquis and was beautifully appointed with gorgeous antiques and ornate portraits. Always the soup lover, I ordered this as my first course, and I was completely blown away by the complexity of flavors in the seemingly simple soup. The beauty of the soup lies in its broth, so this is not one of those "canned broth" soups. It really will be worth your while to make your own *caldo* (broth) for it.

MAKES 12 CUPS (WITHOUT THE NOODLES; 6 LUNCHTIME SERVINGS OR 8 TO 10 FIRST-COURSE SERVINGS) • PREP TIME: 20 MINUTES (PLUS TIME FOR MAKING BROTH) • COOK TIME: 20 MINUTES

Homemade Chicken Broth (page 303)
8 stalks celery (a mix of large outer and pale inner stalks), cut on the diagonal into ¹/₂-inch slices (about 3 cups)
4 carrots, peeled and cut on the diagonal into ¹/₂-inch slices (about 2 cups)
Kosher or fine sea salt and freshly ground pepper

1 pound fideos, other fine egg noodles, or angel hair pasta
1 tablespoon olive oil
2 Hass avocados, halved, pitted, peeled, and cut into ¹/₂-inch cubes
¹/₂ cup chopped fresh cilantro
Juice of 1 lime
1 lime, cut into wedges

1. Make the broth and strain it. Pluck out the chicken pieces and set them aside until they are cool enough to handle. When they are cool, pull off the skin and discard it, then coarsely shred the meat, getting rid of any fat, gristle, etc., as you go. Set the chicken aside. The broth can be made and the chicken shredded up to 2 days ahead; refrigerate them separately.

2. Heat a large pot of salted water to a boil.

3. Meanwhile, bring the strained broth, celery, and carrots to a boil in a large pot. Taste the broth and add salt and pepper if necessary. Adjust the heat so the broth is simmering and cook until the vegetables are tender but not mushy, about 10 minutes. Add the chicken. While the vegetables cook, stir the fideos into the boiling water and cook until tender but with a little bit of bite, about 4 minutes. Drain the noodles and put them in a bowl. Add the olive oil and toss well.

4. When the vegetables are tender, stir the avocado, cilantro, and lime juice into the soup. Bring the pot of soup to the table, along with the noodles and a bowl of the lime wedges. Spoon some of the noodles into each bowl and ladle the soup over them. (Stir the soup with the ladle as you fill each bowl so you're sure to get a good mix of ingredients into each bowl.) Pass the lime wedges separately.

Shrimp Bisque ✎ CHUPE DE CAMARONES

Chupes are the Peruvian equivalent (more or less) of what we think of as bisques. They are smooth, rich, and elegant. This is the blueprint for all *chupes,* whether the ingredient is shrimp, as it is here, or tender, bright green, fresh fava beans (a Peruvian favorite!), or even the everyday potato.

MAKES 8 CUPS (6 LUNCHTIME SERVINGS) • PREP TIME: 30 MINUTES • COOK TIME: 30 MINUTES

¼ cup olive oil

1 large yellow onion, cut into ¼-inch dice (about 1¾ cups)

3 cloves garlic, minced

¼ cup all-purpose flour

2 large ripe plum tomatoes (about 12 ounces), peeled, seeded (see page 38), and cut into ¼-inch dice

One 48-ounce can (or six 8-ounce bottles) clam juice

One 12-ounce can evaporated milk

Kosher or fine sea salt and freshly ground pepper

3 carrots, peeled and cut into ¼-inch rounds (about 2 cups)

2 ears corn, shucked and cut into 1-inch rounds

¼ cup long-grain white rice

2 pounds large shrimp (under 15 per pound), peeled and deveined

1 cup shelled fresh or frozen peas

1. Heat the olive oil in a 4-quart Dutch oven or heavy casserole over medium heat. Add the onion and garlic and cook, stirring, until the onion is softened but not browned, about 4 minutes. Add the flour, reduce the heat to low, and cook, stirring, until smooth and bubbling. Add the tomatoes and stir for a minute. Pour in the clam juice and evaporated milk and bring to a boil, stirring often, paying special attention to the corners of the pan, where the soup might stick or scorch. Season lightly with salt and pepper.

2. Adjust the heat so the liquid is simmering and add the carrots, corn, and rice. Simmer until the rice is very tender, about 20 minutes. The soup can be prepared to this point and kept at room temperature for up to an hour; return to a simmer before proceeding.

3. Stir the shrimp and peas into the soup and simmer until the shrimp are cooked through, about 4 minutes. Season with salt and pepper to taste and ladle into large warm bowls.

Shrimp Bisque and Daisy's Favorite Salad (page 56)

Cuzco, Peru

Sightseeing is a good way to work up an appetite (as if I need an excuse!). On a trip to Peru, we drove up to Sacsayhuaman one particularly busy morning for a panoramic view of the city of Cuzco and the White Christ that looks down benevolently over what the Incas called the "Navel of the World." The shrine of Tambomachay, where ritual purifications took place, and the breathtaking fortress of limestone known as Qenqo were also on our itinerary. Needless to say, by the time lunchtime came around, there was much "grumbly in the tumbly" going on.

One of the fun things about traveling as a family, aside from the obvious, is that when we eat in a restaurant, we have the advantage of tasting a whole bunch of dishes. This was especially serendipitous when we had a fabulous lunch at La Casa del Inka, a beautiful restaurant on a hill overlooking Cuzco. The restaurant has baskets and platters that exhibit the bounty of Peru, including its extraordinary selection of potatoes, *ají* chiles, and legumes.

Between appetizers and entrées, my family and I were able to sample *causa limeña* (page 35), a delicious "jelly roll" of mashed potatoes seasoned with *ají amarillo*, filled with a tuna salad, and served cold. Jerry went with the grilled short ribs, and David tucked into the *ají de gallina*, which he sampled at every restaurant we visited! (My version, made to keep David happy until his next trip to Peru, is on page 273). Angela enjoyed the *chicharrones de pescado*, crispy fried fish "tenders" served with fried potatoes. The *rocoto relleno*, a

fiery pepper stuffed with picadillo and topped with melted cheese, was exactly what I was craving, and it made short work of the racket my stomach had been making. After this Peruvian feast, we wandered outside to the patio to enjoy the views and the delicious breeze and plan our afternoon.

Angie, David, Marc, me, and "Indiana Erik" take a breather.

We wrapped up our tour that day by visiting the Temple of the Sun in the Plaza de Armas, which today is the Santo Domingo Monastery, and then Cuzco Catedral, where the Inquisition House is heralded by a skull and crossbones. Later that evening, while we chatted and recapped the day, we all decided that, even with all the fantastic sightseeing, our lunch at Casa del Inka was one that we would never forget!

Ensalada Rusa (see photo, page 110)

Ensalada rusa is widely enjoyed all over Latin America and Spain—I've had it in Mexico, Buenos Aires, and Barcelona and always considered it a very Latin dish—so I thought it very funny when I found it on the curriculum when I attended The French Culinary Institute, where it was known as *salade russe*. Because it is a home cook's dish in the Latin world, though one saved for special occasions like birthdays, Christmas, and so on, there are as many versions of *ensalada rusa* as there are cooks who make it. Some have shredded chicken, some canned tuna, and others red beans. This one has the addition of pretty red beets, which give lovely sweetness to the salad. The great thing about this is that you can prep and cook the vegetables the day before, then compose the salad right before you serve it, or even before your guests arrive.

MAKES 8 SERVINGS • PREP TIME: 30 MINUTES (INCLUDES MAKING MAYONNAISE) • COOK TIME: 35 MINUTES

1 cup peeled and diced ($\frac{1}{2}$-inch) red waxy potato (about one 6-ounce potato)

1 cup peeled and diced ($\frac{1}{2}$-inch) white turnip (about one 6-ounce turnip)

1 cup peeled and diced ($\frac{1}{2}$-inch) carrots (about 2 medium)

1 cup string beans cut into $\frac{1}{2}$-inch pieces (about 4 ounces)

1 cup shelled fresh or frozen peas

1 cup peeled and diced ($\frac{1}{2}$-inch) red beet (about one 8-ounce beet)

Several pretty leaves romaine lettuce

Kosher or fine sea salt

1 cup Homemade Mayonnaise (recipe follows)

1. Steam the vegetables separately until soft; about 7 minutes for the potato, 5 to 6 minutes for the turnip, about 5 minutes for the carrots, about 4 minutes for the string beans, about 4 minutes for fresh peas (frozen peas need just about 1 minute), and about 8 minutes for the beet. Remove each (except the beet) to a large mixing bowl as it is done and replenish the water in the steamer as necessary; put the beet in a separate bowl and set aside.

2. Line a platter with the romaine lettuce leaves. Toss the potato, turnip, carrots, string beans, and peas together in the bowl and season with salt. Fold in the mayonnaise and turn out onto the platter. Just before serving, scatter the beet over the salad.

(continued)

Homemade Mayonnaise

No one has ever accused me of being fancy when it comes to home cooking, but every once in a while, it's nice to whip up a batch of mayo to spread on sandwiches or to make a truly killer tuna salad. And it's absolutely imperative for making that weekend lunch staple, *ensalada rusa.* Feel free to play with the citrus juice, substituting lime, orange, or grapefruit for the lemon.

MAKES ABOUT 1 CUP • PREP TIME: 10 MINUTES

1 large egg yolk	²/₃ cup grapeseed oil
1 teaspoon Dijon mustard	1 tablespoon fresh lemon juice
Pinch of kosher or fine sea salt	Freshly ground pepper

Whisk the yolk, mustard, and salt together in a small mixing bowl until blended. Whisking constantly, add the oil drop by drop until you've added about half the oil. The mixture should look completely homogeneous and creamy right from the start; if it looks "broken" at any point, start all over again. Whisk in the remaining oil in a slow, thin stream. Whisk in the lemon juice and season with salt and pepper to taste.

TIP: To keep the bowl steady while whisking and to keep both hands free, try this: Dampen a kitchen towel and arrange it in a ring on your work surface. Center the bowl over the towel ring, which should hold it in place through the continuous whisking. If the bowl still wiggles or moves, tweak the placement of the towel and/or dampen it a little more.

Buenos Aires Hearts of Palm Salad

I will never forget the meal I enjoyed with my family and friends at La Cabrera Norte restaurant in Buenos Aires. Talk about a meat-fest! We could barely hear ourselves speak for all of the excitement around us, as the restaurant was packed to the gills. It's a good thing we were a large party, because I ordered one of practically everything on the menu. Alongside the meat, our waiter brought trays of ramekins filled with an assortment of tempting little sides, among them this delicious salad of hearts of palm, tomato, and avocado. Here in the States it is very difficult to find fresh hearts of palm, but you can find a good-quality product in cans or, better yet, in jars with brine. The freshness of this salad and its pretty colors make it a natural with any roasted or grilled meat.

MAKES 4 SERVINGS • PREP TIME: 20 MINUTES

One 14-ounce jar or can hearts of palm, drained

1 large, ripe, juicy tomato

1 Hass avocado

½ cup olive oil

2 tablespoons orange juice

Juice of 1 lime

Kosher or fine sea salt and freshly ground pepper

1. Just before serving, cut the hearts of palm and tomato into ¼-inch slices. Cut the avocado in half, remove the pit, and peel the halves. Cut each half into ¼-inch slices.
2. Arrange the hearts of palm, tomato, and avocado attractively on a platter. Whisk the olive oil, orange juice, lime juice, and salt and pepper to taste together in a small bowl. Drizzle the dressing over the salad.

Daisy's Favorite Salad (see photo, page 50)

Featured here are a varied bunch of greens and vegetables and a dressing that offer a good balance of tart and sweet, bitter and savory. While this makes a good first course or side, it can also double as a light lunch. I love fennel in any guise, but raw and in a salad is my absolute favorite way to eat it. The green Granny Smith apples are pretty and delicious, but a segmented navel orange (see page 182) would also fit the bill quite nicely. The lemon oil in the dressing showcases the haricots verts and asparagus beautifully while gently embracing the pepper of the arugula.

Without a doubt, this is the one salad recipe that people always ask me for . . . now they can all ask you!

MAKES 8 SERVINGS • PREP TIME: 30 MINUTES

FOR THE SALAD

1 heart of romaine, cut crosswise into 1-inch-wide strips down to about 1 inch from the core

2 heads Belgian endive, cut crosswise into $1/2$-inch strips (remove the pieces of core from the strips; about 2 cups)

2 lightly packed cups baby arugula

2 cups trimmed haricots verts or very thin green beans (about 4 ounces)

2 cups pencil-thin asparagus spears cut into 2-inch lengths (see Note)

$1/2$ hothouse cucumber, cut in half lengthwise, then crosswise into $1/4$-inch slices (about $1 1/2$ cups)

1 bulb fennel, cored and cut into $1/4$-inch slices

2 Granny Smith apples, cored, quartered, and cut into $1/4$-inch slices

FOR THE DRESSING

$1/4$ cup olive oil

2 tablespoons lemon-ginger olive oil, homemade (page 155) or store-bought

Juice of 1 lemon

Splash of rice vinegar

Kosher or fine sea salt and freshly ground pepper

1. Wash the romaine, endive, and arugula and spin them dry in a salad spinner. The greens can be prepared up to a day in advance. Refrigerate them, wrapped gently in a paper towel and tucked into a plastic bag.

2. Heat a medium saucepan of salted water to a boil. Set a bowl of ice water nearby. Stir in the haricots and cook just until bright green and softened but still firm, about 3 minutes. Lift them out with a spider (see page 154) or slotted spoon and drop them into the ice water. Repeat with the asparagus. Drain the vegetables thoroughly and blot them dry. The vegetables can be prepared up to a day in advance and refrigerated.

3. Make the dressing: Put the olive oil, flavored oil, lemon juice, vinegar, and salt and pepper to taste in a small jar with a tight-fitting lid and shake vigorously. The dressing can be made up to a day in advance and refrigerated.

4. If necessary, remove the greens, vegetables, and dressing from the refrigerator about 30 minutes before serving. Toss the greens, blanched vegetables, cuke, fennel, and apple gently in a large serving bowl to mix. Shake the dressing very well, pour it over the salad, and toss again.

NOTE: This is a good way to use up asparagus stalks if you happen to have them left over from a recipe that calls for asparagus tips, like the Egg-Stuffed Baked Tomatoes on page 31. If you're starting from scratch, about half a bunch of pencil-thin asparagus, trimmed and cut into 2-inch lengths, will do the trick.

Celery Root, Jicama, and Red Pear Salad

I really love this salad because the celery root and jicama flavors harmonize so beautifully. After discovering jicama in a salad during our trip to Mexico (I drove the waitress crazy asking her about other ways I could prepare it!), I couldn't get enough of it. This keeps nicely in the refrigerator after you dress it—for up to 2 days, which was a very pleasant surprise—so it's a great "make-ahead." And since it has no mayo, it's a perfect salad for barbecues or picnics!

MAKES 6 SERVINGS • PREP TIME: 30 MINUTES

1/4 cup olive oil
Juice of 1 to 2 lemons
1 tablespoon chopped fresh flat-leaf parsley
Kosher or fine sea salt and freshly ground
  pepper

1 small jicama (about 14 ounces; see
  Note)
1 small celery root (about 12 ounces)
2 red Bartlett pears

1. Whisk the olive oil, juice of 1 lemon, the parsley, and salt and pepper to taste in a large bowl. Set aside.

2. Peel the jicama and celery root. Cut them and the pears, down to the core, into long, thin strips (about 1/8 inch wide; see Tip), adding them to the dressing as you go. When all are cut, toss the vegetables and pears in the dressing to coat. Taste and add salt and pepper and/or additional lemon juice if you think the salad needs it. Refrigerate until chilled, for at least 1 hour, or up to 2 days.

NOTE: Jicama is a large round root vegetable with a light tan skin that is removed before eating. Almost always served raw, it has firm white flesh, a crisp texture, and a sweet and slightly starchy taste. You can find jicama in supermarkets with well-stocked produce sections. Look for jicama with unblemished skin and no soft spots.

TIP: There are several ways to get the thin, delicate strands of vegetable and pear that make this salad such a treat. By far the easiest is a little gizmo I picked up somewhere: it resembles a Y-shaped vegetable peeler, but instead of a simple peeling blade, there is a notched blade that cuts the vegetable or fruit into strands simply by dragging the blade over the surface. You can also use a mandoline or one of those inexpensive Japanese cutting tools if you have one, or the thinnest julienne blade for a food processor.

Empanadas with Potato Filling

Potatoes might not be the first thing that crosses your mind when you think of empanadas, but maybe they should be! On a trip to the Dominican Republic, I enjoyed *catabias,* turnovers with a filling similar to this one but encased in a dough made of grated raw yuca, eggs, and flour. They were absolutely delicious, and I figured, "Why not put the same filling inside an empanada?"

I should mention that I wasn't eating just any *catabias,* I was eating Doña Leonora's *catabias,* which are justly famous all over the island. Doña Leonora typically makes six hundred *catabias* at a clip—and when she runs out for the day, that's pretty much it until the next day. When we got to Doña L's in the late morning, she had sold her last *catabia* just moments before. I think she took pity when she saw the look in our eyes, and she whipped up a little batch for us right on the spot. This is my version of her potato filling. Doña L's was made with sofrito (page 305), but mine is made with a "deconstructed" sofrito—I leave the vegetables in larger pieces to add a little texture to the filling.

This very humble filling could be a side dish on its own, next to a roast chicken, grilled fish, or some other simple entrée. It would also, without the final addition of tomato sauce, make a fine topping for *cocas* (see page 202).

MAKES ABOUT 10 EMPANADAS (4 CUPS FILLING) • PREP TIME: 30 MINUTES • COOK TIME: 1½ HOURS (FOR MAKING AND COOLING FILLING AND FRYING EMPANADAS; LONGER FOR BAKING EMPANADAS)

1 large Idaho (baking) potato (about 1¼ pounds), peeled and cut in half crosswise

2 tablespoons extra-virgin olive oil

1 medium yellow onion (about 6 ounces), cut into ½-inch dice (about 1¼ cups)

½ large red bell pepper, cored, seeded, and cut into ½-inch strips (about 1 cup)

2 large cloves garlic, minced

¼ teaspoon ground cumin

¼ teaspoon dried oregano

1 plum tomato, cored and diced (about ½ cup)

Packed ¼ cup chopped fresh cilantro

Kosher or fine sea salt and freshly ground pepper

One 8-ounce can Spanish-style tomato sauce

One 10-ounce package large (about 6-inch) empanada wrappers (see page 61), defrosted if necessary

(continued on page 61)

1. Put the potato halves in a medium saucepan with enough salted cold water to cover and bring to a boil. Adjust the heat so the liquid is at a gentle boil and cook until the potato is tender, about 25 minutes.

2. Drain the potato halves and return to the pan off the heat. When they are cool enough to handle, cut them lengthwise into ½-inch slices. Set aside.

3. Heat the olive oil in a large skillet over medium-high heat. Add the onion, bell pepper, and garlic and cook, stirring occasionally, until you can smell the garlic and the pepper is wilted, about 4 minutes. Add the cumin and oregano and cook for a minute or two. Add the diced tomato and the cilantro and season lightly with salt and pepper. Cook until the liquid given up by the tomato is almost evaporated, 3 to 4 minutes. Add the potato and stir gently until coated with the vegetables. It is fine if the potato breaks up a little, but try to keep from mashing it. Add the tomato sauce and 3 tablespoons water, stir gently, and bring to a boil. Taste and season with salt and pepper as necessary. Remove from the heat and let cool completely. The filling can be refrigerated for up to 2 days.

4. Using a generous ⅓ cup filling for each, form and cook the empanadas as described below.

To Form and Cook Empanadas

Empanada wrappers, either plain or seasoned and/or colored, are available frozen (sometimes refrigerated) in many supermarkets and almost all Latin markets. Goya is the most common brand. A 10-ounce package of 6-inch empanada wrappers usually contains 10 wrappers. For best results, defrost the wrappers overnight in the refrigerator.

TO FORM THE EMPANADAS: Moisten the edges of each empanada wrapper with a fingertip dipped in warm water, and center a generous ⅓ cup of the filling (or the amount called for in the recipe) on the wrapper. Bring the sides of the wrapper together to meet over the filling to form a half-moon shape, and press the edges together to seal.

TO CRIMP THE EDGES: Lay the empanada flat on the work surface. Work your way around the edges of the half-moon, folding the edges to make ½-inch pleats. Press as you go to seal the pleats. Or, if you don't want to mess with crimping, just press down on the edges with the tines of a fork.

TO FRY THE EMPANADAS: Pour enough vegetable or canola oil into a large heavy skillet to come to about ¾ inch. Heat over medium heat until the tip of the handle of a wooden spoon immersed in the oil gives off a lively sizzle (about 360°F). Carefully slip only as many empanadas at a time into the oil as will fit without crowding. Cook until the dough is lightly browned, about 3 minutes. Carefully flip and repeat. Drain briefly on paper towels before serving.

TO BAKE EMPANADAS: Preheat the oven to 375°F. Line a baking sheet with parchment paper (or use a nonstick baking sheet). Brush the empanadas lightly with beaten egg and bake until they are light golden brown, about 25 minutes. Cool for a few minutes before serving.

Spoon the filling (here, Creamy Corn Filling, page 65) over the center of an empanada wrapper.

Moisten the edges of the empanada wrapper with a fingertip dipped in water.

Fold the wrapper in over to enclose the filling, then press the edges firmly to seal.

Crimp the edges by hand or with a fork.

Empanadas with Blue Cheese and Caramelized Onion Filling

In Argentina, where I first tried this filling, the blue cheese of choice is Roquefort. That works for me too, but I have also enjoyed it with Cabrales, Valdeón (see page 244), and even supermarket containers of crumbled blue cheese.

MAKES ABOUT 8 EMPANADAS (2 CUPS FILLING) • PREP TIME: 10 MINUTES • COOK TIME: 1 HOUR (FOR MAKING AND COOLING FILLING AND FRYING EMPANADAS; LONGER FOR BAKING EMPANADAS)

3 large yellow onions (about 3 pounds), cut in half through the core, then crosswise into ¼-inch-wide slices

2 tablespoons olive oil

1 teaspoon sherry vinegar or cider vinegar

Kosher or fine sea salt and freshly ground pepper

2 ounces Valdeón cheese (see page 244) or Cabrales, or the blue cheese of your choice, crumbled (about ⅔ cup)

2 tablespoons chopped fresh flat-leaf parsley

One 10-ounce package large (about 6-inch) empanada wrappers (see page 61), defrosted if necessary

1. Put the onions, olive oil, and ¾ cup water in a large deep skillet and bring to a boil over high heat. Cover the skillet and boil, stirring occasionally, until the onions are translucent and softened and the liquid is nearly evaporated, about 10 minutes. Uncover the skillet and cook until all the liquid is evaporated and the onions are beginning to brown, about 5 minutes. Reduce the heat to low and cook, stirring occasionally, until the onions are very tender and golden brown, about 20 minutes.

2. Remove the onions from the heat, stir in the vinegar, and season very lightly with salt (the blue cheese will add a fair amount) and with pepper to taste. Let cool to room temperature.

3. Stir the blue cheese and parsley into the onions. Form and cook 8 empanadas, dividing the filling evenly among the wrappers, according to the directions on pages 61 and 62.

TIP: The water that goes in with the onions and oil at the beginning of the cooking serves two purposes: it coaxes much of the sugar out of the onions (which lends them a nice caramel color at the end of cooking) and gives the onions a head start toward tenderness.

Empanadas with Bacon-Shrimp Filling

Here I go again, doing my own riff on Latin classics. An empanada can be filled with practically any-thing, as long as the filling isn't too wet. I decided to pair up two of my favorite things—bacon and shrimp—and turn them into an empanada filling.

MAKES ABOUT 10 EMPANADAS • PREP TIME: 20 MINUTES • COOK TIME: 1 HOUR (FOR MAKING AND COOLING FILLING AND FRYING EMPANADAS; LONGER FOR BAKING EMPANADAS)

12 ounces slab bacon, skin removed (if any), bacon cut into $\frac{1}{2}$-inch cubes

1 tablespoon olive oil

2 cloves garlic, finely chopped

1 pound very small shrimp (about 100 per pound), peeled and deveined

1 plum tomato, peeled, seeded (see page 38), and cut into $\frac{1}{2}$-inch dice

Kosher or fine sea salt and freshly ground pepper

2 scallions, trimmed and thinly sliced (about $\frac{1}{4}$ cup)

Large pinch of crushed red pepper flakes

One 10-ounce package large (about 6-inch) empanada wrappers (see page 61), defrosted if necessary

1. Pour enough water into a large skillet to barely cover the bottom. Add the bacon, set over medium-high heat, and cook until the water is evaporated and the bacon is starting to sizzle. Reduce the heat to medium and cook, stirring often, until the bacon is lightly browned, about 5 minutes. Scrape onto a paper-towel-lined plate to drain.

2. Pour the bacon fat from the pan and wipe out the pan. Add the olive oil and garlic, return the pan to medium heat, and cook until the garlic is fragrant, a minute or two. Add the shrimp and stir until they turn pink, then stir in the tomato and continue cooking until the shrimp are cooked through, about 2 minutes. Season with salt and pepper to taste. Remove from the heat and stir in the scallions, crushed red pepper, and bacon. Let cool completely.

3. Using a scant $\frac{1}{3}$ cup filling for each, form and cook the empanadas according to the directions on pages 61 and 62.

Empanadas with Creamy Corn Filling

∽ HUMITAS

When it comes to the names of certain dishes, Latin America can be a very confusing place. If you were to order *humitas* in a restaurant in Ecuador, what you would most likely get is something similar to tamales—dried corn husks filled with a cornmeal stuffing studded with any number of ingredients. However, in Argentina, ask for *humitas*, and you will—very happily, I might add—end up with a plate of empanadas filled with delicious creamed corn. If you have a couple of sprigs of thyme in the vegetable drawer, throw them in with the béchamel sauce (fish them out before adding the corn).

MAKES ABOUT 10 EMPANADAS (3 CUPS FILLING) • PREP TIME: 20 MINUTES • COOK TIME: 15 MINUTES (FOR MAKING AND COOLING FILLING AND FRYING EMPANADAS; LONGER FOR BAKING EMPANADAS)

4 tablespoons unsalted butter

3 tablespoons all-purpose flour

1 cup milk

¼ teaspoon smoked paprika

Kosher or fine sea salt and freshly ground pepper (preferably white)

2 cups fresh or defrosted frozen corn kernels

1 heaping tablespoon chopped fresh flat-leaf parsley

One 10-ounce package large (about 6-inch) empanada wrappers (see page 61), defrosted if necessary

1. Melt the butter in a small saucepan over medium heat. Add the flour and cook, stirring, until the mixture is smooth and bubbly, about 3 minutes. Whisking constantly, slowly add the milk. Bring to a simmer, stirring constantly, paying special attention to the corners of the saucepan. Cook until the sauce is smooth and glossy, about 15 minutes.

2. Add the smoked paprika and salt and pepper to taste, stir in the corn and parsley, and return to a simmer. Scrape the filling into a bowl and let cool completely.

3. Using ⅓ cup filling for each, form and cook the empanadas according to the directions on pages 61 and 62.

TIP: The smoked paprika brings out the sweetness of the corn, a little trick that works equally well with fresh tomato sauce or soup or virtually any shrimp dish.

Penne a la Sirop

This recipe is inspired by Sirop, a wonderful Italian restaurant we visited in Buenos Aires. I don't believe it's a traditional Italian (or Argentinean) dish, but I do believe it's flat-out delicious.

MAKES 6 SERVINGS • PREP TIME: 20 MINUTES • COOK TIME: 15 MINUTES

1 cup dried porcini or other dried
    mushrooms

2 tablespoons extra-virgin olive oil

3 cloves garlic, thinly sliced

4 anchovy fillets

2 tablespoons all-purpose flour

$1/2$ cup heavy cream

$1/4$ cup milk

1 pound penne

One 7-ounce mini wheel of Brie, rind
    removed, cheese cut into $1/2$-inch cubes

One 5-ounce container (6 cups) baby
    arugula, washed and dried in a salad
    spinner

Kosher or fine sea salt and freshly ground
    pepper

1 cup dried sweet cherries

Freshly grated Parmesan cheese (optional)

1. Put the porcini in a small heatproof bowl and pour enough boiling water (about $1 1/2$ cups) over them to cover them. Let soak until softened, 20 to 30 minutes.

2. Meanwhile, heat a large pot of salted water to a boil.

3. Lift out the mushrooms from the bowl, leaving any grit behind. Strain the porcini liquid through a cheesecloth-lined sieve or coffee filter into a measuring cup. Measure $1/4$ cup of the strained mushroom liquid and set aside for this recipe. Reserve the rest for another use if desired. Cut the porcini into thin strips and set aside.

4. Heat the olive oil in a large deep skillet over low heat. Add the garlic and anchovies and cook, stirring occasionally, until the anchovies fall apart and the garlic is very lightly browned, about 4 minutes. Whisk in the flour and cook, whisking, until the mixture is smooth and bubbly, about 2 minutes. Add the cream and milk to the mushroom liquid and, still whisking, pour into the roux. Whisk until the sauce is smooth and thickened, about 3 minutes. Add the Brie in 3 additions, whisking after each until the sauce is completely velvety smooth. Turn off the heat.

5. While the roux is cooking, stir the pasta into the boiling water and cook, stirring occasionally, until tender but with a little bit of bite, about 8 minutes.

6. When the pasta has about 1 minute of cooking time remaining, add the arugula to the pasta pot. When the pasta is done, drain the pasta and arugula. Transfer the pasta and arugula to a large serving bowl.

7. Add the sliced porcini to the Brie sauce and season with salt and pepper to taste. Pour the sauce over the pasta and toss to coat. Sprinkle the dried cherries over the pasta. Serve hot or warm, with grated Parmesan cheese if you like.

Peruvian-Style Chow Fan ∽ CHAUFA (see photo, page 70)

During a visit to a lovely restaurant at the base of Machu Picchu, we were a little stumped when our waitress asked if we would like to try the *chaufa,* as it was very good that day. Having no idea what it was we had ordered, I was somewhat bewildered when we were served a plate of what looked and tasted a lot like Chinese fried rice. When I asked the waitress about the dish, she explained that it was indeed a very traditional Peruvian dish that was introduced generations ago by Chinese immigrants. (Aaahhh, it finally occurred to me—*chaufa,* like the Dominican dish *chaufan,* the local take on the Chinese term for fried rice, *chow fan.*) Whatever the case, *chaufa* is a great way to rid the fridge of odd bits of this and that. It's also economical and, most important, delicious!

MAKES 6 TO 8 SERVINGS • PREP TIME: 15 MINUTES • COOK TIME: 20 MINUTES

Vegetable oil cooking spray

2 large eggs, beaten

3 tablespoons toasted sesame oil

1 smoked pork chop, boned and cut into
    ½-inch dice, or 1½ cups diced (½ inch)
    smoked ham

1 medium Spanish onion, cut into ½-inch
    dice (about 1¼ cups)

1 pound medium shrimp (30 to 40 per
    pound), peeled and deveined

4 cups cooked white rice (leftover is
    perfect; if not, cook the rice far enough
    in advance for it to cool completely)

½ cup dark soy sauce

2 tablespoons cooking sherry

Chopped fresh cilantro, for garnish

1. Heat a small nonstick skillet over high heat and spray it with cooking spray. Pour just enough of the beaten eggs into the pan to coat the bottom, swirling to set the egg. Take the skillet off the heat and flip the egg "tortilla" over. Then cook just until fully set, about a minute. Remove the "tortilla" and repeat until all of the egg is used. Roll each of the "tortillas" into a cylinder and slice into ¼-inch-wide strips. Set aside.

2. Heat the sesame oil in a large skillet over high heat. Add the pork, onion, and shrimp and cook, stirring, until the shrimp are just opaque, 1 to 2 minutes. Add the rice and stir until the pork and shrimp are mixed throughout. Drizzle the soy sauce and sherry into the rice mixture, toss well to season the rice evenly, and cook until heated through. Check for seasoning, turn the rice out into a serving bowl, and top with chopped cilantro.

Shrimp Ceviche "Xni Pec"

Here's something you don't hear every day: this spiced-up version of ceviche that I tried on a trip to Mexico gets its name, *xni pec* ("shnee pek"), from the Mayan for "dog's nose." Odd as that may sound, it begins to make sense when you eat it—the heat from the chiles may cause your nose to run a bit. Making the ceviche and salsa separately, then mixing them together at the last minute, keeps the vegetable and seafood flavors fresh and alive.

MAKES 8 SERVINGS • PREP TIME: 1 HOUR (LESS WITH STORE-BOUGHT PEELED AND DEVEINED SHRIMP)
• "COOK" TIME: 3 HOURS (MOSTLY UNATTENDED FOR THE SHRIMP TO "COOK" IN THE CITRUS JUICE)

FOR THE CEVICHE
2 pounds small (40 to 50 per pound)
   shrimp, peeled and deveined
Juice of 3 lemons
Juice of 3 limes
Juice of 2 oranges

FOR THE *XNI PEC* SALSA
1 large tomato, cored, seeded, and cut into
   medium dice (about 1 1/4 cups)
1/3 cup chopped fresh cilantro

1/3 cup olive oil
1/4 cup finely diced Spanish onion
1 teaspoon finely chopped chile
   (the hotter, the better!)
Juice of 1 lime
Kosher or fine sea salt and freshly
   ground pepper

2 tablespoons olive oil
Good-quality tortilla chips

1. Make the ceviche: Toss the shrimp with the lemon, lime, and orange juices in a large nonreactive bowl. Refrigerate for 3 hours, or until the shrimp have turned opaque, stirring occasionally so the shrimp cure evenly. The shrimp can be marinated the night before.

2. Meanwhile, make the *xni pec:* Toss the tomato, cilantro, olive oil, onion, chile, and lime juice in a bowl to mix. Season with salt and pepper to taste. (The *xni pec* can be made up to 2 hours in advance and left at room temperature.)

3. When the shrimp are ready, drain them and reserve the marinade (see Note). Toss with the *xni pec* and olive oil. Divide among martini glasses or serving dishes and garnish each with a tortilla chip. Pass a bowl of chips separately.

NOTE: The liquid drained from a ceviche is known as *leche de tigre* ("tiger's milk") and is often served chilled in small glasses to accompany the ceviche. It is also wonderful in a Ceviche Bloody Mary (see page 181) or used to enhance a simple glass of tomato juice.

Peruvian Roast Chicken ∞ POLLO "A LA BRASA"

I *know* that I am going to get some flak for this, but I really do believe that a perfectly cooked Peruvian rotisserie-roasted chicken *(pollo a la brasa)* is nothing short of a deeply religious experience. It is no small wonder, then, that Peruvian restaurant owners treat their roast chicken recipes like a matter of national security! While I've eaten plenty of Peruvian roast chicken in Peru and in many of my favorite Peruvian restaurants here in New York City (no two are alike!), I found that my attempts in the kitchen to re-create any one of those delicious birds always fell short of the elusive flavor I was searching for. Roast chicken after roast chicken came out of my oven or the rotisserie, until one of my kids said to me, "Mom, please . . . can we change it up a bit?" So, the train of chickens continued its exodus out of my oven and over to my neighbors (whom I often engage as guinea pigs in quests like this), until I finally came up with a combination that made me happy.

My final assessment? While most of us do not have the luxury of an open-flame rotisserie, we can approximate *pollo a la brasa* in a conventional oven, but there is one procedure that is nonnegotiable: marinate, marinate, *marinate!* This will result in a moist, juicy, flavorful chicken that is well worth the extra attention. The amount of garlic is just enough to make the chicken interesting without being overpowering, and the small amount of grated fresh ginger plays beautifully in contrast to the malty, salty, tart flavors of malta, soy sauce, and lime juice. Try this next time you make roast chicken—it's a different take on an old favorite, and a lot cheaper than airfare to Peru!

MAKES 6 TO 8 SERVINGS • PREP TIME: 20 MINUTES (PLUS UP TO A DAY FOR MARINATING) • COOK TIME: 1½ HOURS

2 tablespoons dry adobo, homemade (page 307) or store-bought
1 teaspoon freshly ground pepper
1 teaspoon dried oregano
Juice of 3 limes
Two 3-pound chickens, rinsed and patted dry

½ cup soy sauce
½ cup malta (see Notes)
4 large cloves garlic, crushed
One 1-inch piece fresh ginger, peeled and grated
Ají Verde (recipe follows)

1. Stir the adobo, pepper, oregano, and lime juice together in a small bowl. Loosen the skin over the chicken breasts and as much of the legs as you can by working your fingers gently in between the meat and skin. Flip the chickens over and do the same to as much of the skin over the back as you can. With the aid of a teaspoon, work about three-fourths of the adobo mixture under the skin of the chickens and inside the cavities. Tie the chicken

Peruvian Roast Chicken and Peruvian-Style Chow Fan (page 68)

legs together with kitchen twine and rub the remaining adobo mixture over the skin of the chickens.

2. Stir the soy sauce and malta together in a small bowl. Divide between 2 gallon-size resealable plastic bags. Add 2 cloves of the garlic and half the ginger to each bag. Put 1 chicken in each bag, seal the bag, pressing out excess air, and squish the liquid around so it coats the chicken evenly. Refrigerate for at least 4 hours, or preferably overnight. Turn and squish the chickens occasionally.

3. Preheat the oven to 400°F.

4. Drain the chickens thoroughly. Put the chickens on a rack in a roasting pan. Tuck the wing tips underneath each chicken to hold the wings firmly against the sides of the chicken.

5. Roast until the juices run clear (not pink) when you pierce the meat between the thigh and the leg, about 1 hour.

6. Let the chickens rest for 10 minutes. Cut each one into 4 to 8 pieces before serving with the *ají verde.*

NOTES: Malta is a malt-based nonalcoholic beverage that is found all over Latin America and the Spanish-speaking Caribbean. It is purported to boost iron levels in the blood (especially when mixed with raw eggs, as I have often seen!). You can find malta in every bodega in every borough of New York City (literally) and in any market that serves even a smallish Latin population. If you cannot find it, beat 2 tablespoons molasses and 3 to 4 tablespoons water together and use that instead.

The traditional way to cook Peruvian chicken is *a la brasa,* on a rotating spit over an open flame, using either coal or wood as fuel. While most of us don't have the luxury of a countertop rotisserie (late-night-television impulse purchase, anyone?), I found that when I tried the recipe on the rotisserie on my gas grill, and added a chunk or two of charcoal to the smoke box, it really brought the bird to another level. This rendition of my recipe, while not strictly *a la brasa,* is a tasty, juicy, easier version that is sure to become a staple in your repertoire.

Ají Verde

Ají verde ("ah-HEE ver-de") is the Peruvian equivalent of Mexican tomatillo salsa (page 103). It is *everywhere,* on practically every table in every restaurant. And no wonder! Besides the Peruvian Roast Chicken, it is wonderful served alongside ceviche, Cumin-Scented Fried Potatoes (page 153), Barbecued Beef Short Ribs (page 88), and Daisy's Grilled Chicken Express (page 92); as a dip for chips; and a whole lot more!

MAKES ABOUT 1¼ CUPS • PREP TIME: 20 MINUTES

1 cup coarsely chopped fresh cilantro

¼ cup sliced scallions

3 jalapeños, coarsely chopped

2 tablespoons grated cotija cheese

2 cloves garlic, minced

½ cup extra-virgin olive oil

Juice of 1 lime

Kosher or fine sea salt and freshly ground pepper

Put the cilantro, scallions, jalapeños, cheese, and garlic in the work bowl of a food processor and process until very finely chopped. With the motor running, drizzle in the olive oil. Squeeze in the lime juice and then add enough water to make a sauce with the consistency of a thick milkshake. Season with salt and pepper to taste. The sauce can be refrigerated for a few days, but bring it to room temperature before serving.

Crabmeat Strudel with Passion Fruit Hollandaise

This, like the Avocado Stuffed with Crab-Mango Salad on page 129, is something I came up with for my mom, Conchita, the Queen of Crab. The toasted bread crumbs lend additional crunch to the crisp phyllo pastry.

MAKES 2 STRUDELS (12 SERVINGS TOTAL; SEE A STITCH IN TIME) • PREP TIME: 30 MINUTES • COOK TIME: 25 MINUTES

FOR THE TOASTED BREAD CRUMBS

2 tablespoons olive oil

1 cup seasoned or plain dried bread crumbs

Kosher or fine sea salt and freshly ground pepper

FOR THE CRAB FILLING

3 tablespoons clarified unsalted butter (see page 75)

1 shallot, minced (about 1½ tablespoons)

1 pound lump crabmeat, picked over for shells and cartilage

2 tablespoons chopped fresh cilantro

Finely grated zest of 1 lime

Juice of ½ lime

Kosher or fine sea salt and freshly ground pepper

30 sheets phyllo dough (12 × 8 inches)

½ cup clarified unsalted butter (see page 75), plus more for brushing the strudels

Passion Fruit Hollandaise (recipe follows)

1. Preheat the oven to 375°F.

2. Toast the bread crumbs: Heat the oil in a large skillet over medium heat. Add the bread crumbs, season them lightly with salt and pepper, and cook, stirring and turning constantly, until they are golden brown and crisp, about 5 minutes. Remove from the pan and cool.

3. Make the crab filling: Heat the clarified butter in a large skillet over medium-low heat. Add the shallot and cook, stirring, just until wilted. Add the crabmeat and cook, stirring very gently to keep the pieces of crab as large as possible, until warmed through. Add the cilantro, lime zest, lime juice, and salt and pepper to taste and stir just to mix. Remove from the heat.

4. Assemble the strudels: Unwrap the phyllo and lay the sheets out flat on your work surface (see page 312 for tips on working with phyllo). Cover the stack of phyllo with a damp kitchen towel. Remove 3 of the sheets and stack them on the work surface with one of the long sides closest to you. Brush the top sheet generously with clarified butter. Sprinkle about 2 teaspoons of the toasted bread crumbs over the butter. Repeat 4 times (using a total of 15 sheets of phyllo), but do not sprinkle the top layer with bread crumbs. Spoon half of the filling lengthwise along the center of the phyllo in an 8 × 3-inch strip. Fold the short ends of the dough over the filling, then fold over the long ends. Flip the strudel over so the seam side is down and carefully transfer it to a lightly greased baking sheet; be sure the ends of the roll are tucked neatly underneath. Repeat with the remaining phyllo, clarified butter, bread crumbs, and filling as needed.

5. Brush the tops of the strudels with clarified butter and bake until they are golden brown and crisp, about 25 minutes. Let stand for 10 minutes before serving.

6. Cut each strudel into 6 equal pieces (or 8 pieces, if yours is a dainty crowd). Drizzle a little of the hollandaise over each and pass the remaining sauce separately.

A STITCH IN TIME: This makes more bread crumbs than you will need for the strudels. Keep them on hand to sprinkle over soups or on top of just about any pasta dish.

Even if you're serving only 4 to 6 people, make both strudels. The strudel freezes beautifully unbaked, and some day when you're caught short for a weeknight dinner or lazy weekend lunch, you'll be glad you did. Let the frozen strudel stand at room temperature for 30 minutes before baking.

Passion Fruit Hollandaise

The little touch of passion fruit in this otherwise classic hollandaise adds a mysterious tart note. Its buttery wonderfulness would pair nicely with any fish off the grill or add zip to a tropical version of eggs Benedict.

MAKES ABOUT 1½ CUPS • PREP TIME: 5 MINUTES • COOK TIME: 10 MINUTES

2 extra-large egg yolks

Pinch of cayenne pepper

1 cup clarified unsalted butter (see below), melted and kept warm

2 tablespoons passion fruit puree (see Note, page 121)

Kosher or fine sea salt

1. Pour 2 inches of water into the bottom of a double boiler and bring to a simmer. If you don't have a double boiler, pour 2 inches of water into a wide saucepan and bring to a simmer, then set over the saucepan a heatproof bowl that will sit on top of the pan without touching the water.

2. Put the egg yolks, cayenne, and 1 tablespoon water into the top of the double boiler or the bowl and whisk over the simmering water until the yolks are pale yellow, lightened in texture, and thickened enough that you can see the bottom of the double boiler (or bowl) as you whisk. Don't be tempted to cheat on the whisking during this stage, or the eggs won't be ready to absorb the butter and you will end up with a mess instead of a sauce. Whisking constantly, dribble in the butter literally a drop at a time until you've added about half of it. Still whisking constantly, pour in the remaining butter, never at more than a very thin trickle. (If you add the butter too fast or slow down the whisking, the sauce will break.) Whisk in the passion fruit puree and season with salt to taste. Serve right away, or cover the sauce with a clean kitchen towel and keep warm for up to 3 hours. A corner of the stove is a good place to keep the sauce warm; a thermos or an insulated coffee carafe is also a good way to keep it warm.

Clarified Butter

Clarifying butter is a simple process: Put as much butter as you need in a microwavable container large enough to hold the butter after it melts. Microwave at medium power until the butter is completely melted. Let the melted butter stand until all the milky white sediment drifts to the bottom, then simply skim off any foam from the surface and pour the clear yellow butter into a fresh container, leaving the milk solids behind. Use clarified butter any time you want the flavor of butter but need it to stand up to higher heat: for example, brushing baked goods before baking to give them a rich buttery flavor and deep golden crust; greasing a griddle for pancakes or French toast; or frying small pieces of food over high heat.

Tortillas with Rajas and Fixin's

I enjoyed this simple but delicious roll-your-own taco dish at a restaurant in Oaxaca. The poblano peppers were deliciously roasted and served with gently caramelized onions and a dollop of queso fresco. These are made with roasted poblanos cut into strips (known as *"rajas"*) and the fixin's listed below, but you can let your imagination run wild and add softly scrambled eggs, or avocado, or tomatillo salsa, or anything else you like along with the *rajas*.

MAKES 6 SERVINGS • PREP TIME: 45 MINUTES

10 poblano peppers (about 1³/₄ pounds), roasted, peeled, and seeded (see page 274), cut into ¹/₂-inch strips

1 tablespoon olive oil

One package (about 16) 6-inch corn tortillas

ANY OR ALL OF THE FOLLOWING FIXIN'S

Coarsely shredded queso Oaxaca

Requesón or ricotta cheese (see Note)

Caramelized Onions (see Empanadas with Blue Cheese and Caramelized Onion Filling, page 63)

Diced tomato

Sour cream

Weeknight Salsa (page 147) or other favorite homemade or bottled salsa

Sliced avocado

1. Preheat the oven to 350°F.

2. Toss the poblano strips with the olive oil and set them aside. Wrap the tortillas securely in aluminum foil and put them in the oven until warmed through, about 15 minutes.

3. Meanwhile, put whichever of the fixin's you choose in bowls and fit each with a spoon. Unwrap the tortillas, spoon a healthy amount of poblano strips onto each one, and top with the fixin's of your choice. Roll up the tortillas and eat.

NOTE: Requesón is a slightly salty Mexican cheese, midway between ricotta and ricotta salata in texture, moist, and perfect for crumbling. It is somewhat difficult to find outside Latin markets but worth picking up if you run across it.

VARIATION: Beat 3 extra-large eggs with 2 tablespoons finely diced tomato and a tablespoon of milk. Scramble the eggs to a very soft texture. Divide the eggs between 6 warmed tortillas and dress them with any of the above fixin's.

Dominican-Style Pressed Salami and Cheese Sandwiches

In the capital city of the Dominican Republic, Santo Domingo, there is an institution known as Barra Payan, open to all twenty-four hours a day. After the opera, a movie, or a night on the town, you'll find everyone from the paperboy to the mayor enjoying the vibe and the food. That's where we tasted these for the first (but obviously not the last) time.

MAKES 6 SANDWICHES • PREP TIME: 10 MINUTES • COOK TIME: 5 MINUTES

6 Portuguese rolls, crusty kaiser rolls, or ciabatta rolls

Deli-style mustard

Mayonnaise

18 thickish slices cooked beef salami (about 1¼ pounds)

6 thickish slices cheddar cheese (6 to 8 ounces)

12 dill pickle slices (sandwich slices work well)

6 thick slices tomato

Kosher or fine sea salt and freshly ground pepper

6 iceberg lettuce leaves

1. Preheat a sandwich or panini press (see Tip).

2. Build the sandwiches: Cut each roll completely in half horizontally. Spread one half lightly with mustard and the other with mayonnaise. Fold the salami slices in half and lay 3 folded slices over the bottom half of each roll. Top with a slice of cheese, 2 pickle slices, and a slice of tomato. Season the tomato with salt and pepper to taste and top with a lettuce leaf. Close up the sandwiches. The sandwiches can be prepared up to several hours in advance. Line them up on a tray, cover with plastic wrap, and refrigerate until ready to grill.

3. Cook the sandwiches in a sandwich press according to the manufacturer's directions until the center is warmed through and the bread is crisp. Cut in half and serve right away.

TIP: If you don't have a sandwich press, try this simple improvisation: Warm a large heavy skillet or griddle (cast iron for either is ideal) over medium-low heat. Lay as many sandwiches in the skillet or on the griddle as will fit comfortably. Weight them with another skillet if using a skillet, or with a baking sheet topped with 2 medium-size cans if using a griddle. In either case, flip the sandwiches once the underside is toasted and cook until the center is warmed through and the bread is crisp on both sides.

Jibaritos

Jibarito ("hee-bah-REE-toh") is a term of endearment in Puerto Rico. The word is difficult to translate exactly, but it represents the people who are the heart and soul of Puerto Rico. There is a song by Rafael Hernández, "Lamento Borincano," in which a poor soul from the country ventures into the city market with the meager offerings from his humble garden plot. *Jibarito* is also the name of a delicious sandwich made with slices of fried plantain in place of bread. Like all food legends—old and new— the origins of the *jibarito* can be a little hard to untangle, although most people credit Jorge "Peter" Figueroa of Chicago with the invention. Peter's original version calls for beef, but I love mine made with leftover *pernil* or even slices of adobo-marinated turkey breast. Any way you cut it, it's a winner.

MAKES 2 SANDWICHES • PREP TIME: 40 MINUTES (INCLUDES TIME FOR THE PLANTAINS TO COOL BETWEEN FRYINGS) • COOK TIME: 5 TO 10 MINUTES

2 green plantains (see page 315)

Canola oil, for frying

4 thickish (about 1/8-inch) slices Swiss cheese

1½ cups shredded leftover *Pernil* (page 268) or Turkey Breast *"Pavochon"* (page 269)

4 dill pickle slices (sandwich slices work well)

4 thin slices deli ham

2 tablespoons deli mustard

1. Peel the plantains (see page 315). Carefully cut them in half lengthwise.

2. Pour 1 inch of oil into a large skillet and heat over medium heat until the tip of the handle of a wooden spoon dipped in the oil gives off a slow stream of bubbles (about 325°F). Fry the plantain halves, turning once, until they are tender when poked with the tip of a paring knife but only just starting to brown, about 5 minutes. Fry only as many plantain halves as will fit into the skillet without touching; if necessary, fry them in batches. If they begin to brown before they are tender, immediately lower the heat. Remove and drain on paper towels until cool enough to handle.

3. Lay a still-warm plaintain half flat side down on a sturdy surface. Pound with a flat-bottomed heavy skillet to an even thickness of about 1/4 inch. Repeat with the remaining plantain halves. The plantains can be prepared to this point up to an hour in advance.

4. Preheat a sandwich or panini press. (See Tip on page 78 for preparing these sandwiches without a press.)

5. Reheat the oil over medium-high heat until the tip of the handle of a wooden spoon dipped in the oil gives off a very lively stream of bubbles (about 375°F). Fry the flattened plantains, turning once, until crisp and golden brown, about 5 minutes.

6. Tear or cut the slices of cheese as necessary to cover 2 of the flattened plantain halves. Top the cheese on each with an even layer of the shredded pork or turkey, then a layer of sliced pickle and 2 slices of ham. Spread the mustard over the ham and top with the remaining 2 fried plantains.

7. Cook the sandwiches in a sandwich or panini press until the cheese is melted and the centers are warmed through. Cut the sandwiches in half and serve immediately.

VARIATION: To make a traditional *cubano* sandwich, use thinly sliced leftover *pernil*. Build and cook the sandwiches as above, substituting two 8- to 9-inch soft-textured rolls for the plantains. Or use sliced turkey for a turkey *cubano*.

Baby Banana Beignets and Dulce de Leche (page 291)

Baby Banana Beignets

Baby bananas *(niñitos)* were such a treat when I was a little girl. Don't confuse *niñitos* with the short, fat bananas often found in Asian markets that redden as they turn ripe. These are shaped like regular bananas, grow in bunches of up to fifteen, and turn yellow as they ripen. To me, they are sweeter and creamier than their grown-up cousins, but that may just be the little girl in me.

MAKES 12 TO 15 BEIGNETS • PREP TIME: 10 MINUTES (PLUS TIME FOR THE BATTER TO REST)

• COOK TIME: 15 MINUTES

1 cup all-purpose flour

1 teaspoon baking powder

$1/2$ teaspoon sugar

Pinch of salt

1 cup milk

1 extra-large egg

Canola oil, for frying

12 to 15 baby bananas

"GO-WITHS" (ANY OR ALL OF THE FOLLOWING)

Confectioners' sugar or cinnamon sugar, for sprinkling

Dulce de leche (see page 291) for dipping

Chocolate syrup

Vanilla ice cream

1. Make the batter: Stir the flour, baking powder, sugar, and salt together in a bowl. Beat the milk and egg until blended, then stir into the dry ingredients until most of the lumps are gone; don't overmix. Cover the bowl and let the batter rest for at least 30 minutes, or up to 2 hours at room temperature. The batter can also be refrigerated for up to 1 day.

2. Just before frying, pour 3 inches of oil into a deep heavy pot. Heat the oil over medium heat until the tip of the handle of a wooden spoon dipped in the oil gives off a lively stream of bubbles (about 360°F).

3. Meanwhile, peel the bananas. Working with 2 forks, roll 1 banana in the batter to coat it completely, then lift out of the batter, let the excess batter drip back into the bowl, and gently lower the banana into the oil. Repeat with as many bananas as will fit in the oil without crowding. Cook, turning once if necessary, until golden brown on all sides, about 4 minutes. Remove with a spider (see page 154) or slotted spoon and drain on paper towels. Repeat with the remaining bananas and batter. Serve warm with your choice of "go-withs."

Cinnamon-Perfumed Custard

✑ CREMA CATALANA

I fell in love with this delicate custard dessert at the restaurant Botafumeiro in Barcelona—and to this day, theirs is my favorite version in Barcelona. The texture of *crema catalana* should be very delicate, much more like a French *pot de crème* than an American-style pudding. If you run across a recipe for *crema catalana* that calls for cornstarch, turn and run the other way. The jiggly, tender, delicious texture of this dessert comes from the fact that it is thickened only (and minimally) with egg yolks.

MAKES 4 SERVINGS • PREP TIME: 20 MINUTES • COOK TIME: 40 MINUTES
(UNATTENDED, PLUS CHILLING TIME)

$1^2/_3$ cups milk

2 large cinnamon sticks

1 teaspoon vanilla extract

4 extra-large egg yolks

$3^1/_2$ tablespoons sugar

1. Preheat the oven to 325°F.
2. Heat the milk, cinnamon, and vanilla in a medium saucepan over low heat just until little bubbles form around the edges. Set aside to steep for 15 minutes or so.
3. Beat the yolks with the sugar in a medium bowl until they turn a pale yellow and the sugar starts to dissolve. Strain in the warm milk a little at a time, whisking well after each addition, then stir until the sugar is completely dissolved.
4. Divide the milk mixture among four 8-ounce ramekins or custard cups. Put them into a baking dish that holds them snugly—a 9 × 9-inch dish works well. Cover each ramekin with a small square of aluminum foil and put the baking dish in the oven. Pour in enough hot water to come halfway up the sides of the ramekins and bake until the centers are barely set—they should jiggle a little when you shake the baking dish gently—about 40 minutes.
5. Let the custards cool to room temperature in the baking dish. Remove them from the water bath and chill until set, at least 2 hours. The custards can be made up to a day in advance.

Dulce de Yuca ∽ SWEET YUCA PUDDING

I can't take credit for this recipe, and I am not ashamed to admit it. I literally begged my friend Kisha Figueroa, a culinary student at The Institute for Culinary Education in New York City, for the recipe after she made some and brought me a piece at an event I did there (it was still warm!). I am a fan of all things yuca, and while I found myself a bit skeptical when I heard *"dulce de yuca,"* I was an instant convert the second I took my first bite. I was so excited that I called *Mami* in Florida and asked her if she had ever heard of this, and she said she hadn't! You can imagine how delighted I was to be the one who made it for her first.

MAKES 9 SERVINGS • PREP TIME: 25 MINUTES (LESS WITH FROZEN YUCA)
• COOK TIME: 45 MINUTES (UNATTENDED)

4 tablespoons unsalted butter, melted, plus more for greasing the baking dish and brushing the top of the *dulce*

1 1/4 pounds yuca or 2 cups thawed and squeezed frozen yuca (see Note)

1 cup canned unsweetened coconut milk

1/2 cup sugar

1 teaspoon vanilla extract

1. Preheat the oven to 350°F. Grease an 8 × 8-inch baking dish.
2. If using fresh yuca, peel it, cut it lengthwise into quarters, and cut out the woody center core. Shred the yuca on the coarse side of a box grater. With your hands, squeeze as much of the liquid from the shredded yuca as possible. (Skipping this step will make for a mushier texture.)
3. Put the yuca, coconut milk, sugar, and vanilla in a blender. Blend at low speed until smooth. With the blender running, drizzle in the 4 tablespoons melted butter and blend until the mixture is very smooth. The batter should be the texture of cooked farina. Pour the batter into the prepared dish and brush the top with melted butter.
4. Bake until the *dulce* is firm in the center, golden around the edges, and lightly browned on top, about 45 minutes. If you can bear it, let the *dulce* cool to room temperature before serving—it will be easier to cut into neat squares that way. (If you do sneak some while it is still warm, pour a little honey or dulce de leche over it before eating.) Cut into 9 squares and serve anywhere from warm to room temperature.

NOTE: Frozen grated yuca is available in some Latin markets and supermarkets. It is a tremendous time-saver. Frozen yuca should be thawed in the refrigerator, then drained. Remove any excess liquid from the thawed yuca by squeezing it dry in a clean kitchen towel before measuring it.

BARBECUES

This chapter draws its inspiration from the Argentine *asados,* known throughout the rest of Latin America as *parrilladas,* those spectacular barbecues featuring a host of grilled meaty entrées and a swarm of varied and delicious side dishes. During a family trip to Argentina over the Christmas and New Year's holiday, we were lucky enough to enjoy the *asado* experience in two very different ways. The first was a Christmas celebration at the house of a dear friend (see page 99) and the second at Estancia La Cina Cina. The *estancia* ("ranch") is a real working farm that offers people a peek into the life of the gauchos, the legendary cowboys of Argentina. We swam, rode horseback, and watched the gauchos put on a show of horsemanship the likes of which I had never seen. But the thing I remember most (of course!) about the trip to Estancia La Cina Cina was the food. No sooner had we stepped off the bus than we were greeted by a young woman in traditional garb with a basket full of warm *empanaditas* with picadillo filling.

The same gauchos who rode horses so beautifully did the cooking for the *asado.* A grill that stretched for what must have been thirty feet was covered, and I mean *covered,* with *morcilla,* chorizo, and *churrasco* (see pages 87, 310, and 90). All this meatiness was supplemented with greens, vegetable salads, and the simple and delicious potato-and-egg salad that one finds all over Argentina (a tip of the hat to the huge German-Argentinean population; page 107). All of this was washed down with cleriquot (my take appears on page 238) and the national beer of Argentina, Quilmes.

Once the gauchos had put down their grilling tools, they picked up their instruments and serenaded us with romantic old tango songs and the traditional folk songs of Argentina. Now that's my idea of a man—someone who cooks me dinner and sings to me while I eat! I'm glad we had all our activity earlier in the day, because after the feast, all we could manage was to lie back on lounge chairs under the shade of the trees and sip our glasses of cleriquot.

Some of the recipes in this chapter are re-creations of memorable dishes culled from that family trip to Argentina, a few are time-tested family favorites, and one or two are my take on the barbecue/*asado* theme. All are fabulous and all owe a debt to the spirit of the *parrillada.*

Hosting an authentic Argentinean *asado* (or your own version of one) doesn't need to be a no-holds-barred blowout: tailor the number of dishes to the size of your crowd, your comfort level around a grill, and the time you have to prepare. A respectable *asado* can be built around grilled Argentinean chorizo, a platter of tangy adobo-marinated chicken, and a couple of side dishes. Or it can grow from there to include empanadas (as is often the case in Argentina; see pages 59 through 65 for recipes); a lighter dish like grilled summer squash with a tart balsamic vinaigrette; or a tried-and-true favorite like buttered sweet corn on the cob, hot from the pot. (See page 296 for a few menus to get your creative juices flowing.) And, of course, even if the spirit of your barbecue is purely Argentinean, that doesn't mean all the dishes have to be. Feel free to pick one or a few from your roster of favorite recipes and liven them up with one of the sauces and side dishes on pages 103 through 115.

A last word: The three sauces featured in this chapter can be served interchangeably with just about any of these recipes or with any grilled meat, fish, poultry, or vegetable you can think of. It would be a shame, though, not to enjoy the classic pairing of crispy-edged grilled skirt steak with herby-zingy chimichurri sauce!

Rounding Out Your Argentinean Barbecue

Here are a few items that appear at almost every *asado*. They don't really require recipes—just a little prep and, of course, a trip to the grill.

MORCILLA is blood sausage, with as many variations in style and flavor as there are butchers who make it. It is generally well seasoned with onion, garlic, and spices and may or may not contain other ingredients, like rice (which is fairly common). Cooked *morcilla* is ready to eat as is, but the uncooked type needs to be cooked before eating. At an *asado,* of course, *morcilla* would be grilled—not over direct heat, which would cause the sausages to burst, but off to the side of the grill, where they can cook gently and thoroughly. Because blood sausages are so well seasoned, there is rarely anything in the way of sauce or salsa served with them.

RIB-EYE STEAK (known in Argentina as *ojo de bife*) and **SIRLOIN STEAK** *(chorizo de bife)* are favorite cuts featured at *asados*. Like other meats at an *asado,* it is all about quality with these two steaks, so a simple rub with salt and pepper is all they get before hitting the grill. Both steaks should be cut thick so they emerge nice and juicy from the grill, and both can be served with chimichurri if you like.

KIDNEYS may not be everyone's cup of tea, but they are an integral part of an Argentinean *asado*. Soak whole kidneys in well-salted acidulated water (vinegar or lemon juice work well) in the refrigerator for several hours, changing the soaking liquid once or twice. After soaking, slice the kidneys in half horizontally and pat them dry. Season them generously with salt and pepper and rub them with enough olive oil to make them glisten, then grill them over moderate heat until cooked through.

Barbecued Beef Short Ribs ⌒ TIRA DE ASADO

With all the other cuts of beef in contention for grilling, short ribs often get overlooked. They aren't the most tender cut of beef, it's true, but when it comes to great grilled-beef flavor, they are hard to beat. A simple rub of salt and pepper and a quick splash of vinegar are all they need by way of prep. This would be superb served with Butter Beans *en Escabeche* (page 164).

MAKES 8 SERVINGS • PREP TIME: 5 MINUTES (PLUS 1 TO 4 HOURS MARINATING TIME)
• COOK TIME: 15 MINUTES

4 pounds beef short ribs, cut across the ribs into 1½-inch slices (see Note)
Kosher or fine sea salt and freshly ground pepper

2 tablespoons red wine vinegar
Tomatillo Salsa (page 103), Cilantro Pesto (page 104), Chimichurri (page 104), or Weeknight Salsa (page 147)

1. Trim any surface fat from the ribs. Rub all surfaces of the meat generously with salt and pepper. Put the ribs into a large baking dish that holds them in a single layer. Drizzle the vinegar over the ribs and turn them over so they are vinegared on both sides. Let the ribs marinate, turning them occasionally, at room temperature for up to 1 hour or in the refrigerator for up to 4 hours. (The longer marinating time may make the surface of the ribs turn grayish-white in spots; that is fine, and the discoloration will disappear when they are grilled.)
2. Heat a gas grill to medium-high or build a strong charcoal fire.
3. Grill the ribs, turning them once, until well browned, even charred here and there, about 6 minutes per side. The ribs should be just a touch rarer than medium—anything less, and they will be very chewy. Let them rest for 4 to 5 minutes before serving.

NOTE: The thickness and the cut are key to enjoying short ribs on the grill. The ribs must be cut across the bones (usually 3 or 4 bones), *not* in between them. This kind of cut for short ribs is sometimes referred to as "short ribs for flanken." Also, the ribs should be cut as close to 1½ inches thick as possible—any thinner, and they will be overcooked by the time the outside is well seared; any thicker, and the surfaces will overcook before the centers reach a shade less than medium.

Barbecued Beef Short Ribs and Weeknight Salsa (page 147)

Grilled Skirt Steak with Chimichurri Sauce

∽ CHURRASCO (see photo, page 110)

I have always loved the beefy flavor of skirt steak and the "tooth" of the meat. My dear friend Alejandro Cantagallo and his dad, Don Francisco, own a butcher shop in Jackson Heights, Queens, that specializes in Argentinean charcuterie, so when I visit his shop for his fabulous chorizos, *morcillas,* and *matambre* (a delicious stuffed breast of veal), I always snap up a couple of skirt steaks to take home and throw on the grill. Don Francisco gave me a personal lesson on how to make chimichurri sauce, and now I can prepare it as the perfect complement to my skirt steak. Skirt steak should be trimmed, so ask your butcher to take care of the silverskin and extra fat for you.

MAKES 12 SERVINGS • PREP TIME: 20 MINUTES (PLUS 30 MINUTES TO 2 DAYS MARINATING TIME) • COOK TIME: 15 MINUTES

Kosher or fine sea salt and freshly ground pepper

4 skirt steaks (about 1 pound each), trimmed of fat and cut in half crosswise

1 teaspoon onion powder

1 tablespoon white wine vinegar

1 tablespoon extra-virgin olive oil

Vegetable oil cooking spray

Chimichurri (page 104)

1. Rub a generous amount of salt and pepper into both sides of the steaks. Rub the onion powder into the steaks, dividing it evenly. Put the steaks into a baking dish or container that holds them comfortably, sprinkle the vinegar over them, and brush them with the olive oil. Marinate the steaks at room temperature for up to 30 minutes, or refrigerate for up to 2 days.

2. Heat a gas grill to medium-high, build a strong charcoal fire, or heat a large grill pan over medium-high heat.

3. Grill the steaks, turning only once, to the desired doneness. Remove from the grill and let rest for 5 minutes.

4. Thinly slice the steaks against the grain before serving. Drizzle some of the chimichurri over the steaks and pass the rest separately.

Sweetbreads on the Grill ⁓ MOLLEJAS

I had never eaten sweetbreads until I was a student at The French Culinary Institute in Manhattan. But once I did, I was hooked for life! Buttery, rich, and delicious, sweetbreads are not an item found in most supermarkets (or even butcher shops), and they do require a bit of a time commitment, especially if cooked the old-school French way. Traditionally that involves soaking the sweetbreads in salted water, blanching them quickly in boiling water, and then weighting them overnight before picking them clean of the connective membranes that hold the lobes together. After visiting Argentina, where I enjoyed sweetbreads that were grilled lightly after minimal preparation, I can tell you that the streamlined prep outlined below, followed by grilling, is my new favorite way to eat sweetbreads. Lightly seasoned and grilled to perfection, they will readily become a part of your mixed grill.

MAKES 8 SERVINGS • PREP TIME: 30 MINUTES (PLUS 45 MINUTES SOAKING TIME AND UP TO 1 DAY MARINATING TIME) • COOK TIME: 12 TO 20 MINUTES

2 pounds veal sweetbreads

1 tablespoon kosher or fine sea salt, plus
more for the soaking water

2 tablespoons olive oil

Freshly ground pepper

1. Soak the whole sweetbreads in well-salted cold water for 45 minutes or so at room temperature.

2. Drain the sweetbreads thoroughly and pat dry with paper towels. Pull them apart gently— they will separate easily into smaller pieces. Pull off any pieces of fat or thick connective tissue, but leave the thinner connective tissue that holds the smaller pieces together. The idea is to keep them in 1½- to 2-inch pieces—any smaller, and they'll slip through the grill.

3. Pat the sweetbreads dry again and toss them with the olive oil, salt, and pepper. Let the sweetbreads stand at room temperature for up to 45 minutes, or refrigerate them for up to a day. If they've been refrigerated, bring them to room temperature before grilling.

4. Heat a gas grill to medium or build a charcoal fire and let it burn until the coals are barely covered with light gray ash.

5. If you like, arrange the sweetbreads in a single layer in a grill basket. Grill the sweetbreads, turning once, until they are grill-marked, are cooked through (no trace of pink remains at the center), and feel firm, 12 to 20 minutes. (For some reason, it seems to take some pieces, even if they are the same size, longer to cook than others.) Serve right away.

NOTE: Feel free to use a stovetop griddle if you don't have a grill.

Daisy's Grilled Chicken Express

I am a working mom who turns to her microwave from time to time to lend a helping hand. In nicer weather, this simple method for speeding up the grilling time for chicken is a once-a-week go-to recipe. (It does take a little up-front time in the microwave, but while the chicken is nuking, the rest of the dinner comes together.) On my way out the door in the morning, I toss the chicken into its marinade to steep for the day. Just before dinner, I cook the chicken most of the way through—still in the marinade—in the microwave. While that's going, I pull together a couple of quick side dishes. When all is ready, we set the table out on the back deck and Jerry mans his station at the grill. By the time the kids (and whoever else!) have drifted in, the chicken is hot and crisp, and we've had a chance to catch up a little on the events of the day.

The same approach works well for a barbecue. Usually you have to grill chicken over low heat for a good long time, watching it constantly, to make sure it cooks all the way through without burning. Par-cooking in the microwave takes much of the pressure off you (or whoever volunteers to do the grilling).

MAKES 10 SERVINGS • PREP TIME: 2 HOURS (OR LONGER, MOSTLY UNATTENDED)
• COOK TIME: 1 HOUR (MOSTLY UNATTENDED)

5 pounds chicken legs and thighs (about
    20 pieces)
¼ cup dry adobo, homemade (page 307)
    or store-bought
2 cups white or cider vinegar

1. Put the chicken in the largest bowl you have. If all the chicken doesn't fit comfortably, use 2 bowls. Sprinkle the adobo over the chicken and toss well to coat. Pour the vinegar over the chicken and toss well again. Let stand at room temperature for at least 1 hour or up to 1½ hours, or refrigerate for as long as overnight. Either way, toss it several times as it marinates.

2. Put half of the chicken pieces in a large microwave-safe bowl that fits in your microwave. Pour half the marinade over the chicken. Cover the bowl tightly with plastic wrap and cook at high power for 10 minutes. Remove the plastic wrap—handle the bowl carefully; it will be hot—and move the chicken around so it cooks evenly. Re-cover the bowl and cook until the chicken is almost completely cooked through, about 10 minutes. Repeat with the remaining chicken and marinade. Once the chicken is microwaved, it should be cooked within an hour.

3. Heat a gas grill to medium or build a charcoal fire and wait for the coals to be covered with fine gray ash.

4. Cook the chicken, turning it often, until golden, even charred in spots, about 10 minutes. Serve hot or at room temperature.

VARIATION: Just as you can customize your adobo (see page 307), you can customize the acidic part of this marinade. Use all white or all cider vinegar or mix the two. Or substitute citrus juice—orange, lemon, and/or lime—for part or all of the vinegar.

Shrimp Without Chorizo Skewers

It seems that almost overnight everyone was making some version of a shrimp and chorizo kabob for grilling. I have nothing against that combo—in fact, I love it!—it's just nice to remind ourselves every once in a while that shrimp has other good buddies too. The juicy tomatoes, mild zucchini, and spicy chiles in this recipe are just a few of them. This is not something that you would see at a traditional Argentinean barbecue. It is something that I came up to serve to those who may not be as crazy about meat as I am. These skewers are dreamy served with the Cilantro Pesto on page 104.

MAKES 12 SERVINGS • PREP TIME: 20 MINUTES • COOK TIME: 6 MINUTES

12 wooden or metal skewers

24 large shrimp (16 to 20 per pound), peeled and deveined

2 medium zucchini (about 1 pound), trimmed and cut into ½-inch rounds

6 big, fat jalapeños, stemmed and cut in half lengthwise, then in half crosswise

12 cherry or grape tomatoes

Olive oil

Kosher or fine sea salt and freshly ground pepper

1. Soak wooden skewers, if using, in water to cover for at least 30 minutes. Drain.
2. Thread the shrimp and vegetables onto the skewers: Start with a round of zucchini and follow with a shrimp, jalapeño, and cherry tomato. Finish up with another zucchini round, shrimp, and jalapeño. The skewers can be assembled up to several hours before being cooked. Put them in a rectangular baking dish, cover with plastic wrap, and refrigerate.
3. Heat a gas grill to medium-high or build a charcoal fire and wait for the coals to just start turning ashy.
4. Brush the shrimp and vegetables lightly with olive oil and season them well with salt and pepper. Grill the skewers, turning them once or twice, until the shrimp are cooked through and the vegetables are softened and lightly browned, about 6 minutes. Serve hot or at room temperature.

Shrimp Without Chorizo Skewers and Cilantro Pesto (page 104)

Grill-Roasted Boneless Pork Shoulder

✏ BIONDOLITO DE CERDO

Paula Strada, a good friend and native of Argentina, took my family out to dinner during our trip to Buenos Aires. Among the many reasons I have to love Paula, not least is that she led us on that evening to Restaurante La Cabrera Norte, where we were treated to a meat-fest unlike anything we had ever experienced. We enjoyed plate after plate of chorizo, grilled *mollejas* (sweetbreads), grilled veal kidneys, and rib-eye steak, surrounded by a dozen little plates of every kind of salad imaginable. I thought we were finished, when the waiter stopped at our table with the sweetest, juiciest, oh-so-mouthwatering grilled pork roast that I had ever had. I have tried, using my memory and my copious notes, to re-create the experience we enjoyed that beautiful night.

MAKES 12 SERVINGS • PREP TIME: 30 MINUTES (PLUS 1 TO 3 DAYS MARINATING TIME)
• COOK TIME: 2 TO 2½ HOURS (MOSTLY UNATTENDED)

FOR THE HERB RUB
5 cloves garlic
¼ cup coarsely chopped fresh flat-leaf
   parsley
¼ cup coarsely chopped fresh basil
1 tablespoon kosher or fine sea salt

1 teaspoon freshly ground pepper
2 tablespoons olive oil

One 4-pound boneless pork shoulder roast
1 pound bacon, the thickest-sliced you can
   find

1. Make the herb rub: Pulse the garlic, parsley, basil, salt, pepper, and olive oil in the work bowl of a food processor until the garlic is finely chopped.

2. Open up the boned pork shoulder. Rub the inside generously with the herb rub. Continue with the recipe or wrap the pork roast well in plastic wrap and refrigerate for at least 1 day, or up to 3 days.

3. Cut twelve 18-inch lengths of kitchen twine. Lay them out about 1 inch apart on a clean work surface. Arrange the bacon slices, overlapping them, over the twine so that each piece of string runs more or less down the middle of a slice of bacon. Set the pork, smooth (nonmarinated) side down, over the bacon. Bring the first slice of bacon and its accompanying string up and around the pork and tie it securely in place. Repeat with the remaining pairs of bacon and string. Depending on the size of the roast, you may not need all the string and bacon. You will end up with a securely tied pork roast encased in overlapping slices of bacon; don't worry if the strips of

Grill-Roasted Boneless Pork Shoulder and Boricua Slaw (page 112)

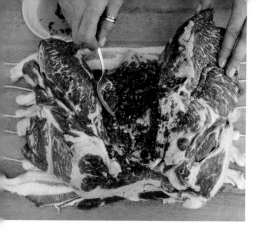

Season the inside of the pork roast with the herb rub.

Lift up the twine and bacon over the roast and tie in place.

The finished pork shoulder, bacon side up.

bacon don't reach all the way around the roast. Let the roast stand at room temperature while the grill is heating.

4. Heat a gas grill to medium-high (see Note). If your grill has a thermometer, the temperature after the grill has heated with the cover closed should read around 375°F.

5. Fill a deep ovenproof skillet halfway with water. Fit a circular cooling rack into the skillet and place the skillet on the grill. Set the pork roast bacon side up on the rack and close the lid. Cook, replacing the water in the pan as necessary, until an instant-read thermometer inserted into the thickest part of the roast registers 150°F, about 2 hours. Carefully remove the pan and roast from the grill. Transfer the roast to a carving board and let stand for 15 to 20 minutes before serving.

6. Snip off the twine, leaving the bacon intact, and carve the roast into ¼-inch-or-so slices.

NOTE: To cook the roast on a charcoal grill, light enough coals to cover the grate evenly. When they are glowing red, use a long metal spatula to divide them in half and push the halves to opposite sides, leaving the center free of coals. Keep an eye on the temperature, and whenever it drops below 350°F, add about 10 fresh coals to each pile. If your grill doesn't have a thermometer, refresh the coals every 30 minutes or so. Cooking time—if temperature is maintained as above—will be approximately the same as for a gas grill.

VARIATION:

OVEN-ROASTED BONELESS PORK SHOULDER: Preheat the oven to 350°F. Put the roast on a rack in a roasting pan and let stand at room temperature while the oven heats. Fill the pan halfway with water, and roast until an instant-read thermometer inserted into the thickest part of the roast registers 150°F, about 2 hours. Let rest for about 15 minutes before serving.

A Christmas Barbecue

When I was a Latina growing up in New York, the words "Christmas" and "barbecue" didn't often come together in the same sentence. There was the occasional *Noche Buena* (Christmas Eve) spent in tropical Puerto Rico, where the feast included a holiday pig roast *(lechón)* at *Tía* Gabriela's, but for the most part, my Christmas holidays were of the "white" variety, with burning Yule logs and lots of *coquito* (coconut-flavored eggnog) to warm folks up.

This all changed during the Christmas of 2007, when, for my family's annual holiday trip, we visited Buenos Aires, Argentina, and were invited to the home of my friend Paula Strada's family for *Noche Buena* dinner. We were presented with a traditional Argentine *asado,* where the men are all in charge of grilling the myriad meats on wood- and coal-burning grills and the ladies supply the

Marc, David, Angela, and Maria Chiquita get their karaoke on in Buenos Aires, Christmas Eve 2007.

side dishes and desserts. The fragrance of juicy grilled Argentinean chorizo wafted through the beautiful backyard, making our mouths water in anticipation of the *choripan* sandwiches on the way. Platter after platter of grilled meats, corn salad, potato salad, and delicious desserts made their way to the table. Somewhere in the midst of all this, we were offered a very traditional *vitello tonnato*—poached veal, sliced thin and served cold, coated with a tuna-caper mayonnaise.

Paula's family embraced mine with open arms and treated us as long-lost relatives. We ate, we sang karaoke, we went swimming, and we made friendships that will last a lifetime! The Strada clan is welcome in my home for Christmas, or any other time of the year. I'll never forget the hospitality they extended to the Martinez-Lombardo family during that truly marvelous holiday.

The table is set for our Christmas Eve asado.

The *Choripan*

Sometimes the simplest things are the best. Take the *choripan,* a deliciously simple chorizo sandwich seasoned with juicy, freshly made salsa. Not surprisingly, given the huge Italian population in Argentina, Argentinean chorizos resemble fresh Italian sausages (minus the fennel seed) more than they do the firm cooked Spanish-style chorizo or uncooked but well-seasoned Mexican chorizo. I am lucky to have access to a great Argentinean butcher in the neighboring borough of Queens (which satisfies my jones for the real thing), but you can capture the spirit of a *choripan* with your favorite hot or sweet Italian sausages.

Here's all there is to it: Find a firm but not crusty sandwich-size roll. In the Northeast, it's easy to find Portuguese rolls, which have exactly the right texture, but in other parts of the country, where such a thing may not exist, you'll do perfectly well with a good-quality kaiser or ciabatta roll. Next, make a simple fresh tomato salsa, like the Weeknight Salsa on page 147 jazzed up with a little extra chile, or the salsa that is part of Shrimp Ceviche *"Xni Pec"* (page 69), which already has enough heat built into it. Pit and peel an avocado, cut it into ½-inch dice, and add it to the salsa of your choice.

Split each link of chorizo or Italian sausage open along the shorter curved side, but don't cut all the way through the sausage. (This is known as "butterflying.") Open the sausage up so it makes a neat rectangular shape. Leaving the casing on keeps the sausage from falling apart, and the butterflying makes it easy to cook the sausage through without burning the outside. Grill the sausages, starting with the casing side down and turning them once, until cooked through and well browned, about 8 minutes. Let them sit for a minute while you split and toast the rolls. Fill the rolls with sausages and a good amount of salsa, and you're off and running!

Choripanes and *"Xni Pec"* Salsa (page 69)

Tomatillo Salsa

This is a standard salsa that you find everywhere in Mexico. Tomatillos have a natural acidic and fresh note that gives them a little sparkle. (They keep that sparkle even after they're cooked, as they are here.) Tomatillo salsa is a natural with the flavors of grilled meats, but it is a great do-ahead, have-on-hand salsa to freshen up just about anything off the grill or out of a skillet.

MAKES ABOUT 4 CUPS • PREP TIME: 15 MINUTES • COOK TIME: 15 MINUTES

1 pound fresh tomatillos

1 large Spanish onion (about 12 ounces), cut into large chunks (about 3 cups)

3 cloves garlic

½ packed cup coarsely chopped fresh cilantro

½ jalapeño (seeds and all if you like heat)

Juice of ½ lime

Kosher or fine sea salt

1. Pull the husks from the tomatillos and wash the tomatillos under cool water until they no longer feel sticky. Cut them into quarters and put them into the work bowl of a food processor. Add the onion and garlic and process until smooth. Add the cilantro, jalapeño, and lime juice and process until the jalapeño is finely chopped.

2. Scrape the mixture into a small saucepan, season lightly with salt, and bring to a boil over medium heat. Cook, stirring occasionally, until most of the liquid is boiled off and the salsa looks relish-y, about 15 minutes. Let cool before using. The sauce can be refrigerated for up to 1 week. If it's been refrigerated, you may want to add a little salt and/or lime juice to the salsa before serving.

Chimichurri

∽ PARSLEY-GARLIC SAUCE FOR STEAK (see photo, page 110)

MAKES ABOUT 1 CUP • PREP TIME: 20 MINUTES

4 cups fresh flat-leaf parsley leaves
  (from about 1 large bunch parsley)
6 cloves garlic
1/2 to 3/4 cup extra-virgin olive oil
1/4 cup red wine vinegar

Kosher or fine sea salt and freshly
  ground pepper
1 heaping teaspoon crushed red
  pepper flakes (optional)

Pulse the parsley and garlic in the bowl of a food processor until finely chopped. Scrape into a bowl and stir in 1/2 cup olive oil and the vinegar. Stir well and taste: if it is too tart, add as much of the remaining olive oil as you like. Season with salt and pepper to taste. Add the red pepper flakes, if using, for a spicy chimichurri. The chimichurri can be made up to 5 days in advance and refrigerated. Bring to room temperature before serving.

TIP: Resist the temptation to plunk all the ingredients into the food processor and whirl away. That will turn this into a bright green, homogeneous sauce instead of what it should be: a tart, garlicky vinaigrette enriched with loads of parsley.

A STITCH IN TIME: Double the recipe; it will keep in the refrigerator for up to 5 days. It is delicious on everything from plain white rice and boiled potatoes to hamburgers and sautéed salmon steaks.

Cilantro Pesto (see photo, page 94)

This is particularly good with the shrimp skewers on page 95 and short ribs on page 88, but it would be equally at home with any simple fish steak or fish fillet off the grill.

MAKES 1½ CUPS • PREP TIME: 15 MINUTES

1 cup extra-virgin olive oil

1 packed cup coarsely chopped fresh
   cilantro (stems and all)

1 packed cup fresh flat-leaf parsley leaves

¼ cup Marcona almonds or blanched almonds

2 teaspoons white wine vinegar

Kosher or fine sea salt and freshly
   ground pepper

Pour the oil into a blender jar. Add the cilantro, parsley, almonds, and vinegar and blend until the herbs are finely chopped and the mixture is fairly smooth. Season to taste with salt and pepper. Scrape into a storage container and press a piece of plastic wrap against the surface to prevent the pesto from turning dark. The pesto will keep for several days in the refrigerator. Bring to room temperature before serving.

Provoletta

In Argentina, provoletta is a part of any typical *asado* (see page 86). Preparing provoletta involves taking a rather large round of slightly aged provolone and grilling it over coals until it turns crisp on the outside and soft in the center. This process must require some kind of Argentinean gene, which I clearly lack—I could never get the vital golden brown crust before the cheese started slipping through the grill. So I improvised. A nonstick pan, a fair amount of heat, and a little bit of patience will reward you with a perfectly delicious representation of the provoletta you would enjoy in Argentina.

MAKES 12 SERVINGS • PREP TIME: 15 MINUTES • COOK TIME: 10 MINUTES

FOR THE DRESSING (OR USE CHIMICHURRI, PAGE 104)

½ cup olive oil

2 tablespoons finely chopped roasted
   garlic, homemade (page 309) or
   store-bought

1 tablespoon chopped fresh flat-leaf parsley

1 teaspoon dried oregano

1 teaspoon white vinegar

Kosher or fine sea salt and freshly ground
   pepper

One ½-inch-thick piece provolone (about
   12 ounces; a young, domestic provolone
   that gives a little when pressed is best
   for this version of provoletta)

Olive oil

Vegetable oil cooking spray

1. Make the dressing: Stir the olive oil, garlic, parsley, oregano, vinegar, and salt and pepper to taste together in a small bowl. Set aside.

2. Brush the cheese generously on both sides with olive oil. Spray with cooking spray a nonstick skillet large enough to hold the cheese comfortably. Heat the skillet over medium-high heat. Lay the oiled provolone into the pan and be patient. When you see the sides of the cheese start to ooze and bubbles start to form around the edges, about 4 minutes, lift an edge of the cheese and peek. If it is golden brown and crisp, turn it over; if not, give it a little more time. Repeat on the second side. Slide the hot cheese onto a serving plate and spoon about half the dressing over it. Serve immediately, with the rest of the dressing on the side.

Provoletta

Potato-Egg Salad

This is the one ubiquitous dish that I encountered during my visit to Buenos Aires. You will find this salad everywhere, from the myriad steakhouses throughout the city to the *estancias* in the countryside. In Argentina, this salad rarely contains anything other than potatoes and hard-boiled eggs, but I have taken the liberty of adding some sweet red peppers. They lend fragrance and sweetness to the sharp vinegar of the salad and the richness of the egg, and a bit of fresh chives gives it some sparkle. It is the perfect accompaniment to the variety of grilled treats at any *asado,* and I especially love it because you can serve it cold or at room temperature. Well, *that,* and because it looks and tastes so very good!

MAKES 8 TO 10 SERVINGS • PREP TIME: 45 MINUTES (PLUS 30 MINUTES MELLOWING TIME)
• COOK TIME: 10 MINUTES

3 pounds Eastern or white new potatoes, peeled and cut into $1/2$-inch dice (about 8 cups)

Kosher or fine sea salt

4 extra-large eggs

2 tablespoons white wine vinegar

$1/3$ cup olive oil

$1/4$ cup minced fresh chives

Freshly ground pepper

1 bottled roasted red pepper, drained and cut into $1/2$-inch dice (optional)

1. Put the potatoes in a large saucepan or Dutch oven, pour in enough cold water to cover, and add a small handful of salt. Bring to a boil over high heat. Adjust the heat so the water is simmering and cook until the potatoes can be easily pierced with a paring knife, about 10 minutes.

2. While the potatoes are cooking, start cooking the eggs: Put the eggs in a saucepan and pour in enough cold water to cover. Bring to a boil over high heat, then adjust the heat to medium-low. Cook the eggs for exactly 10 minutes. Drain the hot water and cool the eggs in the pan under cold running water for several minutes. Peel and set aside.

3. When the potatoes are tender, drain them and put them in a serving bowl. Immediately sprinkle the vinegar over them and toss them gently, then set aside to cool. You don't want to stir the potatoes too much while still hot, as they tend to fall apart and look unattractive.

4. Once the potatoes are cool, add the olive oil and chives and stir gently to coat the potatoes with oil. Season the salad with salt and pepper to taste and toss again. Cut the eggs into quarters and decorate the top of the salad with them and the diced red pepper, if using. Serve at room temperature or chill before serving.

Red Beet and Green Apple Salad

On our trip to Argentina, I was asked by our hostess Maria *Grande* (so named to avoid confusion with her daughter, Maria *Chiquita*) to make an impromptu salad for a New Year's Eve *asado*. I asked Maria *Grande* what she had on hand, as we had left the city for the suburbs and most businesses had closed early for the holiday. Inspired by the fabulous salads served as part of the all-out *asados* we had enjoyed in various restaurants and homes, I came up with this festive-looking salad that made a great impression with Maria's guests and her neighbors. It's a nice combination of earthy sweetness from the beets and tart crunch from the green apple, and it has become a salad that is as welcome at a family barbecue as at a Christmas buffet. I'll let you pick the perfect event to serve this keeper.

MAKES 8 TO 10 SERVINGS • PREP TIME: 20 MINUTES • COOK TIME: 15 MINUTES

8 medium red beets (about 2 pounds), peeled, halved, and cut into ½-inch wedges (about 5 cups)

1 tablespoon white wine vinegar

3 Granny Smith apples, quartered, cored, and cut into ¼-inch wedges (about 2½ cups)

2 tablespoons extra-virgin olive oil

1 tablespoon fresh lemon juice

Kosher or fine sea salt and freshly ground pepper (preferably white)

1. Put the beets in a large saucepan with enough cold salted water to cover. Bring to a boil, then adjust the heat so the water is simmering. Cook until the beets are tender when poked with a paring knife, 10 to 12 minutes. Drain and toss with the vinegar in a large bowl. Let cool, then chill.

2. Toss the apples, olive oil, and lemon juice together in a serving bowl. Stir in the beets. Season the salad with salt and pepper. The salad can be made up to 2 hours ahead and kept at room temperature. The beets will color the other ingredients—don't worry.

VARIATION

BEET SALAD WITH HORSERADISH DRESSING: Omit the apples, olive oil, and lemon juice. Cook and season the beets as described in step 1. Toss the chilled beets with ½ cup sour cream and 2 teaspoons bottled horseradish. Season with salt and pepper to taste and, if you like, scatter ¼ cup thinly sliced fresh chives over the top.

Sweet Corn, Fava Bean, and Fennel Salad

I love fava beans and was so happy when we found them everywhere on our trip to Peru—simply boiled and served as a side dish, mixed with rice, or turned into an elegant bisque. This salad is my take on two South American staples, corn and favas, although I don't know that I've ever run across anything like it in my travels. What I do know is that its sweet, fresh flavor makes it a welcome addition to any barbecue.

MAKES 12 SERVINGS • PREP TIME: 1 HOUR (INCLUDES CORN AND FAVA COOKING TIME)

10 ears corn, shucked and all silk removed
2 1/2 to 3 pounds fava beans, shelled, blanched, and peeled (about 1 1/2 cups; see Note)
1/2 large bulb fennel, outer layer peeled, halved, core removed, cut into 1/4-inch dice (about 1/2 cup)
2 tablespoons chopped fennel fronds
1/4 cup extra-virgin olive oil
Kosher or fine sea salt and freshly ground pepper

1. Bring a large pot of salted water to a boil. Add the corn and cook until tender-firm, about 5 minutes. Drain and let stand until cool enough to handle. Slice the kernels off the cobs.

2. Toss the corn, fava beans, fennel, fennel fronds, and olive oil together in a bowl until the vegetables are coated with oil. Season with salt and pepper to taste. Serve right away, or let stand at room temperature for up to 1 hour.

NOTE: To prepare favas, first remove the beans from the pods: Snap off the stem end of the pod and pull off the string that runs along the seam down the length of the pod. That should make it easy to open the pod with your fingers. (If not, use a paring knife to help open the pod.) Remove the beans. The skin of the beans, which can be very thin or quite thick, must be removed before the favas can be eaten. This is much easier to do if you blanch them first: Drop them into a large pot of boiling water and cook until the beans turn bright green (you'll be able to see the beans right through the skin), 2 to 3 minutes. Drain the beans in a colander, run them under cool water, and drain again. Use your thumbnail to flick open the dark spot in the skin at one end of each bean, then just squeeze out the bean.

VARIATION: If there are no favas in the market, fresh peas, blanched very quickly in boiling salted water, make a fine substitute. So do freshly cooked and shelled or defrosted frozen shelled edamame.

Classic Argentinean Rice Salad

I was very surprised to learn that rice is not the starch of choice in Argentina, as it is in most of Latin America. The large numbers of immigrants from Italy and Germany greatly influenced Argentinean cuisine, swinging the starch pendulum toward pasta and potatoes. So it was with interest that I sampled this room-temperature rice salad, chock-full of tasty vegetables. It is the perfect picnic salad, as it has no mayonnaise or dairy, and it is as light and refreshing as it is delectable. It's also a great way to clean out the refrigerator, so your imagination is the limit when it comes to which vegetables to use. This is my favorite version—I hope it inspires you to come up with your own.

MAKES 12 SERVINGS • PREP TIME: 30 MINUTES • COOK TIME: 30 MINUTES
(INCLUDES COOKING AND COOLING TIME FOR THE RICE)

Basic White Rice (page 159)

2 medium carrots, peeled and cut into 1/4-inch dice (about 1 cup)

Kosher or fine sea salt

5 tablespoons extra-virgin olive oil

1 tablespoon red wine vinegar

1/2 teaspoon dried oregano

Freshly ground pepper

Kernels cut from 1 ear of corn

1 cup shelled fresh baby peas or defrosted frozen peas

2 stalks celery, cut into 1/4-inch dice (about 1 cup)

1 red bell pepper, cored, seeded, and cut into 1/4-inch dice (about 1 1/4 cups)

1 small red onion, cut into thin slivers (about 1 1/4 cups)

Finely grated zest of 1 lemon

1. Make the rice and set aside to cool to room temperature.

2. Meanwhile, put the carrots in a medium saucepan of cold water, add salt to taste, and bring to a boil over high heat. Cook until barely tender, about 2 minutes. Remove the carrots with a spider (see page 154) or a slotted spoon, letting them drain well, and put them in a large serving bowl. (Keep the boiling water on the heat.) Add 2 tablespoons of the olive oil, the red wine vinegar, oregano, and salt and pepper to taste to the bowl. Toss well and set aside to cool.

3. Blanch the corn and peas separately in the boiling water until tender, about 3 minutes for the corn, 4 minutes for the peas (or just 1 minute if using frozen peas). Add them to the bowl with the carrots.

4. Add the cooled rice, celery, bell pepper, and onion to the bowl with the carrots, corn, and peas. Add the lemon zest and the remaining 3 tablespoons olive oil, and toss to mix. Serve warm, or let stand at room temperature for up to 2 hours. Check the seasoning again before serving.

Clockwise from bottom left: *Churrasco* (page 90); Sweet Corn, Fava Bean, and Fennel Salad (page 109); Classic Argentinean Rice Salad; Chimichurri (page 104); *Ensalada Rusa* (page 53)

Boricua Slaw (see photo, page 96)

This recipe was given to me by my favorite Jew-yoriquen, Jason Perlow, who is a foodie par excellence and the man behind the Off the Broiler blog (www.offthebroiler.com). When Jason started to eat more greens, vegetables, and fruits, he began to meld his love of Latin flavors with a wide variety of vegetable salads. He came up with a slaw similar to this to complement a turkey breast that he made, which was seasoned similarly to the Turkey Breast *"Pavochon"* on page 269, but that was smoked instead of roasted. The slaw turned out to be the perfect accompaniment for the turkey, but you could serve it with anything at a barbecue, from hot dogs and hamburgers to a whole suckling pig! Oh, one more thing: If you can, make this when you make the Spicy Shredded Pork Tacos on page 208 and pass the slaw around the table, letting folks spoon a little of the slaw into the tortillas. The contrasts in flavor, texture, and temperature are a blast.

MAKES 12 SERVINGS • PREP TIME: 20 MINUTES (PLUS 1½ TO 2 HOURS SITTING TIME)

1 small head red cabbage (about 4 pounds)

1 pound carrots, peeled and coarsely shredded (about 3½ cups)

½ cup cider vinegar

2 teaspoons kosher or fine sea salt

½ cup chopped fresh cilantro

2 scallions, trimmed and thinly sliced (about ¼ cup)

Vinagre (page 308)

1. Peel off any wilty leaves from the head of cabbage. Cut the head in half through the core. Set half the head aside for another use. Cut the remaining half in half through the core, then cut out the core. Cut the quarters crosswise into ¼-inch-wide shreds. You will have about 12 cups.

2. Toss the cabbage and carrots together in a large bowl. Sprinkle the vinegar and salt over the vegetables and toss again. Let stand until the cabbage is wilted, about 1½ hours.

3. Stir in the cilantro, scallions, and *vinagre* to taste. Serve right away, or let stand at room temperature for up to 30 minutes or chill before serving.

Napa Cabbage Slaw

I am always fascinated by the fact that when I travel—no matter what the country—sooner or later I can recognize the influence immigrants to that country have had on its cuisine. The cooking of Peru, for instance, is rich with Asian influences, especially Japanese and Chinese. During a very upscale dinner at the Monasterio Restaurante in Cuzco, I was served a delicious grilled kingfish *(peje rey)* on a bed of warm pickled Napa cabbage, and the "Daisy bells" chimed loud and clear—it was not far removed from the Japanese salads I have come to love, or even Korean kimchi! I came home and developed this recipe from the flavors of that memorable meal in Peru. I like to prep my cabbage the day before and leave it in plastic bags, so that an hour before I serve it, I can dress it and return it to the fridge so that it will be well chilled and refreshing. There is never any left over!

MAKES 12 SERVINGS (ABOUT 14 CUPS) • PREP TIME: 20 MINUTES (PLUS 1 HOUR SITTING TIME)

1 head Napa cabbage (about 3 pounds)
1 cup chopped fresh cilantro
1/4 to 1/3 cup toasted sesame oil
Juice of 2 lemons
Juice of 1 lime

Kosher or fine sea salt and freshly ground
    pepper (preferably white)
1 jalapeño (or other chile of choice; see
    page 314), finely chopped (optional)

1. Trim any wilted or discolored leaves from the cabbage. Cut it crosswise into thin strips. (Cut the head in half lengthwise and remove the core first to make slicing easier.) You will have about 20 cups.

2. Toss the shredded cabbage and cilantro together in a large serving bowl. The cabbage and cilantro can be prepped up to a day in advance, but don't dress the salad until an hour before serving.

3. Whisk together 1/4 cup sesame oil, the lemon and lime juices, salt and pepper to taste, and the chile, if using, in a separate small bowl until the salt is dissolved. Taste and add more sesame oil if you like. Pour the dressing over the cabbage and toss to coat. Refrigerate for up to an hour, tossing occasionally. Serve cold.

Grilled Vegetable Salad ✑ ESCALIVADA (see photo, page 43)

Grilled vegetables are always a hit, but in Spain they are an art form, as we discovered during our trip to Barcelona. On an unusually balmy December day, we headed to the port of Barcelona and dined al-fresco on *fideuá* (a sort of noodle paella), *chipirones* (fried baby squid), and a breathtakingly beautiful large platter of this grilled vegetable salad. Dressed with just fragrant extra-virgin Spanish olive oil and a squeeze of lemon, it was perfection on a plate. (My version uses sherry vinegar, but feel free to use lemon juice instead.) I wish I had a picture of the smile on my face as I watched my children return to that platter over and over until it was wiped clean! The vegetables require constant attention while they are on the grill, but they can be grilled well before the main course.

MAKES 12 GENEROUS SERVINGS • PREP TIME: 30 MINUTES • COOK TIME: 45 MINUTES

4 small zucchini (about 5 ounces each)

2 large (preferably long) red bell peppers (about 8 ounces each)

1 large bulb fennel (about 1¼ pounds)

3 medium yellow onions (about 6 ounces each)

1 head radicchio (about 1 pound)

1 medium eggplant (about 1¼ pounds)

¾ cup olive oil, plus more as needed

Kosher or fine sea salt and freshly ground pepper

2 teaspoons sherry or other vinegar

1. Prepare the vegetables: Trim the ends from the zucchini and cut each one lengthwise into 3 slices (about ⅓ inch thick). Cut the ends off the bell peppers and cut them in half length-wise. Scoop and scrape out the cores and seeds, leaving the halves intact. Trim the stalks of the fennel flush with the bulb. Trim the root ends flush with the bottom of the bulb, and cut the fennel into ½-inch wedges through the core. Peel the onions, leaving the roots intact (to keep the pieces together during grilling), and cut them into quarters through the root. Cut the radicchio into 8 wedges through the core. Cut the ends off the eggplant and slice the eggplant into 1-inch rounds.

2. Put all the vegetables into a very large bowl (there should be room to toss the veggies; if not, work in batches). Drizzle ½ cup of the oil over the vegetables, season them liberally with salt and pepper, and toss until the vegetables are coated—if there is not enough oil to give the vegetables a nice gloss, add a little more oil.

3. If using a gas grill, heat one side to high and one side to medium-low. If using a charcoal grill, light the coals, then bank them (rake them out so the layer of coals is thick on one side and ta-pers gradually to thin on the other side). Grill denser vegetables, like the onions and fennel, over

medium-low heat (or the thinner layer of charcoal); medium-dense vegetables, like eggplant and radicchio, in the center, over moderate heat; and more delicate vegetables, like bell pepper and zucchini, over high heat (or the thicker layer of coals). It is difficult to gauge exact times, but the bell peppers and zucchini will take about 10 minutes; the skin of the peppers should be well charred, and the zucchini should be very tender, well browned, and even charred in places. The radicchio and eggplant will take 15 to 20 minutes and should be well browned, even charred in spots, on both sides. The onions and fennel will take the longest—about 30 minutes—and should be crisp-tender at the very center and charred in spots on the surface. Turn the vegetables occasionally as they cook (see Tips). If any of the vegetables start to char before they begin to soften, move them to a cooler part of the grill. Arrange the vegetables on a large serving platter as they are done. The vegetables can be grilled up to several hours before serving. Cover and keep at room temperature.

4. Just before serving, whisk the remaining ¼ cup olive oil and the sherry vinegar together in a small bowl. Season generously with salt and pepper and drizzle over the vegetables.

TIPS: Turn the vegetables occasionally, but not continually, as they grill. Turning them occasionally will help them cook and color evenly; turn them too frequently, and they won't brown or cook evenly.

This is quite a lot of vegetables—feel free to edit, using only some of the vegetables or fewer of some, like the onions, peppers, or zucchini.

Sparkling Mexican Limeade ✌ LIMONADA

Whether on the high plains of central Mexico in summer or in your own backyard, nothing beats this spritzy, tart, lightly sweet drink for flat-out, thirst-quenching goodness.

MAKES 8 SERVINGS (ABOUT 8 CUPS) • PREP TIME: 10 MINUTES

1 cup fresh lime juice (about 7 limes)
1 cup superfine sugar
$\frac{1}{2}$ teaspoon vanilla extract

Three 750-ml bottles or two 1-quart bottles
    sparkling mineral water or seltzer, chilled
Lime slices (optional)

1. Stir the lime juice, sugar, vanilla, and $\frac{1}{2}$ cup water together in a large pitcher until the sugar is dissolved. Chill thoroughly. The syrup can be made up to several hours before serving.
2. Just before serving, pour the sparkling water into the syrup and stir. Serve over ice, with a lime slice tucked into each glass if you like.

Michelada

This idea for a supercharged beer came to me from Carolina Penafiel, who tried something like this on a trip to Mexico. The smoke from the chipotle hot sauce, the tang of lime, and the unique zing of Worcestershire sauce make for an incredibly refreshing drink. You may not flip for this at your first sip the way I did, but I can pretty much guarantee that you have never tasted anything like it before. The amounts given here are just a suggestion—this needs to be fine-tuned to personal taste.

MAKES 1 DRINK

Juice of $\frac{1}{2}$ lime
$\frac{1}{2}$ teaspoon chipotle hot sauce
Big dash of Worcestershire sauce

One 12-ounce bottle light-bodied beer
    (Corona is a good start)

Put the lime juice, hot pepper sauce, and Worcestershire sauce in a large tumbler. Fill the tumbler halfway with ice and slowly pour in the beer. Find a hammock.

Borinquen Sunset ✑ PASSION FRUIT AND MANGO
PANNA COTTA WITH RASPBERRY SAUCE

Before Christopher Columbus visited the island of Puerto Rico in 1492—in fact, before it was *called* Puerto Rico—the islands were settled by Arawak Indians who originated in the Orinoco valley in South America, down around the region of what is now Venezuela. The Arawak who settled the island of Puerto Rico referred to themselves as *Tainos,* meaning "noble" or "good." The name for their island home, *Boriken,* means "Great Land of the Valiant and Noble Lord." The name "Boriken," although not used by the occupying Spanish, survived, along with other English words that were derived from the Taino language like "tobacco," "hammock," "hurricane," and, my favorite, "barbecue"

When my children were small, they loved to hear stories of my summers in Puerto Rico visiting my grandmother Clotilde, especially how my cousins and I would climb to the roof of the house to gather mangoes and avocados the size of footballs. I was able to travel to PR with my family a few years ago, and one evening I was contentedly sipping a passion fruit cocktail on the beach in Rio Mar, watching my kids frolic in the water as the sun was setting. The sky appeared to be ablaze, and it was beautiful enough to take my breath away. I reached over and took Jerry's hand and felt delirious happiness. When I came home, I whipped up this recipe as part of a romantic dinner. Its colors remind me of the sunset on that incredibly happy evening. Needless to say, Jerry totally got it!

MAKES 8 SERVINGS (ABOUT 1 CUP SAUCE) • PREP TIME: 20 MINUTES (PLUS 4 TO 24 HOURS CHILLING TIME)

FOR THE PANNA COTTA

1/2 cup sugar
1 tablespoon powdered gelatin
1 1/2 cups mango puree (see Note, page 121)
1/2 cup passion fruit puree (see Note, page 121)
2 cups heavy cream

FOR THE RASPBERRY SAUCE

One 10-ounce bag frozen raspberries
2 to 3 tablespoons sugar
Juice of 1/2 lime, or to taste

1. Make the panna cotta: Heat 3/4 cup water and the sugar in a small saucepan over medium heat, stirring, until the sugar is dissolved and the syrup is boiling. Remove from the heat.

2. Sprinkle the gelatin over 1/4 cup cool water in a small bowl. Let stand until softened, then stir the gelatin mixture into the sugar syrup until the gelatin is completely dissolved. Let cool to room temperature.

3. Stir the mango puree, passion fruit puree, and heavy cream together in a large bowl. Stir in the gelatin mixture thoroughly. Divide the mixture among eight 6-ounce ramekins or custard cups. Set the filled cups on a tray, cover them with a single sheet of plastic wrap, and chill until completely set, at least 4 hours. The panna cotta can be made up to a day in advance.

4. Make the sauce: Heat the raspberries, sugar to taste, and ¼ cup water in a small saucepan, stirring, until the mixture is simmering and the sugar is dissolved. Pass the mixture through a fine sieve into a small bowl, scraping the fruit with the back of a spoon to pass as much sauce through while keeping the seeds and pulp behind. Stir in lime juice to taste. Let cool and chill before serving.

5. To serve, invert each ramekin or custard cup over a dessert plate. Wait a few seconds, and the panna cotta will slip right out and onto the plate. Spoon some of the raspberry sauce around each serving and pass the remaining sauce separately.

Passion Fruit Tart with Fresh Berries

I'm not a sweets person, I'm a savory girl, but I know that some of my people love their sweets. I know that you can get by with a few trusty dessert recipes in your arsenal. Pâte à choux—French puff paste—which can be turned into everything from *churros* (see page 22) to cream puffs and éclairs, is a good example. This sweet pastry crust is another. Once made and baked "blind" (without any filling), it can be filled with pastry cream (another simple and versatile addition to your dessert repertoire!) flavored with just about any manner of fruit, chocolate, or nut you can think of. Top the cream with fruits that are *simpático* with the filling, and you've got an excellent make-ahead dessert.

The inspiration for this tart came from a passion fruit mousse I had at Social Paraiso, a restaurant in Buenos Aires where I had the most amazing lunch on the restaurant's patio on a gorgeous summer-in-December day.

MAKES 8 SERVINGS • PREP TIME: 45 MINUTES (PLUS CHILLING TIME FOR THE CRUST AND PASTRY CREAM) • COOK TIME: 45 MINUTES

FOR THE PASTRY
1³/₄ cups all-purpose flour
2 tablespoons sugar
Pinch of salt
7 tablespoons unsalted butter
1 extra-large egg, beaten with
   1 tablespoon ice water

FOR THE PASTRY CREAM
2¹/₄ cups milk
1 teaspoon vanilla extract
Pinch of salt
¹/₄ cup sugar

2 tablespoons all-purpose flour
2 tablespoons cornstarch
2 extra-large egg yolks
2 tablespoons passion fruit puree (see Note)

FOR THE TOPPING
1 pint blueberries
1 pint strawberries, hulled and cut
   in half lengthwise
¹/₂ pint raspberries
2 tablespoons seedless raspberry jam

1. Make the pastry: Put the flour, sugar, and salt in the work bowl of a food processor. Add the butter and pulse until the mixture looks sandy and there are no big pieces of butter. Add the egg–ice water mixture and process until the dough pulls away from the sides of the work bowl and is smooth. Shape into a disk, wrap the dough in plastic wrap, and refrigerate for at least 30 minutes, or up to a day.

2. Make the pastry cream: Heat the milk, vanilla, and salt in a medium saucepan over medium-low heat just until bubbles form around the edges. Remove from the heat.

3. Meanwhile, beat the sugar, flour, cornstarch, and egg yolks together in a medium bowl until smooth. Drizzle about ½ cup of the hot milk mixture into the flour mixture while whisking constantly. Scrape the flour mixture into the saucepan and cook, stirring constantly—especially in the corners of the pan—until the mixture is thickened and one or two bubbles break on the surface. Immediately remove from the heat and scrape the pastry cream into a clean bowl. Whisk in the passion fruit puree. Cover with a sheet of plastic wrap pressed directly onto the surface of the pasty cream and let cool to room temperature, then refrigerate until chilled. The pastry cream can be made up to 2 days in advance.

4. Preheat the oven to 375°F.

5. On a lightly floured work surface, roll the dough out to a 12-inch circle. Roll the dough up around the rolling pin and unroll it over a 9½ × 1-inch fluted tart pan with a removable bottom. Gently edge the dough into the corners of the pan and press the dough gently against the sides to keep it in place. Trim the overhanging dough by rolling over the rim with the rolling pin. Poke the bottom of the tart shell all over with the tines of a fork. Line the tart shell with a sheet of parchment and fill the shell with pie weights, dried beans, or rice.

6. Put the tart pan on a baking sheet and bake until the top edges start to brown, about 20 minutes. Remove the foil and weights and cook the shell until it begins to pull away from the sides of the pan and is light golden brown on the bottom, 5 to 10 minutes. Remove from the oven and let cool completely.

7. To assemble the tart, rinse the berries briefly under cool water and dry them well. Spoon the chilled pastry cream into the shell and spread it into an even layer. Arrange the berries over the top in any way that looks nice to you. (Scatter any extra berries over each serving of the tart when you serve it.)

8. Heat the jam and 2 tablespoons water in a small saucepan, stirring, until liquidy and well blended. Strain the glaze and brush over the berries. The tart should be served within 2 hours so the bottom crust doesn't become soggy.

NOTE: Goya (and other companies) make tropical fruit purees that are sold in the frozen fruit section of many supermarkets. Defrost the puree overnight in the refrigerator, or in a bowl of cold water. Another option is the line of excellent fruit purees produced by The Perfect Puree of Napa Valley. You can order their passion fruit puree online at www.perfectpuree.com.

"Fatback from the Heavens" ✏ TOCINO DEL CIELO

What is there left to say about a dessert whose name, literally translated, means "fatback from the heavens"? (Or "bacon from the heavens" or "lard from the heavens," depending on which corner of the Spanish-speaking world you happen to be in.) On our trip to Spain, my son David made sure he sampled *tocino* whenever it was on the menu. The texture of this dessert is the stuff dreams are made of, reminiscent of French pots de crème. When we had it in Spain, it was served in small pieces in little paper muffin liners with the corners mitered square, but I don't think the *tocino* police will give you any grief for using round muffin liners.

MAKES 16 SMALL SERVINGS • PREP TIME: 30 MINUTES (INCLUDES MAKING CARAMEL)
• COOK TIME: 50 MINUTES (PLUS 2 TO 24 HOURS CHILLING TIME)

FOR THE SYRUP

1¼ cups sugar

Zest of 1 orange, removed with a vegetable
   peeler

1 cinnamon stick

FOR THE CARAMEL

1¼ cups sugar

FOR THE CUSTARD

3 extra-large eggs

8 extra-large egg yolks

1 teaspoon vanilla extract

1. Make the syrup for the custard: Heat the sugar and ½ cup water to a boil in a medium saucepan over medium heat, to dissolve the sugar. Add the orange zest and cinnamon stick. Put a candy/deep-frying thermometer into the syrup, adjust the heat so the syrup is boiling gently, and cook until the temperature reaches 234°F; this can take anywhere from 10 to 15 minutes. Remove the syrup from the stove and let cool to room temperature.

2. While the syrup is cooling, make the caramel with the 1¼ cups sugar and ¼ cup water (see Caramelicious, page 124) and line the bottom and sides of a 9-inch square glass baking dish with it.

3. Preheat the oven to 350°F.

4. When the syrup for the custard is cool, make the custard: Beat the eggs, egg yolks, and vanilla in a mixing bowl until smooth. Strain the syrup into the egg mixture, whisking constantly.

5. Pour the custard into the caramel-lined dish. Pull out the oven rack and set a roasting pan on the rack. Put the baking dish in the roasting pan and pour in enough warm water to come halfway up the sides of the dish. Bake until the center is barely set—it should jiggle slightly when the baking dish is shaken gently—about 50 minutes. Let cool completely, then chill for at least 2 hours, or up to 1 day, before serving.

(continued)

6. To serve, run the blade of a table knife around the edges of the custard. Center a large serving plate over the baking dish and, with one bold move, invert the custard onto the dish. Give it a second, and the custard will slip easily from the dish onto the plate. (The longer the custard chills, the easier it will be to unmold.) Cut into 16 squares and serve, in small paper muffin liners if you like. Keep the serving size small—it is a very rich dessert.

Caramelicious

For the home cook, caramel is sometimes an ordeal. Even I, who have made a flan or two in my day, went on a little streak where the sugar kept seizing—crystallizing—no matter what I did. To end my little slump, I came up with this method, which has worked every time I've used it. There are two big differences between this method and the traditional method: I use a wide skillet instead of a saucepan and I start out with much more water than is usual. The first eliminates the need to fuss with the syrup by washing down the sides of the pan with a brush dipped in water (as directed in most caramel recipes), and the second ensures that the sugar will melt completely before starting to color. I hope this simple method encourages people who are leery about making caramel to give it a shot. It will open the door to all kinds of simple desserts, from flans to the incredibly delicious "Fatback from the Heavens" on page 123.

To make the caramel, first set yourself up: Have ready the baking dish or other equipment called for in the recipe and a pair of thick pot holders or oven mitts. Mound the amount of sugar called for in the recipe in the center of a large heavy skillet. Pour the water called for around the sugar and place the skillet over medium heat. Swirl the pan to completely dissolve the sugar as the liquid heats. Then cook, swirling the pan gently but not stirring, until you see the sugar start to color. Continue cooking, swirling the pan gently so the caramel cooks evenly, until the caramel is a deep copper color. Immediately pour the caramel into the baking dish. Grasp the edges of the dish with pot holders or mitts—caramel is incredibly hot and will heat up the dish in no time flat—and carefully tilt the dish to cover the bottom and sides until it is well and evenly coated. As the caramel starts to cool, it will move more slowly. Set the dish down on a heatproof surface and be careful—it will stay hot for quite some time.

Pan-Seared Cod with Lentils and Chorizo (page 226)

The evening meal is the one that I can always look forward to sharing with my family, whether we are traveling or not, and if I can fit a few friends at the table, well, the more the merrier! Evening dining doesn't have to be complicated, because, let's face it, as a working mom, I don't have a lot of spare time during the week, but you will find some really delicious, uncomplicated recipes, like Pan-Seared Cod with Lentils and Chorizo, or the Artichoke, Potato, and Serrano Tortilla, that make for inspired weeknight dining.

When I have the luxury of time on my hands and really want to rock the pots and pans, I put a few nibbles together, like Rice Croquettes or Twice-Fried Plantain Cups, and serve something fun to sip, and I have all the makings of a cocktail party. Dinner parties are the perfect opportunity to really flex my cooking muscles in the kitchen, and you will find mouthwatering recipes in this section that will have you running to the kitchen to perform some culinary calisthenics of your own!

NIGHT

WEEKNIGHT DINNERS

Everyone who is faced with the challenge of putting dinner on the table after a hectic workday approaches it a little differently. To some, the solution is a revolving door of take-out options; to others, it's the can-of-soup casserole approach. Having raised four kids (and played mom to a slew of their friends), I know the time constraints are real. I also know I am not going to compromise on flavor or quality. So my approach is a little different: I spend a couple of hours in the kitchen every Sunday putting a few trusty basics in the "bank" and then make withdrawals from my account during the week. These couple of hours don't seem like work to me—it is my time to relax. Usually on a Sunday, the kids are off doing their own thing, Jerry might be making rounds at the hospital or conked out on the couch, and I have the kitchen to myself.

This approach pays big-time dividends. But let me make it clear that it doesn't have to be Sunday, it doesn't have to take two hours, and it doesn't even have to be every week. Most of the secret weapons called for in the recipes in this chapter (chicken broth, sofrito, and achiote oil, for example) can be refrigerated for at least a couple of days or frozen for much longer. So, if you find yourself with an hour or two to spare one day, why not put together some of these basics to streamline your weeknight meals for a couple of weeks? Even if you have only half an hour every other week to spare, you can still make sofrito and achiote oil and be that much ahead of the game.

A STITCH IN TIME: One more note about getting a leg up on weeknight dinner prep: Throughout the book, you will see the heading "A Stitch in Time." These simple suggestions are tips on how to get two meals out of one stint at the stove. Double a batch of the plain rice that you serve with Braised Chicken with Coconut Milk and Curry (page 139), for example, and turn the leftovers into a 15-minute Peruvian version of fried rice (page 68) later in the week. Make a double batch of Spanish Blue Cheese Dressing (page 130), serve half over iceberg lettuce with a roast chicken dinner one night, and spoon the rest over baked potatoes later in the week. Once you start thinking like this, you'll be surprised at the amount of time you can save.

Sundays in the Kitchen with Daisy

You've heard the expression "There is no such thing as a free lunch." If you ask me, there's no such thing as a free dinner either. The secret to putting delicious homemade meals on the table fast during a hectic workweek is to spend a little—and I mean a little—of your spare time in the kitchen to stock your larder.

Here is how a typical Sunday might go:

1. Shoo out anybody who is hanging around the kitchen. Put a little Willie Colón on the CD player.

2. Put up a pot of Homemade Chicken Broth (page 303), and heat the oven to 375°F.

3. While waiting for the stock to come to a boil, prep 4 heads of garlic and start them roasting (page 309). Then make enough Achiote Oil (page 306) to get through the week—it keeps beautifully at room temp.

4. Once the stock is skimmed and the garlic is roasting, they won't need any attention for an hour or so. Put up a pot of dried beans (page 161), either black beans to turn into a soup later in the week or any other kind that tickles your fancy. (Here's where my soakless method of cooking beans comes in handy!) Then just reheat the beans a day or three later, and you've got a side dish. Or a way to stretch yellow rice (page 157) into a meal. Or the makings of a batch of New-Style "Refried" Beans (page 162).

5. While the beans and broth are perking, it's on to my lifeline (and one you won't find on *Who Wants to Be a Millionaire*): Sofrito (page 305). In 15 minutes, you can have eight freezer bags, with 1 cup of sofrito in each, tucked into the freezer. Frozen assets to spark off a big potful of yellow rice, kick some chicken curry into high gear, or even "Daisify" a batch of spaghetti and meatballs.

6. After just an hour or two, the garlic is cooling, the beans are almost done, and the chicken broth is about ready to be strained. The cut-up chicken that enriched the stock is another shortcut, ready to be shredded back into the broth for a head start on Mexican Chicken-Lime Soup (page 213) or to turn into a panful of Arroz con Pollo (page 270), Chicken Braised in Peruvian Yellow Pepper Puree (page 273), or a batch of croquettes (page 198).

Didn't that feel good?

Avocado Stuffed with Crab-Mango Salad

This lively little salad spiked with red onion and chile makes a nice fresh starter for a weeknight meal. Follow it up with something simple—the Pigeon Peas in Coconut Milk on page 163 and plain white rice would be perfect. Especially in warmer weather, it also makes the move to lunch or brunch nicely. Here's a little confession: when the kids were young and I needed my mother to babysit in a pinch, this salad was the draw. It has all her favorites in one dish: buttery avocado, juicy-tart mango, and sweet crab.

MAKES 6 SERVINGS • PREP TIME: 25 MINUTES

1 lime

2 tablespoons olive oil

2 tablespoons chopped fresh cilantro

$1/2$ mango, peeled and cut into $1/4$-inch dice (about 1 cup)

$1/3$ cup diced ($1/4$-inch) red bell pepper

$1/3$ cup diced ($1/4$-inch) red onion

$1/2$ jalapeño, cut into small dice (about 2 tablespoons)

$1/2$ pound jumbo lump crabmeat, picked over for shells and cartilage

3 Hass avocados

Kosher or fine sea salt and freshly ground pepper

1. Finely grate the zest of the lime; set aside. Halve the lime and squeeze the juice from one half into a bowl. Add the olive oil, cilantro, and lime zest and whisk well. Add the mango, bell pepper, onion, and jalapeño and toss to coat. Stir in the crabmeat gently, to keep it from breaking up. Set aside.

2. Cut the avocados in half and remove the pits. Peel the avocado halves if you like. Squeeze the juice of the remaining lime half over the avocado flesh, using the lime half to paint it evenly over the avocados, to keep them from turning black.

3. Toss the crab salad and season with salt and pepper to taste. Mound the crab salad in the avocado halves, dividing it evenly. (Use an ice cream scoop for neat, even rounds if that's your thing.) Serve right away.

TIP: To keep the avocados from sliding around the plates, cut a thin sliver of skin (or flesh) from the rounded side of each half before filling them. That flat side will help keep the avocado steady on the plate.

Simple Salad with Spanish Blue Cheese Dressing

When people think Spanish + blue cheese, they usually come up with Cabrales. I have nothing against Cabrales, but if you run across Valdeón in your travels, don't pass it by. Valdeón is a wonderful blue-veined cheese made from goat's and cow's milk. It is wrapped in leaves (sycamore or chestnut) before aging, which lends the cheese an herby, earthy scent.

MAKES 6 SERVINGS • PREP TIME: 15 MINUTES

FOR THE DRESSING (MAKES ABOUT 2¼ CUPS)

1 cup crema Mexicana or sour cream

¾ cup store-bought mayonnaise

Juice of 1 lime

½ cup chopped fresh chives

1 cup crumbled Valdeón or other blue cheese

Pinch of cayenne pepper

Kosher or fine sea salt and freshly ground pepper

1 large head iceberg lettuce or 2 hearts of romaine or 6 romaine rings (see Note)

1. Whisk the crema, mayonnaise, and lime juice together in a medium bowl. Fold in the chives and cheese. Season with cayenne and salt and pepper to taste. The dressing can be made up to 1 week in advance and refrigerated. Remove from the refrigerator about 30 minutes before serving.

2. If using iceberg lettuce, strip off any wilted or brown leaves. Hold the lettuce, core side down, and whack the core lightly on the counter—this should loosen the core and make it easy to pull right out. Cut the head into 6 more or less equal wedges. If using romaine, pull off any wilty leaves from the outside and cut each head into 3 wedges through the core.

3. Set each serving of lettuce on a plate and drizzle some of the dressing over it. Pass the remaining dressing separately.

NOTE: To make romaine rings, strip any wilted outer leaves from good-size firm heads of romaine. Keeping the heads intact, spread the leaves back gently and rinse the leaves under cool running water. Shake out as much of the water as you can. Starting about 2 inches from the base, tie the romaine snugly at 2-inch intervals with kitchen twine. Cut the romaine crosswise between the twine into 2-inch rounds. Set them cut side down on a serving plate and gently remove the twine. All right, so maybe you won't do this on a weeknight, but keep it in mind as a way to dress up your next romaine salad.

Calabaza and White Bean Soup

I can thank my mother for the inspiration for this soup—it is pretty much her recipe for calabaza and white beans, thinned out with a little broth and reinforced with little pasta shapes. You can bolster yours with rice or thin egg noodles instead, if that's what floats your boat. This is a nice cold-weather starter, but it can certainly be the main event, especially when made with a little less broth for an even denser soup. And if there is some leftover cooked chicken, pork, or beef lurking in your fridge, coarsely shred it and stir it in just to heat it through. One note: This is not the place for limp store-bought broth. You need a broth with some oomph. If you don't have the real thing, use my quick method for doctoring canned broth.

MAKES 6 SERVINGS • PREP TIME: 10 MINUTES • COOK TIME: 25 MINUTES

12 cups Homemade Chicken Broth (page 303) or "Paging Doctored Broth!" (page 305)

3 cups diced ($\frac{1}{2}$-inch) calabaza (see Note)

2 cups ditalini or other little pasta shape

One 15$\frac{1}{2}$-ounce can white beans, drained and rinsed

Kosher or fine sea salt and freshly ground pepper

$\frac{1}{4}$ cup finely chopped fresh cilantro

Vinagre (page 308) for serving

1. Bring the chicken broth to a boil in a 5-quart pot over medium heat. Add the calabaza and return to a boil, then adjust the heat so the stock is simmering. Skim any foam that rises to the surface. Cook until the squash can be easily pierced with a fork, about 10 minutes.

2. Stir in the pasta and beans. Cook, stirring often so the pasta doesn't clump together, until the pasta is tender but with a little bit of bite—usually a minute or two less than the package directions call for. Season with salt and pepper to taste. Stir in the cilantro.

(continued)

3. Ladle the soup into warm bowls and drizzle a tablespoon or so of *vinagre* over each. Pass the *vinagre* at the table too, for those who are feeling frisky!

NOTE: Calabazas are very large squashes. Most places that sell whole calabazas also sell wedges cut from whole squash. You will need a wedge weighing about 1¼ pounds to yield 3 cups peeled and seeded diced squash. Half a 2½-pound butternut squash can be substituted for the calabaza.

Calabaza and White Bean Soup

Tuna "Chilindron" with Penne

Think of *chilindron* as a Spanish version of the Italian classic cacciatore. Like cacciatore, *chilindron* is often made with rabbit or other kinds of game. This is my own take on the theme, which I developed on one of those "Crikey, I need dinner on the table in a hurry" nights. The only wild game on hand was the canned tuna I hunted down in the pantry. The smoked paprika lends a very nice aroma, and the fresh peppers (always on hand in the veggie drawer) keep their shape and bite through the brief cooking. Bottled roasted peppers have their place, as in the Oven-Roasted Halibut with Black Olive Tapenade on page 224, but for this dish, fresh is the only way to go.

This is a win/win/win recipe: it's easy on the pocketbook, kids love it, and it lands on the table in about half an hour.

MAKES 6 SERVINGS • PREP TIME: 20 MINUTES • COOK TIME: 15 MINUTES

¼ cup extra-virgin olive oil

1 medium Spanish onion, cut in half lengthwise, then into ½-inch-wide strips

4 cloves garlic, thinly sliced

2 teaspoons chile powder

1 teaspoon smoked paprika

1 teaspoon dried oregano

1 red bell pepper, cored, seeded, and cut into ½-inch-wide strips

1 yellow bell pepper, cored, seeded, and cut into ½-inch-wide strips

1 orange bell pepper, cored, seeded cut into ½-inch-wide strips

One 28-ounce can crushed tomatoes

Two 12-ounce cans chunk light or solid white tuna (your choice) packed in water, drained

6 large fresh basil leaves, finely shredded (see Tip)

Kosher or fine sea salt and freshly ground pepper

1 pound penne

Chopped fresh flat-leaf parsley (optional)

1. Bring a large pot of salted water to a boil over high heat.
2. Meanwhile, start the sauce: Heat 2 tablespoons of the olive oil in a large skillet over medium-high heat until hot but not smoking. Add the onion and garlic, lower the heat to medium, and cook, stirring, until the onion is soft, about 4 minutes.
3. Sprinkle the chile powder, paprika, and oregano over the onion and toss to incorporate. Add the bell peppers, raise the heat to high, and cook, stirring, until the peppers start to soften

(continued on page 135)

133

(you don't want them sad, just relaxed), 2 to 3 minutes. Stir in the crushed tomatoes, tuna, and basil. Adjust the heat so the sauce is simmering and season lightly with salt and pepper. Cover the skillet and cook just until the sauce is heated through and bubbly. The peppers should have a little tooth. Keep warm over very low heat.

4. Stir the penne into the boiling water and cook, stirring occasionally, until it is tender but with a little bit of bite, usually about 1 or 2 minutes less than the package directions call for.

5. Ladle out a cup or so of the pasta cooking water and set aside. Drain the pasta, return it to the pot, and stir in the sauce. If the sauce is a bit tight, add enough of the reserved pasta water to loosen it up.

6. Drizzle the remaining 2 tablespoons olive oil over the pasta, turn the pasta out onto a serving platter, and sprinkle chopped parsley, if using, over the top.

TIP: The fastest way to turn basil leaves into a beautiful, finely shredded "chiffonade" is to pull off the larger stems and stack half a dozen or so leaves. If the leaves are large, roll them up into a compact roll and slice them crosswise into thin ribbons. If the leaves are small, just leave them flat and slice them crosswise. This stacking-and-rolling trick works well for other large-leaf herbs like sage and mint, and for leafy greens like chard, collard greens, arugula, and spinach.

Linguine with Artichoke–Serrano Ham "Bolognese"

Pull the boxes of artichokes from the freezer and pop them into the fridge on your way out the door to work in the morning, and the prep for this delicious pasta can be done by the time the water comes to a boil.

MAKES 6 SERVINGS • PREP TIME: 20 MINUTES • COOK TIME: 30 MINUTES

2 tablespoons olive oil

1 medium Spanish onion, chopped

2 stalks celery, trimmed and cut into
  1/4-inch dice

1 carrot, peeled and cut into 1/4-inch dice

6 cloves roasted garlic, homemade (page
  310) or store-bought, minced

Two 9-ounce boxes frozen artichoke hearts,
  defrosted and drained

1/4 pound serrano ham or prosciutto, cut
  into 1/4-inch dice

6 fresh basil leaves, finely shredded (see
  Tip, page 135)

One 28-ounce can crushed tomatoes

2 cups heavy cream

1/8 teaspoon ground nutmeg, preferably
  freshly grated

Kosher or fine sea salt and freshly ground
  pepper

1 pound linguine

1. Bring a large pot of salted water to a boil over high heat.

2. Meanwhile, start the sauce: Heat the olive oil in a large deep skillet over medium-high heat. Add the onion, celery, carrot, and garlic and cook until the onion is soft and translucent and the other vegetables are softened, about 5 minutes.

3. In the meantime, pulse the artichoke hearts in a food processor until well chopped. Stir the artichokes into the onion-garlic mixture, lower the heat, and cook for a minute or two. Stir in the ham and basil, raise the heat to high, and cook just until the ham is fragrant, a minute or two. Pour in the crushed tomatoes and cream. Add the nutmeg and season lightly with salt and pepper. Bring the sauce to a boil, then adjust the heat so the sauce is simmering and cook until slightly thickened, about 20 minutes. The sauce can be made up to 2 days in advance and refrigerated. Bring to a simmer before proceeding.

4. When the sauce has been simmering for about 10 minutes, stir the linguine into the boiling water. Cook, stirring occasionally, until tender but with a little bit of bite—usually a minute or two less than the package directions.

5. Ladle out about 1 cup of the pasta cooking water and set aside. Drain the pasta and return it to the pot. Add the sauce and stir over low heat until the pasta is coated and the sauce is bubbling. If the sauce is too thick to coat the pasta evenly and smoothly, stir in some of the reserved pasta cooking water a tablespoon at a time.

6. Turn the pasta out onto a serving platter and serve hot.

A STITCH IN TIME: The sauce freezes beautifully, so if you are cooking for 2 or 3 (not 6), make the full batch and freeze half.

Work-Night Chicken Breasts

The only trick to this dish is to brown the chicken in a really hot pan—it should sing when it hits the skillet. While the chicken bakes, I finish my side dish or toss a salad.

MAKES 6 SERVINGS • PREP TIME: 10 MINUTES • COOK TIME: 25 MINUTES

1 cup orange juice (freshly squeezed is nice but not mandatory)

Juice of 3 lemons

2 tablespoons dry adobo, homemade (page 307) or store-bought

6 boneless, skinless chicken breasts (about 2½ pounds)

1 cup all-purpose flour

Grapeseed or vegetable oil

¾ cup dry white wine

¼ cup chicken broth, homemade (page 303) or store-bought

¼ cup chopped fresh cilantro

1. Stir the orange juice, two-thirds of the lemon juice, and the dry adobo together in a large baking dish or bowl. Add the chicken breasts and turn to coat with the marinade. Marinate at room temperature for a minimum of 15 minutes, or refrigerate for up to 2 hours, turning once or twice.

2. Preheat the oven to 375°F.

3. Drain the chicken breasts and discard the marinade. Pat the chicken breasts dry. Spread the flour out on a wide plate. Drizzle enough grapeseed oil into a heavy ovenproof skillet (cast iron is ideal) to coat the bottom generously and heat over medium-high heat. Dredge the chicken in the flour to coat all sides and shake off the excess flour. Lay as many breasts in the skillet as will fit comfortably and cook, turning once, until golden brown on both sides, about 6 minutes. (The chicken will not be cooked through, just browned well.) Transfer the chicken to a platter and repeat with the remaining chicken if necessary, adding a little more oil to the pan.

4. When all the chicken is browned, pour the wine into the skillet and stir to scrape up the brown bits sticking to the bottom. When the wine is reduced by about half, add the chicken broth. Return the chicken breasts to the skillet and add the cilantro and the remaining lemon juice.

5. Cover the pan loosely with aluminum foil, transfer to the oven, and bake until no trace of pink remains in the thickest part of the breasts, about 15 minutes.

TIP: Finishing the chicken in the oven instead of on the stovetop ensures that it will cook evenly and gently, without drying out—or the need to turn it! Plus, it clears a little room on the stovetop in case you need it.

Work-Night Chicken Breasts and Basic Yellow Rice (page 157)

Braised Chicken with Coconut Milk and Curry

You will see variations on a coconut-curry-tomato theme all over Puerto Rico and the Dominican Republic. This combo is used to braise goat, simmer eggplant, and make a seafood stew. In my take, the tomato, and a whole lot more, comes from my trusty sofrito. All you'll need to round out the meal is some plain rice—but the Spinach Rice on page 159 would be nice too.

MAKES 6 SERVINGS • PREP TIME: 10 MINUTES (WITH ALREADY-MADE SOFRITO, 25 MINUTES WITHOUT) • COOK TIME: 45 MINUTES

2 small (about 3-pound) chickens, each cut into 10 pieces (see Note, page 304)

Kosher or fine sea salt and freshly ground pepper

Vegetable oil

1 cup Sofrito (page 305)

1½ teaspoons curry powder

¼ teaspoon ground cloves

¼ cup all-purpose flour

1 cup chicken broth, homemade (page 303) or store-bought

One 13½-ounce can unsweetened coconut milk

1. Pat the chicken pieces dry with paper towels. Season them generously on all sides with salt and pepper. Pour enough vegetable oil into a large Dutch oven (or other heavy pot with a lid) to cover the bottom of the pot. Heat over medium-high heat. Lay as many pieces of chicken in the pan as will fit without bumping up against each other and cook, turning as necessary, until browned on all sides, about 10 minutes. Adjust the heat as necessary during browning to keep up a lively sizzle, not an out-of-control sputtering. Remove the chicken from the pot and repeat with the remaining pieces.

2. Pour or spoon off all but ¼ cup of the fat from the pot. Add the sofrito, curry powder, and cloves and cook until the liquid has evaporated and the sofrito is sizzling. Lower the heat and whisk in the flour, then continue whisking until the flour absorbs all the oil. Slowly pour in the chicken broth and coconut milk while continuing to whisk. Season lightly with salt and pepper and bring the sauce to a simmer over medium heat.

3. Return the chicken to the pot, cover, and cook until the chicken is very tender (almost falling from the bone), about 25 minutes. Check the chicken a few times while it cooks to make sure the sauce stays at a gentle simmer. While you're at it, turn the chicken pieces over and move them around so everything cooks evenly.

(continued)

4. Spoon the chicken into warm serving bowls or set the Dutch oven on the table and serve from it.

A STITCH IN TIME: Like most stews, this curry gets better if it sits for 2 or 3 days. So even if you're cooking for fewer than 6, go ahead and make the whole batch with an eye toward reheating the leftovers later in the week. And if you get carried away and eat more than half the chicken, just cook up some Chinese-style egg noodles or angel hair pasta and serve the stew over them the second time around to stretch it out a bit.

Braised Chicken with Coconut Milk and Curry and Spinach Rice (page 159)

Faster-Than-Take-out Chicken in Green Sauce

For years, my take on shellfish in green sauce *(mariscada en salsa verde)*, the Spanish classic, has been a weeknight staple. In one of those "aha!" moments, I thought of making essentially the same dish with seared boneless chicken breasts standing in for the shellfish. This is extra saucy—be sure to have some rice, like the Basic Yellow Rice on page 157, on hand. Or boil up some angel hair pasta or linguine while the chicken is simmering and serve the chicken and all its delicious sauce over the pasta.

MAKES 4 SERVINGS • PREP TIME: 20 MINUTES • COOKING TIME: 20 MINUTES

4 large boneless skinless chicken breasts (about 2 pounds)
Kosher or fine sea salt and freshly ground pepper
⅓ cup extra-virgin olive oil
6 to 8 cloves garlic, chopped
1 chile of your choice (see page 314), finely chopped (optional)

2 bunches flat-leaf parsley, leaves only (or leaves from 1 bunch parsley plus 1 bunch cilantro, stems and all), chopped
½ cup dry white wine
½ cup chicken broth, homemade (page 303) or store-bought
2 teaspoons cornstarch
⅓ cup milk

1. Pat the chicken dry with paper towels. Season them generously with salt and pepper. Heat the olive oil in a wide shallow pan (a paella pan works perfectly) over medium-high heat. Lay the chicken breasts in the pan and cook, turning once, just until deep golden brown on both sides, about 6 minutes. (The chicken will finish cooking in the sauce.) Transfer the chicken to a plate.

2. Add the garlic and chile, if using, to the oil left in the pan and cook for a minute or two, until soft but not colored. Stir in three-quarters of the chopped parsley or the parsley-cilantro mix and wine, raise the heat to high, and cook until almost all of the wine is evaporated. Pour in the chicken broth.

3. Stir the cornstarch and milk together in a small bowl until the cornstarch is dissolved. Whisk the cornstarch mixture into the pan and lower the heat. Return the chicken to the pan, cover, and cook, turning the chicken once, until no trace of pink remains at the thickest part of the chicken breasts, about 12 minutes. Stir in the remaining parsley or parsley-cilantro mix. Check the sauce and adjust the seasoning, adding salt and pepper as you like.

Panfried Breaded Veal, Turkey, Pork, Beef, or Chicken Cutlets *∽ MILANESAS*

Here is the master plan for making juicy *milanesas* with a crisp coating. Virtually any fresh herb or ground spice—oregano, sage, parsley, basil, cumin, or coriander, to name a few—can be added to the bread-crumb coating. A little finely grated Parmesan cheese makes a nice addition too. See opposite for a few serving ideas or, better yet, come up with a few of your own.

MAKES 6 SERVINGS • PREP TIME: 10 MINUTES • COOK TIME: 10 MINUTES

Six 3- to 4-ounce veal, turkey, pork, beef, or
    chicken cutlets (see opposite page for a
    description of options)
Kosher or fine sea salt and freshly ground
    pepper

4 extra-large eggs
1 cup all-purpose flour
2 cups fine dry bread crumbs
Canola oil, for frying
Lemon wedges, for serving

1. Pound out the cutlets: Tear off 2 good-size pieces of plastic wrap. Center a cutlet over one of the sheets and top with the other sheet. With a meat mallet or the bottom of a small heavy saucepan, pound the cutlet to an even ¼-inch thickness (or as close as you can manage). Use good, firm whacks, but try not to tear holes in the cutlet. Put the pounded cutlet on a baking sheet and repeat with the remaining cutlets. Season them well with salt and pepper.

2. Set up a breading station: Beat the eggs with a few drops of water in a wide shallow bowl. Spread the flour and bread crumbs on separate plates. One at a time, dredge each cutlet in the flour to coat both sides and shake off the excess flour. Dip the floured cutlet in the egg until it is coated, and hold it over the bowl for a few seconds to let the excess egg drip back into the bowl. Lay the cutlet flat in the bread crumbs and turn once or twice, patting the crumbs onto the cutlet to help them stick. Shake off the excess crumbs and lay out the cutlet on a clean baking sheet (or wire rack; see Tip).

3. Pour about ½ inch of canola oil into a large skillet and heat over medium-high heat. The oil should be hot enough to give off a very lively sizzle when an edge of a breaded cutlet is dipped into it, but not smoking. Add as many cutlets as will fit in the pan without overlapping, lower the heat to medium-high, and cook until the undersides are crisp and golden, about 2 minutes. Turn the cutlets over to brown the other sides, 2 to 3 minutes. Drain on paper towels. Fry any remaining cutlets, replacing the oil in the pan and giving it time to reheat as necessary. Serve the cutlets with lemon wedges.

Milanesa

Everywhere you go in Argentina, you will run into *milanesa,* a breaded and panfried cutlet of chicken, pork, turkey, veal, or—this is Argentina we're talking about, after all—beef. *La milanesa* makes its appearance for breakfast on a roll with a fried egg, for lunch as a light entrée, or for dinner with all sorts of side-dish possibilities. It is not unusual to be offered a large *milanesa* cut into strips as a tapa with drinks in someone's home. Below are some pointers for starting out with the right cuts of meat or poultry for breading and frying. The simple recipe for breading and frying the cutlets and a handful of serving ideas are on pages 142 and 144.

Just about any kind of meat or poultry can be turned into a milanesa. But it helps, especially with beef and pork, if the cutlets are cut across the grain. That ensures a fork-tender consistency in the finished result, not to mention easier pounding. Turkey and chicken cutlets are easy to prepare at home. If you have a cooperative butcher or access to a supermarket with a real person behind the meat counter, pork, beef, or veal will be a snap too. Regardless of which type of *milanesa* you are preparing, start with something in the neighborhood of a 3- to 4-ounce cutlet that measures about ¼ inch thick before it is pounded out.

PORK—Use very thin (about ¼ inch), even slices cut across the grain from a center-cut loin of pork roast.

BEEF—Use very thin (about ¼ inch), even slices cut across the grain from an eye round roast, or look for cubed steak in the prepackaged meat section of the supermarket.

VEAL—A lot of things are sold under the name "veal scaloppine" or "veal cutlets" in supermarket cases. Most of them will work for preparing a *milanesa*. Ideally, though, the veal for *milanesa* (like the beef and pork) should be cut across the grain from a single muscle to make for easy flattening and tender results.

CHICKEN—"Chicken cutlets" are sold in most supermarkets. Take a look at the package, and if they appear to be ¼ inch thick or so and in nice, large pieces, go ahead and buy them. Then simply pound them out according to the directions in the recipe. If they look superthin and/or ratty, buy whole boneless chicken breasts and slice them horizontally in half before pounding them out. The sliced chicken breasts may be thicker than ¼ inch, but they will be easy to pound out to ¼ inch as described in the recipe. If any of the little "fillets" underneath become detached while you are prepping the chicken breasts, just set them aside, then make "mini *milanesas*" with them and fry them up along with their bigger brothers.

TURKEY—Finding turkey cutlets that work for *milanesa* is a relatively easy task in most supermarkets. Look for boneless turkey breasts that have been thinly sliced across the grain and are labeled "turkey scallops" or "turkey cutlets." Like sliced chicken breasts, the turkey cutlets may be thicker than ¼ inch, but they will pound out nicely.

TIP: If you own a wire cooling rack (or two), this is a good place to use it. After the cutlets are breaded, lay them on the rack(s) while the oil is heating. This will firm up the coating and help keep the crumbs in place during frying, and it will also prevent the breading from getting soggy.

How to Serve a *Milanesa*

Would you like a side of fries with that? The Cumin-Scented Fried Potatoes on page 153 would go very nicely. If that sounds like too much fried for one plate, top the *milanesas* with a salad of baby greens tossed in a light vinaigrette, or serve the Simple Salad with Spanish Blue Cheese Dressing (page 130) alongside. In Argentina, any of the *milanesas* might be served on top of a chopped salad of onion, tomato, lettuce, and portobello mushrooms. They might also be served *a la napolitana*, that is, topped with a light napping of tomato sauce, a slice of prosciutto or ham, and one of mozzarella cheese and heated until the cheese is melty and delicious.

Chicken *milanesa* with a little green salad

Shrimp Tacos with Tomato-Avo Salsa (see photo, page ii)

MAKES 6 SERVINGS • PREP TIME: 30 MINUTES (INCLUDING MAKING THE *MOJO*)
• COOK TIME: 5 MINUTES

12 wooden or metal skewers

FOR THE SALSA

1 large tomato (about 8 ounces), cored and
  cut into $1/2$-inch dice

1 Hass avocado, halved, pitted, peeled, and
  cut into $1/4$-inch dice (about $1 1/4$ cups)

$1/2$ small red onion, cut into $1/4$-inch dice
  (about $1/2$ cup)

$1/4$ cup chopped fresh cilantro

1 clove garlic, minced

Juice of 1 lime

Kosher or fine sea salt and freshly ground
  pepper

12 corn tortillas

12 U-10 shrimp (see Note), peeled and
  deveined

Kosher or fine sea salt

$1/3$ cup Spicy Ancho Chile *Mojo* (page 308),
  plus more for serving

1. Heat a gas grill to high or build a strong charcoal fire. Preheat the oven to 300°F. Soak the wooden skewers, if using, for 30 minutes in warm water to cover.

2. Make the salsa: Stir the tomato, avocado, red onion, cilantro, and garlic together in a bowl. Add the lime juice and season with salt and pepper to taste. Refrigerate while you prepare the shrimp.

3. Wrap the tortillas in aluminum foil and place in the oven to warm while you grill the shrimp.

4. Skewer the shrimp (1 per skewer): Holding the shrimp straight (not in its natural C shape), pass a skewer through the center of each shrimp from the tail to the head end. When all the shrimp have been skewered, season them with salt and brush generously with the *mojo*. Grill the shrimp, turning once, just until they are opaque at the center of the thickest part, 2 to 3 minutes on each side. Brush with additional sauce when you turn them, if you like.

5. To serve, slide each shrimp off the skewer onto a tortilla, and spoon on some of the salsa. Pass additional *mojo* at the table.

NOTE: Shrimp are sold (and priced) according to size. Many supermarkets and fish stores have started to post these sizes instead of vague terms like "jumbo" or "large." When a range is given, "16–20" or "30–40," for example, that is the number of shrimp in a pound. Often larger shrimp are labeled "U-12" or "U-15," which means there are under 12 or under 15 shrimp per pound. Labeling shrimp this way is definitely more helpful than calling them "super colossal."

Pan-Seared Red Snapper with Weeknight Salsa

When the kids and I were traveling throughout Puerto Rico, we drove to the beautiful beach town of Naguabo, which boasted numerous oceanside "restaurants" (more like stands, really!). They specialized in serving up the catch of the day, which in Puerto Rico is usually red snapper or, as the Boricuas call it, *chillo*. The snapper is usually fried whole, head and tail included, until crispy and delicious, then served with *ensalada* (page 152), *tostones* (page 189), and a bottle of spicy *vinagre* (see page 308) on the side. I washed the whole thing down with an ice-cold India beer, and I can guarantee you that nothing in the world ever tasted so good!

MAKES 6 SERVINGS • PREP TIME: 20 MINUTES • COOK TIME: 15 MINUTES

FOR THE SALSA

2 tomatoes, seeded and chopped (about 2 cups)

1 small Spanish onion, chopped (about ½ cup)

2 tablespoons chopped fresh cilantro

Juice of 1 lime

1 tablespoon olive oil

Minced chile of your choice (see page 314)

Kosher or fine sea salt and freshly ground pepper

Canola oil, for frying

6 red snapper fillets (about 6 ounces each), skin on

Kosher or fine sea salt and freshly ground pepper

All-purpose flour, for dusting

1. Make the salsa: Stir the tomatoes, onion, and cilantro together in a small bowl. Stir in the lime juice, olive oil, and chile. Season with salt and pepper to taste. Place in the refrigerator to chill while you prepare the fish.

2. Preheat the oven to 200°F.

3. Pour enough canola oil into a large frying pan to generously coat the bottom and heat over medium-high heat until hot but not smoking. While the oil is heating, season as many of the fillets as will fit in the pan comfortably with salt and pepper. Dredge the seasoned fillets in flour to coat both sides and shake off the excess flour. Carefully slip the coated snapper into the hot oil, give the pan a little shake to prevent sticking, and cook until lightly golden on the underside, about 3 minutes. Flip the fillets over and cook until the thickest parts of the fillets are opaque at the center, 2 to 3 minutes. Transfer to a baking sheet and keep warm in the oven. Repeat with the remaining fillets, adding more oil to the pan if necessary.

4. Serve the fish warm, passing the tomato salsa separately.

Pan-Seared Red Snapper with Weeknight Salsa and vegetarian version of Spicy Kale with Turkey Sausage (page 280)

"Soupy Rice" with Pigeon Peas

ASOPAO CON GANDULES

This is the ultimate weeknight meal: it is delicious, easy to make, and endlessly adaptable. A word of warning: *asopao* requires the best, most flavorful broth you can make. If you've made some ahead (see Sundays in the Kitchen with Daisy, page 127), you've got what it takes. Even if you haven't, you can start some "Paging Doctored Broth!" (page 305) and have the sofrito and achiote oil made by the time the broth is ready. You'll still have dinner on the table in under an hour, not to mention sofrito, achiote oil, and delicious broth to spare for another fantastic meal.

When I think of *asopao,* I think of heat. You could add chiles to the rice as it cooks, but I prefer to mash a little chile of choice in the bottom of each bowl for those who want it. That way, everybody gets the amount of heat (or not) they like.

MAKES 6 SERVINGS • PREP TIME: 5 MINUTES (WITH ACHIOTE OIL, SOFRITO, AND CHICKEN BROTH ON HAND, 35 MINUTES WITHOUT THOSE INGREDIENTS AND USING DOCTORED BROTH) • COOK TIME: 30 MINUTES

2 tablespoons Achiote Oil (page 306)

2 cups diced (1/2-inch) smoked pork butt (about 12 ounces)

1 cup Sofrito (page 305)

Kosher or fine sea salt and freshly ground pepper

1/4 cup alcaparrado or coarsely chopped pimiento-stuffed olives

2 bay leaves

1 teaspoon ground cumin

1 teaspoon dried oregano

One 14-ounce bag frozen pigeon peas *(gandules),* defrosted, or one 15 1/2-ounce can pigeon peas, drained and rinsed

1 cup long-grain white rice

6 cups Homemade Chicken Broth (page 303) or "Paging Doctored Broth!" (page 305)

Chiles of your choice (see page 314), halved or quartered lengthwise, seeds left in for more heat

1. Heat the achiote oil in a 4- to 5-quart Dutch oven or other heavy pot over medium heat. Add the diced pork and cook, stirring, until sizzling and coated with oil. Stir in the sofrito, season lightly with salt and pepper, and cook, stirring, until the liquid has evaporated and the sofrito is sizzling. Stir in the alcaparrado, bay leaves, cumin, and oregano and cook for a minute or two.

2. Stir in the pigeon peas and rice and cook until the rice turns chalky and absorbs the color of the achiote oil. Pour in 4 cups of the broth and bring to a boil. Adjust the heat so the liquid is at a gentle boil and cook until the level of the liquid meets the rice and peas. The rice will still have "bones"—be chalky-white at the center—at this point. Stir in the remaining 2 cups broth and cook just until the ends of the grains of rice start to split, about 20 minutes. Remove the bay leaves and season with salt and pepper to taste.

3. Bring the pot of rice to the table. Encourage people to take as much or as little chile as they like and mash it against the bottom of their empty bowls to start the heat flowing. Ladle the *asopao* over the chiles and enjoy!

VARIATIONS: Seafood *Asopao:* Delicious, and simple, too. Try either a pound of medium shrimp, peeled and deveined, or firm fish fillets (like tilapia), cut into 1-inch cubes. Stir into the *asopao* during the last 5 minutes of cooking. Or, if you have the know-how, cut up a live 1¼-pound lobster (or two) and stir into the *asopao* about 5 minutes before the rice is done.

For a truly delicious *asopao*, make Homemade Chicken Broth (page 303) with a stewing fowl. Cook the broth for as long as it takes to tenderize the bird. Strain the stock and use it for the *asopao*. Stir the chicken pieces into the rice during the last 5 minutes, just to heat them through.

Stovetop "Wrinkled" Potatoes

You will see these in just about every tapas bar and restaurant in Spain, which just goes to show that you can make delicious tapas from very humble ingredients. These wrinkled little beauties require virtually no work, but you do have to keep an eye on them toward the end of cooking, so they are the perfect side dish to make while you've got something else for dinner cooking away on the stovetop. Try these with really small (about ¾-inch) potatoes for a cocktail party. Skewer the potatoes and pass them around, along with a small bowl of Spicy Ancho Chile *Mojo* (page 308) for dipping.

MAKES 6 SERVINGS • PREP TIME: 5 MINUTES • COOK TIME: 30 MINUTES

1½ pounds small (about 1½-inch,
    sometimes labeled "B") Red Bliss
    potatoes, scrubbed clean
2 tablespoons kosher salt

1. Put the potatoes and salt in a large deep heavy skillet (cast iron is ideal) in which the potatoes will fit comfortably. (The size of the pan is important: it should be as deep as the potatoes are wide, and there should be room for them to roll around a little when you shake the pan.) Pour in enough water to cover the potatoes halfway and bring to a boil over high heat. Adjust the heat so the water is at a good steady boil and cook, shaking the pan every few minutes to cook the potatoes evenly, until the water has almost evaporated and the potatoes look ashy, about 25 minutes.

2. Lower the heat and cook just until all the water is evaporated, 2 to 3 minutes. Remove the pan from the heat and cover with a clean damp kitchen towel. Let sit for 10 to 15 minutes, then serve the potatoes right from the pan.

Ensalada

Throughout my childhood, the simple *ensalada*—shredded iceberg lettuce topped with a few slices of tomato and avocado—was present at most of the meals we ate, elaborate family get-togethers and everyday dinners alike. Sometimes the simplest dishes are the ones we take for granted. I know that was the case with me and *ensalada*. A trip to Puerto Rico changed all that.

I decided to take *Mami* and *Papi* on a tour of Puerto Rico, traveling to parts of the island that were significant to them and introducing them to some places they had never seen. My brother Pete and I planned the whole trip, crisscrossing the island from north to south and then from east to west. The east-west drive took us along the mountainous *cordillera* (spine) of the island. That road is said to have 365 turns, one for every day of the year. The *cordillera* is not the kind of drive to take if you're prone to car sickness, as my son Marc can verify. But it is a beautiful drive, full of vistas and landscapes that you won't find anywhere else. I remember in particular one stretch: the almond trees that lined the road had grown so huge that the overhead branches joined to form a canopy. None of us will ever forget the light streaming through their branches and the smell of the almonds that hung from above and littered the roadside.

We visited the house on the beach in Aguadilla where *Papi* was born and lived until he was four years old. His father ran a business out of that house, hand-rolling cigars, a business he brought with him to Spanish Harlem when the family left the island for New York. And we visited two of *Mami*'s houses—one set in the middle of acres of wonderfully fragrant coffee fields and a two-story house in the town of Arecibo. *Mami*'s father ran a general store on the ground floor and the family lived above it.

Throughout our trip, we ate at roadside *fondas* (family-run restaurants) and *lechoneras*, where whole roasted pig was the main (and pretty much only) attraction, to savor the flavors of the island. Anywhere we stopped for lunch or dinner, our meal was accompanied by an *ensalada* identical to those of my childhood. I guess I'd always known it, but on that trip it really hit home how, when dressed with a sparkle of lime and some good oil, those simple ingredients are the perfect accompaniment to so much of "our" food.

I have wonderful memories of that trip: the tears that welled up in my mother's eyes under the canopy of almond trees and the look on my father's face as he stood on the beach in front of his childhood home are among them. I also have a newfound respect for and understanding of the pleasures of simple dishes like *ensalada*.

Mami and Papi go on an underground expedition at Las Cuevas de Camuy in Puerto Rico.

Cumin-Scented Fried Potatoes

Make these once, just once, and you will ask yourself, "Why did I ever buy a frozen French fry?" These are a treat for dinner; save them for a day when someone brings home a good report card or news of a big raise.

A logistical note: These will fit into weeknight dinners if you fry the potatoes for the first time and let them soak up the seasoning while you take care of the main course, say a roast chicken, a simple steak on the grill (page 90), or a *milanesa* (page 142). Just before serving, reheat the oil and give the potatoes their last trip through the oil. The second frying takes only a few minutes.

MAKES 6 SERVINGS • PREP TIME: 10 MINUTES • COOK TIME: 10 MINUTES

Canola oil, for frying

3 large Idaho (baking) potatoes, peeled and cut into 1-inch cubes (see Tips)

1 1/2 teaspoons kosher or fine sea salt

1/2 teaspoon ground cumin

1/4 teaspoon freshly ground pepper

1. Pour 3 inches of oil into a large deep skillet or a Dutch oven. Using a deep-frying thermometer for accuracy, heat the oil over medium-high heat to 300°F. Meanwhile, drain the potatoes if necessary and pat them as dry as possible with a clean kitchen towel. When the oil reaches the proper temperature, lower only as many potatoes into the oil as will fit in a single layer. A spider (see Tips) is ideal for doing this safely, but you can also use a slotted spoon. Fry until the potatoes are softened but haven't taken on any color, 4 to 5 minutes. Scoop the potatoes out with the spider or slotted spoon onto a paper-towel-lined baking sheet. Repeat with the remaining potatoes, waiting for the oil to return to temperature if necessary before adding each batch.

2. When all the potatoes have drained, remove the paper towels from the baking sheet. Stir the salt, cumin, and pepper together in a small bowl. Sprinkle the spice mix liberally over the potatoes, tossing the potatoes to coat them evenly. The potatoes can be made to this point in advance and held for a couple of hours at room temperature, covered with a towel; remove the pan of oil from the heat.

3. Just before serving, heat the oil over medium-high heat to 400°F. Lower the potatoes into the oil as before, in batches if necessary, and fry until golden brown and crisp, 3 to 4 minutes. Scoop the potatoes out with the spider or slotted spoon onto a baking sheet lined with clean paper towels. Serve immediately.

TIPS: The potatoes can be peeled and diced in advance. Keep them in a bowl with enough salted cold water to cover at room temperature for up to an hour or in the refrigerator for up to 3 hours. Drain them very well and pat them dry with a clean kitchen towel before frying.

There are small, inexpensive pieces of kitchen equipment that make a world of difference in day-to-day cooking. A spider (see below), also known as a skimmer, is one of them. Spiders come in all shapes and sizes, from brass skimmers with wooden handles that can be had for a few bucks in Chinatowns from coast to coast to more expensive stainless steel mesh skimmers with elegant stainless handles. Whatever the type, they all have one thing in common—they have a larger surface area and drain oil (or any other liquid) much faster than a slotted spoon.

String Beans with Rosemary (see photo, page 275)

Rosemary is huge in Spanish cooking, and sometimes it turns up in unexpected places, like this side dish of string beans tossed with oil perfumed with rosemary, garlic, and lemon. (Lemon-scented olive oil is available in many grocery stores now, but it can be pricey. If you're up for it, try my homemade version, which follows this recipe.) These beans are delicious at room temperature, so they can be made a little ahead, which, together with the fact that there is no mayo in the recipe, makes them a lovely dish for a picnic or barbecue on a hot day.

MAKES 6 SERVINGS • PREP TIME: 10 MINUTES • COOK TIME: 20 MINUTES

1 pound string beans, ends trimmed

2 tablespoons lemon olive oil, homemade (see below) or store-bought, or plain extra-virgin olive oil

2 sprigs fresh rosemary

2 large cloves garlic, minced

Finely grated zest of 1 lemon

Kosher or fine sea salt and freshly ground pepper

1. Bring a large pot of salted water to a boil. Slip in the beans and cook until bright green and crisp-tender, about 3 minutes. Drain the beans in a colander.

2. Gently heat the lemon olive oil or plain olive oil and rosemary in a large deep skillet over low heat until the rosemary is softened and very fragrant, 4 to 5 minutes. Raise the heat to medium-low, add the garlic, and cook until the garlic is softened and fragrant, about 4 minutes. Be careful not to burn the garlic.

3. Remove the rosemary sprigs, raise the heat to medium, and add the string beans. Toss until coated with the rosemary-garlic oil and heated through. Stir in the lemon zest and season with salt and pepper to taste. Serve warm or at room temperature.

Lemon- and/or Ginger-Infused Olive Oil

Put the grated zest of 1 lemon and/or a 1-inch piece of peeled fresh ginger in a small saucepan and pour in 2 cups extra-virgin olive oil. Heat over low heat to 250°F. (Check with a thermometer; the temperature is important to prevent the growth of toxins that causes botulism.) Steep for 15 minutes. Let cool completely, and transfer to a jar with a tight-fitting lid. Keep tightly sealed in the refrigerator for up to 1 week. When tomatoes are in season, a simple dish of sliced tomato dressed with this oil and a sprinkling of oregano is a meal unto itself.

Basic Yellow Rice (and Variations)

If making achiote oil and sofrito ahead of time (see Sundays in the Kitchen with Daisy, page 127) is like putting money in the bank, this is the time to make a withdrawal. Yellow rice is, hands down, the most bang-for-the-buck weeknight side dish. It pumps up everything from pork chops off the grill to panfried fish fillets. With some simple additions—like Vienna sausages, lump crabmeat, or canned beans—it is a meal in itself; see the variations on page 158.

MAKES 6 SERVINGS • PREP TIME: 5 MINUTES (WITH ALREADY-MADE SOFRITO AND ACHIOTE OIL, 20 MINUTES WITHOUT) • COOK TIME: 30 MINUTES

½ cup Achiote Oil (page 306)

1 cup Sofrito (page 305)

¼ cup alcaparrado or coarsely chopped pimiento-stuffed olives

2 tablespoons kosher or fine sea salt, or to taste

1 teaspoon freshly ground pepper

1 teaspoon ground cumin

2 bay leaves

3 cups long-grain white rice

5 cups chicken broth, homemade (page 303) or store-bought (see Tip), plus more as needed

1. Heat the achiote oil in a Dutch oven or other heavy 4- to 5-quart pot with a tight-fitting lid over medium-high heat. Stir in the sofrito and alcaparrado and cook until the liquid has evaporated and the sofrito is sizzling. Season with the salt, pepper, and cumin and toss in the bay leaves. Raise the heat to high and add the rice. Cook, stirring, until the rice is coated with the achiote oil–sofrito and the grains begin to turn chalky, about 3 minutes.

2. Pour in enough chicken broth to cover the rice by 1 inch. Bring to a boil and boil until the level of the broth meets the level of the rice.

3. Lower the heat to very low, stir the rice thoroughly but only once, cover, and cook until the rice is tender but with a little bite and all the liquid is absorbed, about 20 minutes. Do not uncover the pot or stir the rice while it cooks. Fluff with a fork before serving.

Three-Bean Paella (page 158)

TIP: If you're using store-bought broth for this or any rice that calls for sofrito, up the amount of sofrito by about ¼ cup or so to make up for any flavor lacking in the broth.

VARIATIONS

YELLOW RICE WITH VIENNA SAUSAGES: Add two 5-ounce cans of drained Vienna sausages to the rice just before adding the chicken broth.

YELLOW RICE WITH CRAB: Substitute bottled clam juice for the chicken broth. Add 2 cups (about 10 ounces) lump crabmeat, picked over for shells and cartilage, and a large can (about 15 ounces) of corn kernels, drained, or 2 cups frozen corn kernels to the rice just before adding the clam juice.

THREE-BEAN PAELLA (see photo, page 156): Drain and rinse one 15½-ounce can each of chickpeas, pink beans, and black-eyed peas. Add the beans, along with 2 teaspoons smoked paprika, after tossing the rice in the oil-sofrito mixture. If you or someone you love is vegetarian, substitute vegetable broth for the chicken and make a meal of it.

MEXICAN RICE: Add 1 red bell pepper, cored, seeded, and finely diced; one 8-ounce can corn kernels, drained, or 1 cup fresh or frozen corn kernels; one 8-ounce can Spanish-style tomato sauce; and 1 cup pitted small black olives along with the sofrito.

YELLOW RICE WITH PIGEON PEAS: Add 1½ pounds smoked pork neck bones to the sofrito mixture before adding the rice, and stir until coated. Just before adding the broth, stir one 14-ounce bag frozen pigeon peas or one 15½-ounce can pigeon peas, drained and rinsed, into the rice.

Basic White Rice (and Variations)

This is the recipe for those of you who have difficulty making rice. Follow these instructions to the letter and you will be rewarded with fluffy, light rice every time you make it.

MAKES 6 TO 8 SERVINGS • COOK TIME: 30 MINUTES

$\frac{1}{4}$ cup vegetable oil

4 cups long-grain white rice

2 tablespoons kosher or fine sea salt

1. Heat the oil in a Dutch oven or other heavy 3- to 4-quart pot with a tight-fitting lid over medium-high heat. Add the rice and salt and stir to coat the rice with the oil. When the rice starts to look chalky, pour enough water into the pot to cover the rice by 1 inch. Raise the heat to high, bring the water to a boil, and boil until the level of the water meets the level of the rice.

2. Reduce the heat to very low, give the rice one very thorough stir, and cover the pot. Cook until the rice is tender but with a little bite, about 20 minutes. Do not uncover the pot or stir the rice while it cooks. Fluff with a fork before serving.

VARIATIONS:

MUSHROOM-ONION RICE: Add 2 cups sliced button mushrooms and 1 chopped onion to the oil before adding the rice. Cook, stirring, until the vegetables are softened, then proceed as above.

CURRIED RICE WITH ALMONDS AND RAISINS: Add 2 tablespoons curry powder, $\frac{1}{2}$ cup sliced almonds, and $\frac{1}{2}$ cup raisins to the oil before adding the rice and salt. Cook until the almonds are lightly toasted. Add 2 bay leaves along with the rice, and proceed as above.

SPINACH RICE (see photo, page 140): Make the rice as above. While it is cooking, heat $\frac{1}{4}$ cup olive oil in a medium skillet over medium heat. Stir in 3 cloves minced garlic and cook until fragrant. Add one 10-ounce box frozen chopped spinach, defrosted and squeezed dry, and cook just until the water from the spinach is evaporated. Season with kosher or fine sea salt and freshly ground pepper to taste. Stir the spinach into the finished rice. If you like, drizzle a little extra-virgin olive oil over the rice just before serving.

WEEKNIGHT BEAN RECIPES (STARRING CANNED BEANS)

Mango and Black Bean Salad

This is a delicious way for me to sneak more fruit and vegetables into our family dinners. If you can't find jicama (see page 58), which adds an apple-y note to the salad, substitute a large green apple. Core the apple, but leave the skin on, and dice it as you would the jicama. More than a 15-minute side dish, this can be dressed up by spooning it into radicchio-leaf cups for a first course, pressed into service as a salsa to complement the next batch of salmon fillets or steaks off the grill, or taken along on your next picnic.

MAKES 6 SERVINGS • PREP TIME: 20 MINUTES

¹/₄ cup extra-virgin olive oil

2 tablespoons cider vinegar

¹/₄ cup chopped fresh cilantro

Kosher or fine sea salt and freshly ground
    pepper

One 15¹/₂-ounce can black beans, drained
    and rinsed

1 mango, peeled, flesh removed from
    the pit, and cut into ¹/₂-inch dice
    (2 generous cups)

1 small jicama (about 1 pound), peeled and
    cut into ¹/₂-inch dice (about 2 cups)

1 small red onion (about 4 ounces), cut in
    half through the root, then into thin
    slivers (about ¹/₂ cup)

1. Whisk the olive oil, vinegar, and cilantro together in a large bowl until blended. Season lightly with salt and pepper. Add the beans, mango, jicama, and onion and toss gently to mix and coat with the dressing. Season with salt and pepper to taste.

2. Serve right away, or let stand at room temperature for up to 30 minutes. Toss and check the seasoning before serving.

Cooking Dried Beans

This section of the book celebrates the convenience of canned beans. (And not only their convenience, but also their nutritional benefits and adaptability.) Let's not forget, though, that cooking dried beans is the opposite of a big deal—even if yours, like mine, is a pretty hectic life. If you don't have time to get freshly cooked beans on the table on a work night (most types of beans take about 2 hours to cook), remember this: a pot of beans, whether plain black beans or a delicious concoction like the Red Beans with Salchichon and Potato on page 284, is actually better a day or two later, which makes it a perfect addition to your weekend plan-ahead cooking spree (see Sundays in the Kitchen with Daisy, page 127).

Let's start with one thing: I never, and I mean *never,* soak dried beans, which many good cooks insist is necessary. And I never have a problem with the end result. My beans are always creamy in texture, without any "bones" (or hard bits) in the middle, and the cooking liquid is delicious too. Here's all you need to know, regardless of what kind of beans you're cooking:

First, pick over the beans. It's rare, but you might find the odd stone, and you'll almost always find shriveled or damaged beans. (Not the end of the world, but it's nice to pick them out before cooking.) Put the beans in a pot large enough to hold three times their volume—a 3-quart pot works well for a pound of beans. Pour in enough water to cover the beans by 2 inches, toss in a bay leaf, and, if you like, add a smoked ham hock or a smoked turkey wing. Bring to a boil, then adjust the heat so the liquid is simmering, and cook until the beans are tender. This can take as little as 1½ hours for small white beans or as much as 3 to 4 hours for chickpeas. Check the heat every once in a while to make sure the liquid stays at a steady simmer, and, while you're at it, make sure there is enough liquid to cover the beans. The goal is tender-but-not-mushy, evenly cooked beans with just enough liquid left in the pot to coat them with a syrupy "sauce." Remove the beans from the heat, add a fair amount of salt, and stir gently. Let them sit for at least 15 minutes to soak up the salt, then serve them. Or let them stand for up to several hours, or refrigerate them for up to 3 days. In either case, reheat them over gentle heat and add a little water if necessary to return them to their original creamy deliciousness. Check the salt and pepper too before serving reheated beans.

New-Style "Refried" Beans

I love the creamy texture of classic refried beans, but nowadays nobody (including me) is wild about the lard that is such an important part of traditional refried bean recipes. This method cuts way back on the fat but delivers a creamy texture by pureeing the beans with a little of their cooking liquid. They are delish.

MAKES 6 SERVINGS • PREP TIME: 10 MINUTES • COOK TIME: 30 MINUTES (MOSTLY UNATTENDED)

1 tablespoon olive oil

$^{1}/_{2}$ large Spanish onion, cut into $^{1}/_{2}$-inch dice

2 cloves garlic, crushed and peeled

1 smoked ham hock or smoked turkey wing

2 cups chicken broth, homemade (page 303) or store-bought

1 bunch cilantro, tough stems removed

2 bay leaves

Two 15$^{1}/_{2}$-ounce cans black beans, drained and rinsed

Kosher or fine sea salt and freshly ground pepper

Good-quality tortilla chips

1. Heat the olive oil in a medium saucepan over medium-high heat. Add the onion and garlic and cook, stirring, until softened but not browned, about 4 minutes. Add the ham hock and pour in the chicken broth. Add the cilantro and bay leaves and bring to a boil. Adjust the heat so the liquid is simmering and cook for 20 minutes; skim the foam off the top of the broth as it forms.

2. Pass the broth through a strainer. Reserve the ham hock (or turkey wing) for another batch of beans (it will keep for a good week or so) and discard the bay leaves and cilantro. Scrape the onion and garlic back into the same saucepan and add the beans. Pour in just enough of the strained broth to cover the beans. Bring to a boil over medium heat, and cook just until the beans are heated through.

3. With a spider (see page 154) or a slotted spoon, transfer the beans to the work bowl of a food processor. (Reserve the cooking liquid; see Tip.) Process, gradually adding the cooking liquid a little at a time, until the beans are the consistency of mashed potatoes. Season with salt and pepper to taste.

4. Serve the beans right away, or return the "refried" beans to the saucepan and keep warm over very low heat for up to 20 minutes. Serve with crispy tortilla chips.

TIP: Reheat leftover beans in a heavy saucepan over very low heat. If the beans are too thick, thin them down by adding more of the cooking liquid, if you saved it (or water in a pinch), a little at a time.

Pigeon Peas in Coconut Milk

Here is an unlikely combination, but one that is so delicious and so full of flavor that this, with a side of steaming plain white rice, is all you need for dinner. The peas can easily be done in the 20 minutes it takes the rice to cook after covering the pot.

MAKES 4 MAIN-COURSE SERVINGS • PREP TIME: 5 MINUTES (WITH ALREADY-MADE SOFRITO; 20 MINUTES WITHOUT) • COOK TIME: 20 MINUTES

2 tablespoons olive oil

1 cup Sofrito (page 305)

¼ cup alcaparrado or coarsely chopped pimiento-stuffed olives

½ teaspoon ground cumin

One 8-ounce can Spanish-style tomato sauce

One 13½-ounce can unsweetened coconut milk

One 14-ounce bag frozen pigeon peas (*gandules*) or two 15½-ounce cans pigeon peas, drained and rinsed

Kosher or fine sea salt and freshly ground pepper

1. Heat the olive oil in a heavy 3-quart saucepan over medium heat. Add the sofrito and alcaparrado and cook, stirring, until the liquid has evaporated and the sofrito is sizzling. Stir in the cumin, then the tomato sauce. Add the coconut milk and pigeon peas (straight from the freezer is fine) and bring to a boil, stirring. Season lightly with salt and pepper. Adjust the heat so the liquid is simmering and cook until the peas are softened and the liquid is slightly thickened, about 15 minutes.

2. Check seasoning and serve hot.

Butter Beans *en Escabeche*

En escabeche is a phrase that, loosely translated, means "vinegared." Travel across Puerto Rico, and in every little roadside *fonda* you will see jars of pickled beans similar to these, as well as string beans, green (as in unripe) bananas, and on and on. If fact, throughout the Caribbean, simple bean dishes like this—seasoned with a little vinegar, onion, and cilantro—are a mainstay.

Dried beans, when freshly cooked and still warm, soak up the vinegary dressing and keep their firm texture. I was really surprised to find that certain canned beans work just as well when given the *escabeche* treatment. Beans prepared like this don't need a whole lot of time to absorb the dressing, but they do need a little. The trick is to dress the beans first, before you start the rest of the dinner. While you're doing your thing, the beans are doing theirs, and by the time dinner is on the table, the beans will have soaked up some of the delicious dressing. These are perfect for weeknight meals not only because they are so quick to put together, but also because they go with just about anything. Try them with steak, pork chops, or fish off the grill; or simple sautéed chicken breasts; or in lettuce-leaf cups as a first course.

MAKES 6 SERVINGS • PREP TIME: 15 MINUTES (PLUS 20 TO 30 MINUTES STANDING TIME)

Two 15½-ounce cans butter beans, drained and rinsed

½ small red onion, thinly sliced (about ½ cup)

1 ripe tomato, cored, seeded, and cut into ½-inch dice (about 1 cup)

¼ cup chopped fresh cilantro

2 bay leaves

¼ cup olive oil

2 cloves garlic, finely chopped

¼ cup cider vinegar

¼ cup white vinegar

Kosher or fine sea salt and freshly ground pepper

1. Put the beans, onion, tomato, cilantro, and bay leaves in a serving bowl.
2. Heat the oil in a small saucepan over medium heat. Add the garlic and cook, stirring, until softened and lightly browned, 1 to 2 minutes. Remove the pan from the heat and pour in the cider and white vinegar—carefully; it will sputter a little at first. Add salt and pepper to taste. Pour the dressing over the beans and let stand for 20 to 30 minutes, tossing every once in a while. Discard the bay leaves and serve the beans at room temp.

A STITCH IN TIME: These beans are delicious the next day, so make plenty. Drain a can of tuna, flake it, and stir it into the leftover beans. Lunch in a minute!

Strawberry Delicia

Think of this as a Latin trifle—cubes of tender cake layered with cream cheese, whipped cream, and a double dose of strawberries, fresh and preserves. This was another recipe thoughtfully shared with me by Ninoschtka Estevez (see page 251).

MAKES 12 SERVINGS • PREP TIME: 25 MINUTES (PLUS 1 HOUR CHILLING TIME)

One store-bought 9-inch angel food cake, preferably a day or two old

2 cups heavy cream, well chilled

$1/2$ cup confectioners' sugar

1 tablespoon vanilla extract

One 8-ounce package cream cheese, at room temperature

2 pints strawberries, hulled and sliced (save 3 whole berries for decoration)

1 cup strawberry jam

1. Choose a serving bowl or, ideally, a glass trifle dish that holds about 10 quarts. Set aside. Cut the angel food cake horizontally into thirds, then cut into 1-inch (or so) cubes.

2. With an electric mixer or whisk, beat the heavy cream in a large, cold mixing bowl until foamy. Gradually add the confectioners' sugar and continue to beat until the cream holds stiff peaks. Stir in the vanilla.

3. Beat the cream cheese in a medium bowl until smooth and creamy. Stir about 1 cup of the whipped cream into the cream cheese to lighten it, then stir that mixture into the rest of the whipped cream.

4. Build the *delicia:* Spread enough of the whipped cream mixture over the bottom of the trifle dish or bowl to make an even $1/2$-inch layer. Cover that with a layer of half the cake and half the sliced berries. Dot half of the jam in between the cake and berries. Cover with half of the remaining whipped cream mixture and smooth it into an even layer. Repeat, using the remaining cake, sliced berries, jam, and whipped cream mixture.

5. Chill for at least 1 hour before serving. Decorate with the reserved 3 whole berries. (The *delicia* can be made up to a day in advance. Leftovers will keep for up to 2 days.)

TIP: Cover the *delicia* well with plastic wrap before refrigerating. Delicate items like this easily pick up strong refrigerator odors.

Guava–Cream Cheese Turnovers

All over Latin America, fruity-sweet guava paste is paired with soft, mildly salty cheeses like queso blanco or queso fresco as a snack. (I like to think of the pairing as the "PB&J" of Latin America.) Often a square of the fruity-sweet guava paste is simply stacked on top of a square of cheese and popped into the mouth. Here guava paste and tart cream cheese team up to make a dynamite, 10-minute dessert that is perfect for a weeknight.

MAKES 8 TURNOVERS • PREP TIME: 15 MINUTES
• COOK TIME: 30 MINUTES (UNATTENDED, INCLUDES COOLING TIME)

FOR THE TURNOVERS

1 tablespoon granulated sugar

One 17.3-ounce package frozen puff
    pastry, thawed (see Tip)

One 8-ounce package cream cheese, cut
    into 8 equal pieces

Eight 1 x 1-inch squares guava paste
    (about 4 ounces)

1 extra-large egg, beaten with 1 teaspoon
    water

FOR THE GLAZE

1/4 cup confectioners' sugar

1 teaspoon milk

1/4 teaspoon vanilla extract

1. Preheat the oven to 400°F.
2. Make the turnovers: Sprinkle the sugar on the work surface to prevent the dough from sticking. Roll out each sheet of puff pastry to an 8-inch square. Using a pizza cutter or sharp knife, cut each sheet into 4 squares.
3. Set a pastry square in front of you with one of the corners pointing toward you. Center 1 piece of cream cheese over the bottom half of the square. Top with a piece of guava paste. Brush the edges of the pastry square with the beaten egg. Fold the upper half of the square over the filling to make a neat triangle. Crimp the edges with a fork. Repeat with the remaining turnovers, placing them on a parchment-paper-lined or nonstick baking sheet as you go.
4. Brush the tops of the turnovers lightly with the remaining beaten egg. Bake for 20 minutes, or until golden brown and puffy.
5. While the turnovers are baking, mix the confectioners' sugar with the milk and vanilla in a small bowl, stirring to dissolve any lumps. Set aside.

6. Let the turnovers cool on a rack for 10 to 15 minutes, then drizzle the glaze over them. Serve warm or at room temperature.

> **TIP:** The best way to defrost puff pastry is to move it to the refrigerator the day before you plan to use it. This slow, steady defrosting will help keep the dough from breaking or tearing when you roll it out.

Coconut Kisses (see photo, page 40)

This is the first dessert I learned to make when I was a little girl. My cousin and I almost burned down the kitchen, but that's another story. . . . Coconut kisses are moist, chewy, and delicious. The almond flour isn't something we used when I was a kid, but it really adds a nice touch.

MAKES ABOUT 30 KISSES • PREP TIME: 15 MINUTES • COOK TIME:
50 MINUTES (UNATTENDED, INCLUDES COOLING TIME)

3 packed cups sweetened shredded coconut

1 packed cup light brown sugar

½ cup almond flour

½ teaspoon ground ginger

½ teaspoon ground cinnamon

2 extra-large eggs

2 extra-large egg yolks

1. Position one rack in the top third and one in the bottom third of the oven and preheat the oven to 350°F. Line 2 baking sheets with parchment paper. (If you have only 1 baking sheet or oven rack, bake the kisses in batches.)

2. Combine the coconut, brown sugar, almond flour, ginger, and cinnamon in a large bowl, and rub together with your hands until the coconut is fluffy and the sugar, flour, and spices are evenly distributed throughout. Add the eggs and yolks and stir until the mixture is evenly moistened.

3. Scoop up about 2 tablespoons of the mix and roll lightly between your hands to make a round ball with an irregular surface; place on a lined baking sheet. Repeat with the remaining mixture, lining the kisses up in 3 rows of 5 on each baking sheet. Bake for 15 minutes. Rotate the baking sheets from rack to rack and back to front. Bake until the kisses are golden brown and feel light when picked up, about 15 minutes. Let cool completely. The kisses will keep in a covered container for 4 to 5 days, unless they're in my house, then good luck with that!

COCKTAIL PARTIES

I've taken you all over in the travelogues scattered throughout this book, but I want to make this chapter introduction a special stop: Casa Daisy! I'll also let you in on a little secret: I don't usually have cocktail parties—not the way "normal" people have cocktail parties, anyway! I always have a cocktail *hour* (or *hour and a half!*) as an opener to the "main event": when I make a commitment to entertain, I like to keep my guests around for more than a bit. . . . But that's just me.

Last year, my dear friend Loni's older daughter, Sara, got married to a lovely boy from the UK, Martin. I consider Loni my "sister from another mister" and her daughters were like my daughters before I had Angela. I have seen them grow up from little girls, and we have shared Christmases, birthdays, and, in fact, every holiday and special occasion I can think of. I wanted to do something special for Sara and Mart, and I asked Loni if I could have a little party for them the day after their wedding. I put together a menu that I thought would be appropriate for an early Sunday afternoon—not too brunchy—and, since the guest list was fairly long, I wanted a lot of variety, and dishes that didn't require me to spend last-minute time in the kitchen.

I set up a bagel and lox station with an assortment of cream cheeses, capers, and red onion, and a ceviche station with tortilla chips. One table held a crabmeat strudel and a sauceboat of passion fruit hollandaise, and another was laden with assorted tortillas cut into bite-size pieces.

My guests arrived and dove into the food with enthusiasm. (Mart and his brothers have very healthy appetites!) While Jerry took care of the coats and Erik got busy pouring wine, I mingled with the guests, always checking the tables to make sure that everything was being replenished (thank you, Marc, David, and Angela!). After about an hour and a half, I started setting up a hot-meal station in the dining room. As I started setting up the chafing dishes, I saw Mart, out of the corner of my eye, ask Sara what I was doing. Sara, having grown up across the street, and no stranger to my house, replied that I was setting out the meal. "What meal?!" inquired Mart, his eyes as big as saucers, and his hands rising to cover his belly. "You mean that wasn't it?" he asked, pointing to the living room. Sara smiled, winked at me, and said, "Welcome to Daisy's, Mart!"

Funky Shrimp with Plantain–Sweet Potato Mash and Pineapple-Rum Dipping Sauce (page 193), Spicy Gazpacho Shooters (page 179), and Black Bean and Queso Fresco Tostaditas (page 176)

I cannot tell you how many lovely thank-you notes I received from the guests at Sara and Mart's party, from both here and abroad!

I'm not going to tell you that that is the way you should entertain. What passes for "cocktail hour" in my house could easily be a quick get-together before the theater, after work, or even on a Sunday afternoon at yours. What I can tell you is that a cocktail party is a delightful way to spend a little time with friends, sharing a nibble and a sip, and creating some terrific memories of your own.

The recipes in this chapter are fun, festive, and very user friendly. Mix and match, and feel free to look through the other chapters for inspiration. I am sure that not only will your cocktail party be a success, but you'll be receiving some pretty terrific correspondence as well!

Piquillo Peppers with Creamy Crab Filling (page 177)

DRINKS AND COLD DISHES

Daisytini

While visiting Chicago, I was invited to dinner with my good friend and fellow chef Art Smith. Art, who is famous for his hospitality, brought Phillipe, a charming friend from Santa Barbara who was his houseguest. Philippe and I became fast friends over dinner. I learned that he ran an event-planning business, and he told me that he would be happy to concoct a cocktail that would reflect my passion for Latin food. A week after I returned home, I found this recipe in my e-mail in-box. Thank you so very much, Philippe!

MAKES 1 COCKTAIL

2 shots silver tequila (Patrón or Herradura would be nice)

1 shot Alizé Gold Passion liqueur

1 shot agave nectar (see Note)

Juice of 1 lime

Fresh mint leaves and a sprig

(continued)

Fill a cocktail shaker halfway with ice. Add the tequila, Alizé, agave nectar, and lime juice and shake well. Pour, ice and all, into a double old-fashioned glass. Bruise a leaf or two of mint and rub them around the rim of the glass. Tuck a mint sprig into the ice cubes.

NOTE: Agave nectar comes from the heart, or *piña*, of the agave plant—the same plant that gives us tequila and *mezcal*. In color and sweetness, it resembles honey. It is available in specialty and health food stores and many supermarkets.

Cava Sangria

Several years ago, my husband, Jerry, and I started a new tradition—taking the whole family on a holiday trip to some part of the Spanish-speaking world. On our first New Year's Eve abroad, I was a little nervous about how the kids would react to being away from home instead of in familiar surroundings to see the old year out. Everyone was all dressed up—and even more dressed up when we got into the party hats and disguises that each of us received at our place settings. (I have a picture of Jerry with his old-fashioned priest hat on and the kids with fake glasses with big noses attached.) To kick things off, we were served a glass of this sangria with an *amuse-bouche* of quail eggs stuffed with *jamón ibérico* mousse. Unforgettable!

MAKES 12 SERVINGS • PREP TIME: 10 MINUTES

2 cups seltzer or sparkling mineral water, well chilled
1 cup peach brandy, well chilled
1 cup superfine sugar
Two 750-ml bottles cava (Spanish sparkling wine), well chilled

About 4 cups assorted berries, such as blueberries, blackberries, and raspberries, rinsed briefly and drained

Stir the seltzer, brandy, and sugar together in a punch bowl or pitcher. When the sugar is dissolved, uncork the sparkling wine and pour it gently into the bowl. Float about half the berries in the sangria and use the rest to decorate the individual glasses of sangria.

Lettuce, Tomato, and Onion Tostaditas (or Tostadas)

This is nothing more than a very simple chopped salad, but that's what makes it so appealing. In addition to using it for topping tostaditas, try it in a taco, next to a burger (or anything off the grill), or as the ultimate no-hassle hot-weather starter.

MAKES ABOUT 3 CUPS, ENOUGH FOR ABOUT 30 TOSTADITAS OR 4 TOSTADAS OR 4 FIRST-COURSE SALADS • PREP TIME: 15 MINUTES

3 cups chopped romaine lettuce (about half a heart of romaine)

2 ripe medium tomatoes (about 12 ounces), cored, seeded, and cut into ½-inch dice (about 1¾ cups)

½ small red onion, cut into ¼-inch dice (about ½ cup)

2 tablespoons olive oil

Juice of 1 lime

Kosher or fine sea salt and freshly ground pepper

½ cup crumbled queso fresco or ricotta salata

About 30 corn chips for tostaditas, homemade (see opposite) or store-bought; or four 6-inch corn tortillas, fried or baked (see opposite) for tostadas

1. Toss the lettuce, tomatoes, and onion together in a mixing bowl. This can be done up to a day in advance; refrigerate in a plastic bag.

2. Add the olive oil and lime juice and toss again, then season with salt and pepper to taste.

3. Divide the topping among the tostadita chips or tortillas and top each with some of the cheese. Serve at once. Or if serving as a first-course salad, simply divide the salad among 4 plates and scatter the cheese evenly over it.

VARIATIONS: Add a little heat in the form of finely minced jalapeño or use *Vinagre* (page 308) in place of the lime juice to dress the salad.

Take the topping on a trip to Puerto Rico by adding finely diced grilled or roasted pineapple or diced avocado.

Tostaditas and Tostadas

Tostadas are the perfect Mexican street-food lunch: a crunchy fried corn tortilla topped with any number of hot or cold toppings—sort of like an open-faced sandwich made on very crunchy, corn-scented bread. Miniaturized, they go by the name *tostaditas*, and they make great cocktail party food.

TOSTADITAS: The easiest way to serve tostaditas is to open a bag of good-quality corn chips and plunk a little topping on each one. Pick round chips if you can—their shape is closer to a mini corn tortilla. But even triangular chips will do.

To make your own chips for tostaditas, start with regular (about 6-inch) corn tortillas and either cut them into wedges or use a biscuit cutter to cut them into circles. Pour about ¼ inch of vegetable oil into a wide heavy skillet and heat the oil over medium heat until the tip of the handle of a wooden spoon dipped in the oil gives off a steady, but not frantic, stream of bubbles (about 350°F). Slip as many wedges or circles into the oil as will fit without touching and cook, turning once, until lightly browned on both sides and crisp, about 4 minutes. Drain on a baking sheet lined with paper towels and repeat with the remaining tortillas, replenishing the oil as necessary.

For "lighter" chips, preheat the oven to 350°F. Lightly grease a baking sheet or two with vegetable oil. Pour a little oil into your palm, pat your palms together, then pat the tortilla pieces to give them a little gloss. Bake until crisp and lightly browned, about 10 minutes. The chips can be baked or fried up to several hours before serving.

LUNCHEON-SIZE TOSTADAS: For these, simply fry or bake whole corn tortillas as described above. Even if the topping is cold, these are delicious served right out of the skillet or oven.

Black Bean and Queso Fresco Tostaditas (or Tostadas)

Simple, especially when made with canned beans, this bean salad can double as a side dish for a busy weeknight or a grill-centric meal.

MAKES 2 CUPS, ENOUGH FOR 24 TOSTADITAS OR 2 TOSTADAS • PREP TIME: 10 MINUTES (WITH CANNED BEANS, MORE WITH FRESHLY COOKED BEANS) • COOK TIME: 0 WITH STORE-BOUGHT CHIPS

One 15½-ounce can black beans, drained and rinsed, or 1½ cups cooked black beans (see page 161)

¼ cup finely chopped red onion

¼ cup finely chopped fresh cilantro

2 tablespoons olive oil

2 teaspoons fresh lime juice

½ teaspoon smoked paprika

Kosher or fine sea salt and freshly ground pepper

½ cup crumbled queso fresco or cotija cheese

About 24 corn chips for tostaditas, homemade (see page 175) or store-bought, or two 6-inch corn tortillas, fried or baked (see page 175) for tostadas

Up to 2 hours before serving, toss the beans, onion, cilanto, olive oil, lime juice, and smoked paprika together in a bowl until the beans are glossy. Season with salt and pepper to taste. Spoon a little of the bean salad onto each chip. Top with a little of the cheese and serve right away. Or divide the salad between the tortillas, top with the cheese, and serve.

Pa Amb Tomaquet

To make *pa amb tomaquet* (Catalan for "bread and tomato"), cut a baguette or loaf of country bread into ½-inch slices. Grill the bread on a lightly oiled hot charcoal or gas grill until grill-marked and toasted, about 3 minutes per side. The bread can also be oven-toasted: Preheat the oven to 375°F. Lay the bread out in a single layer on a baking sheet. Bake, turning once and moving the slices around on the baking sheet for even cooking, until light golden on both sides, about 12 minutes.

Cut a very ripe tomato in half and squeeze out the seeds and goop. Rub the cut sides of the tomato vigorously on both sides of the warm bread. Season with salt and the best Spanish olive oil you can find. These are best rubbed, seasoned, and eaten while still warm, but the toasts can be grilled or toasted ahead and rewarmed just before serving.

Creamy Crab Dip or Filling

This is best eaten when freshly made, but it can be made ahead and refrigerated, then brought up to room temperature. The natural sweetness of the crab and the tang of cream cheese give the dip a good all-around balance. It can stand up to just about anything you choose to use as dippers.

MAKES 3½ CUPS, ENOUGH TO SERVE 16 (EASILY) AS A DIP • PREP TIME: 20 MINUTES

1 cup heavy cream
1 clove garlic, crushed and peeled
2 bay leaves
Half an 8-ounce container chive-onion
    whipped cream cheese
2 tablespoons chopped fresh flat-leaf
    parsley or chives
Finely grated zest of 1 lemon
Kosher or fine sea salt and freshly ground
    pepper

1 pound lump crabmeat, picked over for
    shells and cartilage

ANY OR ALL "DIPPERS"
Celery boats
Triangles of red bell pepper
Sliced crusty bread
"Party" pumpernickel bread
Pita wedges

1. Bring the cream, garlic, and bay leaves to a boil in a small saucepan. Adjust the heat so the cream is at a lively simmer and cook until the cream is reduced to ½ cup.

2. Pick out the bay leaves and garlic and pour the reduced cream into a bowl. Beat in the cream cheese, parsley, lemon zest, and salt and pepper to taste. Fold in the crab gently, to keep the lumps as large as possible. Let cool to room temperature and serve. The dip can be refrigerated for up to 1 day. Bring to room temperature before serving, about an hour.

3. Spoon into a bowl, place the bowl in the center of a platter, and surround with any of the "dippers" you like.

VARIATION

PIQUILLO PEPPERS WITH CRABMEAT FILLING: To use as a filling for piquillo peppers, make the dip without the reduced heavy cream. Drain the peppers and blot them dry with paper towels. (Figure on about 10 whole, usable piquillo peppers per 10-ounce jar.) Fill the peppers with the crab dip. If you like, you can take the pepper pieces not fit for stuffing, chop them fine, and fold them into the crab mixture before stuffing the peppers. And, if you have some on hand, sprinkle some toasted bread crumbs (page 73) over the filling.

Spicy Gazpacho Shooters

This recipe came about in a rather funny way. I have a catering business called The Passionate Palate, and I often serve gazpacho as an elegant first course. On one particular occasion, I had a huge surplus of gazpacho left over, not exactly a tragedy, as I was expecting guests for brunch at my home the next day. With a little ingenuity, and as a person who is loath to waste, I put my leftover gazpacho to good use (along with a little "zing" from the liquor cabinet) and transformed it into something really special! Then I got to thinking—it might be fun to do a "juiced" gazpacho, spiking the juice, and have *real* shooters. So I did. Here is a rendition that requires no leftover gazpacho. (*Note:* You'll need a juicer to make these.)

MAKES 6 CUPS (ABOUT 24 SERVINGS) • PREP TIME: 20 MINUTES

One 32-ounce bottle tomato juice (spicy, if you like)

1 large Spanish onion, cut into large dice (about 1$^1/_2$ cups)

1 medium cucumber, peeled, seeded, and cut into $^1/_2$-inch dice (about 1$^1/_2$ cups)

1 red bell pepper, cored, seeded, and cut into large dice (about 1$^1/_2$ cups)

$^1/_2$ jalapeño, seeds and all

2 cloves garlic

Kosher or fine sea salt

$^3/_4$ cup gold tequila

Juice of 1 lime

$^1/_4$ teaspoon ground cumin

Scallions, trimmed to 3- to 4-inch lengths (depending on the size of your glasses), or long thin slices or $^1/_2$-inch cubes of avocado (optional)

1. Pour the tomato juice into a 2-quart pitcher. Pass the onion, cucumber, bell pepper, jalapeño, and garlic through a juicer and add to the tomato juice. Season with salt to taste and stir in the tequila, lime juice, and cumin. Chill for at least 1 hour, or as long as overnight.

2. Serve in chilled shot glasses or cordial glasses, with a scallion or avocado slice stuck into each, if you like.

Bloody Mary Ceviche

Here's a fun idea for a cocktail party, or brunch for that matter: use all the ingredients for a Bloody Mary—tomato, spice, celery, and citrus juice—to season a refreshing bowlful of shrimp ceviche. The ceviche returns the flavor by lending a mysterious kick to a Bloody Mary cocktail by way of the "tiger's milk," or *leche de tigre*, the South American term for the liquid drained from the ceviche; see page 69.

MAKES ABOUT 4 CUPS (ABOUT 12 COCKTAIL PARTY SERVINGS) • PREP TIME: 20 MINUTES • "COOK" TIME: 4 TO 24 HOURS (TO "COOK" THE SHRIMP IN THE CITRUS JUICE)

1 pound small shrimp (40 to 50 per pound), peeled and deveined

$^1/_2$ cup diced ($^1/_2$-inch) seeded tomato

2 scallions, trimmed and thinly sliced (about $^1/_4$ cup)

Packed $^1/_4$ cup chopped fresh cilantro

Juice of 4 large lemons, plus more as needed

Chiles for heat—anything from a seeded jalapeño or two for mild heat to a small habanero, seeds and all, for blazing heat (see page 314)

Kosher or fine sea salt

1 stalk celery, trimmed and cut into $^1/_2$-inch dice (about $^1/_2$ cup)

$^1/_2$ large seedless cucumber, cut into $^1/_2$-inch dice (1 generous cup)

2 tablespoons olive oil

Tortilla chips (optional)

1. Toss the shrimp, tomato, scallions, cilantro, lemon juice, and chiles together in a bowl. Season with salt to taste. Transfer the ceviche to a tall storage container. There should be enough lemon juice to cover all the ingredients. If not, squeeze in a little more. Chill until the shrimp are opaque all the way through, at least 4 hours, or as long as overnight.

2. Drain the ceviche and reserve the liquid for Ceviche Bloody Marys (recipe opposite; there will be about $^1/_2$ cup of liquid). Put the drained ceviche in a serving bowl, add the celery and cucumber, drizzle with the olive oil, and toss well. Put a serving spoon in the ceviche.

3. To serve, there are two options: Set a stack of small plates and forks next to the ceviche, or put a basket of tortilla chips next to it and let guests spoon a shrimp and some of the vegetables onto the chips.

Ceviche Bloody Mary

This is equally delicious if made without any booze at all.

MAKES 10 DRINKS • PREP TIME: 10 MINUTES (NOT INCLUDING TIME FOR CEVICHE TO "COOK")

One 46-ounce bottle V8 juice (regular or "Spicy Hot")

2 cups vodka or tequila (or more or less, as you prefer)

Reserved liquid from Bloody Mary Ceviche (opposite; about ½ cup)

2 dashes Worcestershire sauce

2 teaspoons bottled horseradish

Juice of 1 lime

Kosher or fine sea salt and freshly ground pepper

FOR THE VEGETABLE GARNISH

Ten 6-inch cucumber spears, 10 celery stalks (inner stalks with leaves are nice), and/or 10 trimmed scallions

1. Stir all the ingredients (except the vegetable garnish) together in a large pitcher. Chill for at least 2 hours, or up to 1 day.
2. Serve the drinks chilled on the rocks, with the cucumber spears, celery, and/or scallions.

Smoked Trout and Endive Canapés

On a lunchtime trip to the restaurant Botafumeiro in Barcelona, our main course was a platter of smoked trout and smoked mackerel, served with capers and grainy mustard. I hadn't thought of Barcelona as smoked fish country, but both were delicious. For dessert, our waiter suggested that we try sections of Valencia oranges with almond tuile cookies—that was it. After the smoked fish plate, the flavor and juiciness of the oranges really hit the spot. That got me thinking, so I blurred the line between main course and dessert and came up with these easy-to-handle hors d'oeuvres. These are my idea of cocktail party food—substantial, beautiful, and full of flavor. This works with any kind of smoked fish: mackerel or sable, to name just two.

MAKES 3 CUPS, ENOUGH FOR ABOUT 30 CANAPÉS • PREP TIME: 30 MINUTES

3 navel oranges

$^1\!/_2$ small red onion, cut into thin slivers (about $^3\!/_4$ cup)

2 tablespoons drained capers ("nonpareil" are best for this)

$1^1\!/_2$ tablespoons chopped fresh flat-leaf parsley

2 smoked trout fillets (about 6 ounces)

2 tablespoons olive oil

$1^1\!/_2$ teaspoons champagne or white wine vinegar

Kosher or fine sea salt and freshly ground pepper

2 large heads Belgian endive

1. Cut the tops and bottoms from the oranges, and cut off the peel, removing as much of the white pith as possible. Cut the sections from between the membranes with a paring knife, working over a bowl to catch the juice. Drain the juice into a small bowl and reserve it. Cut the orange segments crosswise in half and return them to the bowl.

2. Add the red onion, capers, and parsley to the oranges. Peel the skin off the trout and coarsely flake the trout into the bowl.

3. Beat 1 tablespoon of the reserved orange juice, the olive oil, vinegar, and salt and pepper to taste in a small bowl. Pour over the salad and toss gently. The salad can be made up to several hours in advance and refrigerated. Bring to room temperature before serving, about 30 minutes.

4. Cut the root ends off the endives and pull off the outer leaves. When the leaves no longer pull off easily, cut off another small bit of the root end and continue in the same way. You want nice big leaves for this, so stop when the leaves get smaller than 3 inches and keep the smaller leaves for a salad; you should have about 30 large leaves.

5. Line up the endive leaves on a serving platter. Taste the smoked trout salad and season with salt and pepper if you think it needs it. Mound a heaping tablespoonful of the salad onto the wide end of each endive leaf. Use the pointy ends of the leaves as little handles.

VARIATIONS: Serve the salad as an appetizer in a radicchio cup. Serves 6.

Serve the salad in a bowl surrounded by *pa amb tomaquet* (page 176) or plain sliced and toasted baguette or rounds of cucumber. Plunk a spoon in the bowl and let guests make their own canapés.

Crab and Roasted Pineapple Phyllo Triangles

The land crab of Puerto Rico is deliciously sweet and similar in texture to Jonah or peekytoe crab. My *tía* Gabriela would "cleanse" the live crabs by feeding them dry corn and water for three days and nights before cooking them. Knowing *Mami*'s enthusiastic love of her native crab, I wanted to come up with a crab salad that was a little different and a bit special, substituting lump crabmeat (which is more readily available) for the land crab. So I mixed these ingredients and served them in lettuce cups for a gorgeous first course for *Mami*'s birthday dinner. The leap as a filling for crispy, buttery phyllo triangles wasn't far behind. You are going to love these, and the best part is that you can make them ahead and keep them in your freezer!

MAKES ABOUT 40 TRIANGLES • PREP TIME: 1 HOUR • COOK TIME: 20 MINUTES (UNATTENDED)

1 small pineapple (see Note)

Olive oil

1 pound lump crabmeat, picked over for shells and cartilage

1 jalapeño, minced (seeds left in for more heat), or the amount and type of chile you like (see page 314)

2 to 3 tablespoons (or more) chopped fresh cilantro

Juice of 1 lime

Kosher or fine sea salt and freshly ground pepper

Half a 1-pound package frozen phyllo sheets (12 × 8 inches), defrosted

8 tablespoons (1 stick) butter, melted, or as needed

1. Preheat the oven to 400°F.
2. Trim and peel the pineapple as described in the recipe for Caribbean Breeze (page 32). Cut the pineapple into quarters. Cut out the core from 2 of the quarters. Set the remaining half pineapple aside for another use. Cut the trimmed quarters in half lengthwise.
3. Brush the pineapple spears with oil and lay them on a baking sheet. Bake, turning once, until well browned on both sides, about 20 minutes. Remove and let cool.

(continued)

4. Cut the cooled pineapple into ¼-inch dice. Gently toss the pineapple, crab, jalapeño, cilantro, and lime juice together in a bowl until well mixed. Season with salt and pepper to taste.

5. Unwrap the phyllo (see notes on working with phyllo, page 312) and lay the stack of sheets out on a cutting board with one of the short ends closest to you. Cut the sheets lengthwise into thirds. Cover the stack of phyllo strips with a sheet of plastic wrap and top it with a lightly dampened kitchen towel. Remove 2 strips of phyllo and lay them on the work surface, keeping them stacked. Brush the top sheet with melted butter. Mound a heaping teaspoonful of crab filling on the end of the strip closest to you. Fold the bottom edge of the strip over the filling so it is even with the left-hand side of the strip, and continue this "flag fold" until you have a neat triangular package. Tuck any overhanging edges underneath the triangle. Repeat with the remaining filling, phyllo, and butter, lining up the triangles on a parchment- or waxed-paper-lined baking sheet as you go. Brush the tops of the triangles with butter. If you do not plan to bake them right away, it is best to freeze the triangles as soon as they are made. Freeze them right on the baking sheet, then transfer them (gently) to resealable plastic bags or airtight containers once they are frozen solid. (The triangles can be frozen for up to 2 months.)

6. When ready to serve, preheat the oven to 375°F. Arrange the freshly made or frozen triangles on a buttered or nonstick baking sheet and let them stand at room temperature while the oven heats.

7. Bake until the phyllo is crisp and golden brown and the filling is heated through, about 15 minutes for freshly made triangles and 20 minutes for frozen triangles. Let cool for 5 minutes before serving.

NOTE: A 1-pint container of diced pineapple, available in most supermarkets, can be substituted for the whole fresh pineapple. Oil and bake the pineapple as directed above, adjusting the roasting time depending on the size of the chunks.

La Boqueria

Marc and David taste a little of this and that . . .

I often hear my guests say that when they receive an invitation for dinner at my house, they skip breakfast and lunch to be well prepared for the feast ahead. I could not feel more complimented. Meals at my house can last upwards of five hours, and that is no exaggeration!

On my family's first "culinary" trip, when we visited Barcelona, I fell in love with the whole tapas experience, and how much fun it is to sample many different little bites, instead of the traditional appetizer, entrée, and dessert template that we are used to. No other venue lends itself so perfectly to this idea as the cocktail party.

When visiting the phenomenon in Barcelona known as La Boqueria, we wandered through aisle after aisle, marveling at the beauty of the arrangements of seafood, produce, charcuterie, cheeses, and sweets. We snaked through the wondrous market, stopping for little bites of *jamón,* or a bit of cheese, a cup of hard cider, some beautifully roasted piquillo peppers, or any variety of deliciously just-fried croquettes. Jerry passed me half a ham and cheese croquette as I traded off a cup of cider, and he said, jokingly, "This is just like a cocktail party!" That's all it took for the little bell to go off in my head, and I made a mental note to re-create our rainy afternoon in La Boqueria for friends and family as soon as we got home.

Of course, we have done a lot more traveling since then, and I have culled many recipes from those trips that work exceptionally well for a cocktail party. Mexican *botanas* (sampler plates) with mini tostadas and ceviche bars that are good enough to make a meal from conform quite nicely to the tapas theme, but there is never a time when I have friends or family over for a few bites and a drink that Jerry doesn't catch my eye and, with a little wink, remind me of our wonderful memories of Barcelona's Boqueria.

Angela enjoys the delicious mushroom and truffle aroma.

Twice-Fried Plantain Cups

Tostones, fried slices of green plantains, are a staple of the Spanish-speaking Caribbean. They are made—like the best French fries—by frying the plantains twice, once at a lower temperature to cook them through and a second time at a higher temperature to crisp them up. (See the Variation below for more about making *tostones*.) By using the same technique, thick slices of plantain, and a handy little gizmo called a *tostonera*, you can make little cups of fried plantain goodness that are the perfect vehicle for spiced-up fillings. Needless to say, they make perfect cocktail party fare—easy to handle and satisfying enough to count as "real" food.

MAKES ABOUT 16 FRIED CUPS (DEPENDING ON THE SIZE OF THE PLANTAINS)
• PREP TIME: 45 MINUTES • COOK TIME: 15 MINUTES

FOR THE CUPS
4 green plantains
Vegetable oil, for frying

FOR THE FILLING (ANY OR ALL)
Crab Filling for *Pastelón* (page 259)
Filling for Spicy Shredded Pork Tacos
  (page 208)

Xni Pec Salsa (page 69)
Salt cod filling for Salt Cod and Japanese
  Eggplant Napoleons (page 206)
Any of the empanada fillings on pages
  59 through 65

1. Peel the plantains (see page 315). Cut each plantain crosswise into 4 more or less even (about 1½-inch) lengths. If you do not plan to cook the plantains right away, put them in a bowl with cold salted water to cover for up to 2 hours. Drain and pat dry thoroughly before continuing.

2. Pour 3 inches of oil into a Dutch oven or other heavy pot and heat until the tip of the handle of a wooden spoon dipped in the oil gives off a slow stream of bubbles (about 325°F). Carefully slip only as many of the plantain pieces into the oil as will float freely. Fry, turning them over now and then, until tender when poked with the tip of a paring knife, about 5 minutes. Remove them with a spider (see page 154) or a slotted spoon and drain on paper towels. Repeat with the remaining plantains.

3. When all the plantains have been fried, start making the cups with the plantains that were fried first (they will have cooled enough to work with). Stand a piece of plantain up in the well of a *tostonera* and close the lid, using a little gusto. The plantain will form a little cup. Take it out of the *tostonera* and turn the rest of the plantain pieces into cups in the same

Twice-Fried Plantain Cups filled with Weeknight Salsa (page 147)

way. The cups can be made to this point up to an hour in advance. Set them aside at room temperature.

4. Just before serving, reheat the oil until the tip of the handle of the wooden spoon dipped in the oil gives off a lively stream of bubbles (about 360°F). Carefully slip as many of the cups into the oil as will fit without crowding and fry until golden brown and crisp, about 4 minutes. Remove with the spider or slotted spoon and drain on paper towels. Fry the remaining plantain cups. Mound the filling of your choice into the fried *tostón* cups. Serve within 5 minutes.

VARIATION

TOSTONES: Peel as many green plantains (see page 315) as you like. One medium green plantain will yield about 12 *tostones.* Cut the plantains on a slight diagonal into ½-inch slices. Fry them in 325°F oil as described above and then, while they are still warm, smash them with a meat mallet or the bottom of a small heavy saucepan to flatten them to about ¼ inch. The *tostones* can be prepared to this point up to an hour or so before serving. Just before serving, fry them a second time in the hotter oil as described above until golden brown and crisp, about 2 minutes per side. Serve hot.

Fry the green plantains in moderately hot oil until softened.

Put each warm fried plantain cut side up in the *tostonera* and press down firmly.

Remove the pressed plantain cup from the *tostonera*.

Fry the plantain cups in the hot oil until crisp.

Chorizo-Stuffed Mushrooms

Every time, and I mean *every time,* I serve these mushrooms, I am besieged by my family and friends with pleas for more, more, more! The mushrooms available in Spain—*roellos, trozos,* and *llenguas* among them—are earthy and meaty and, sadly, unavailable here in the States. But white or cremini mushrooms make a very good stand-in. The fragrance of the chorizo combines with the nuttiness of the toasted bread crumbs and the umami of the mushrooms to produce an unbelievable burst of flavor.

MAKES 6 SERVINGS • PREP TIME: 30 MINUTES • COOK TIME: 25 MINUTES

1 link Spanish chorizo (about 4 ounces), casing removed (see Note)

18 large (about 2½- to 3-inch-wide) white mushrooms or cremini, if you can find them that large

⅓ cup plus 1 tablespoon olive oil

⅓ cup finely diced onion

½ cup plus 2 tablespoons bread crumbs

¼ cup chicken broth, homemade (page 303) or store-bought

2 tablespoons chopped fresh flat-leaf parsley

⅓ cup coarsely grated Manchego cheese

1. Preheat the oven to 400°F.
2. Cut the chorizo into 1-inch pieces and put them in the bowl of a food processor. Pulse until the chorizo is finely chopped. Scrape the chorizo into a small bowl and set aside. Hang on to the work bowl.
3. Remove the stems from the mushrooms. Mince half the stems in the food processor. Reserve the remaining stems for another use or discard them. Brush the mushroom caps with 1 tablespoon of the olive oil and set stem cavity up on a baking sheet. Set aside.
4. Pour the remaining ⅓ cup olive oil into a large skillet and heat over medium-high heat. Add the onion and minced mushroom stems and cook, stirring, just until softened, 2 to 3 minutes. Add the bread crumbs and toss and stir until toasted and golden brown. Scrape the bread crumb mixture into a bowl and set aside.
5. Wipe the skillet clean with paper towels and add the minced chorizo. Cook over high heat, stirring, until fragrant and glossy, about 3 minutes. Add to the bread crumb mixture. Add the chicken broth and parsley and fluff with a fork. Stir in the Manchego cheese.
6. Use a spoon to fill the mushroom caps, mounding the stuffing attractively. The mushrooms can be stuffed up to a day in advance. Line them up on a baking sheet, cover well with plastic wrap, and refrigerate.
7. Bake the mushrooms until the stuffing is lightly browned, 20 to 25 minutes. Serve hot or warm.

Funky Shrimp Wontons with Plantain–Sweet Potato Mash and Pineapple-Rum Dipping Sauce

White sweet potatoes (aka *boniatos* or *batatas*) are not nearly as sweet as the orangey sweet potatoes that are a Thanksgiving staple, but they have a wonderful creamy texture when cooked, and a flavor that is halfway between a potato and a yam. Green plantains are firm, with a mild, fruity-starchy appeal. Together they make a delicious mash that is wonderful as a side dish and unexpected tucked inside a wonton wrapper with a plump shrimp.

The sweet-tart pineapple dipping sauce is the perfect accompaniment. The pairing is a guaranteed huge hit at any cocktail party.

MAKES ABOUT 36 HORS D'OEUVRES, PLUS ENOUGH PLANTAIN–SWEET POTATO MASH TO SERVE 4 TO 6
• PREP TIME: 1 HOUR • COOK TIME: 40 MINUTES (10 FOR THE SHRIMP, 30 FOR THE SAUCE)

FOR THE DIPPING SAUCE
½ cup diced (¼-inch) pineapple
1½ cups orange juice
1 tablespoon sugar
1 star anise
¼ cup white rum

FOR THE PLANTAIN–SWEET POTATO MASH
3 green plantains
2 medium white sweet potatoes (aka *batatas* or *boniatos*; about 1½ pounds)

3 cloves garlic, pressed
Kosher or fine sea salt and freshly ground pepper

1 package (50) wonton skins
3 pounds jumbo shrimp (12 to 15 per pound), peeled (tails left on) and deveined
Canola oil, for frying

1. Make the sauce: Bring the pineapple, orange juice, sugar, and star anise to a boil in a medium saucepan over high heat. Adjust the heat so the liquid is simmering and cook until it is syrupy and reduced to one-fourth its original volume, about ½ cup. Add the rum and cook for 2 to 3 minutes. Remove from the heat and let cool. The sauce can be made up to a week in advance. Rewarm gently before serving.

2. Make the plantain–sweet potato mash: Peel the plantains (see page 315) and sweet potatoes. Cut both into 1-inch dice and put into a pot large enough to hold them comfortably. Pour

in enough cold water to cover generously, add the garlic, and bring to a boil. Cook until the plantains and potatoes are soft, about 20 minutes. Drain thoroughly.

3. Transfer the plantains, potatoes, and garlic to a bowl, add salt and pepper to taste, and mash with a potato masher until fairly smooth. If you are serving part of the mash as a side dish, you can serve it right away or let it cool and then refrigerate for up to 1 day. To reheat, bring ½ inch of water and a tablespoon of olive or vegetable oil to a boil in a heavy pot. Add the refrigerated mash and stir until softened and heated through. Check the seasoning before serving.

4. Wrap the shrimp: Lay a wonton wrapper on the work surface with one of the corners pointing toward you. Center a shrimp over the wrapper with the tail overhanging the point closest to you. Moisten the edges of the wrapper with a fingertip dipped in water. Spread a tablespoon of the mash over the shrimp, coating the top of it evenly. Fold the corner farthest from you over the shrimp, then fold the two side corners over the shrimp to encase it, leaving the closest corner unfolded, with the tail of the shrimp sticking out. Press all the edges gently to seal the shrimp good and tight. Line the shrimp wontons up on a parchment- or wax-paper-lined baking sheet as you form them. Repeat with the remaining wrappers, shrimp, and mash. The wontons can be refrigerated for up to 3 hours or frozen for up to 1 month. Freeze them right on the baking sheet until solid, then transfer them to freezer containers. Defrost them in the refrigerator for a few hours before frying them.

5. Fry the wontons: Pour ½ inch of oil into a large heavy skillet. Heat over medium heat until the tip of the handle of a wooden spoon dipped into the oil gives off a fairly steady sizzle (about 350°F). Slip only as many wontons into the oil as will fit comfortably and fry, turning as necessary, until evenly browned on all sides, about 5 minutes. If the wonton wrappers start to color too fast, turn down the heat, or the wrappers will brown before the shrimp have a chance to cook through. Drain on paper towels. The wontons can be kept warm in an oven heated to 200°F or "Warm" while you fry the rest. Serve hot with the dipping sauce in a bowl on the side.

A STITCH IN TIME: This recipe yields a bonus side dish—about 4 cups (4 to 6 servings) of plantain–sweet potato mash. Or look at it from the other side: Make the mash as a side dish for friends or family, then use whatever is left to make these delicious hors d'oeuvres and pop them into the freezer. Money in the bank.

Clam Fritters

Jicama is definitely not traditional, but fritters like these often have a little crunch in the way of celery or raw onion.

MAKES ABOUT 24 FRITTERS • PREP TIME: 30 MINUTES (INCLUDES STEAMING THE CLAMS) • COOK TIME: 4 MINUTES PER BATCH

2 dozen cherrystone or other small hard-shell clams, scrubbed

1 cup all-purpose flour

1 teaspoon baking powder

$1/2$ teaspoon crushed red pepper flakes

2 extra-large eggs

$1/2$ cup coarsely shredded jicama or finely diced celery (or even water chestnuts)

3 tablespoons chopped fresh cilantro

Canola oil, for frying

1. Pour enough water into a large heavy pot to cover the bottom generously. Bring to a boil, add the clams, and cover the pot. Steam just until the clams open, 6 to 7 minutes. Drain the clams and reserve the liquid. As soon as the clams are cool enough to handle, remove from the shells; discard the shells. Chop the clams coarsely.

2. Stir the flour, baking powder, and red pepper flakes together in a medium bowl. Beat the eggs and $2/3$ cup of the reserved clam cooking liquid together in a separate bowl. Pour the egg mixture into the dry ingredients; add the chopped clams, jicama, and cilantro; and stir just until the clams are evenly distributed and the dry ingredients are moistened. Let stand while you heat the oil.

3. Heat 2 inches of oil in a large deep skillet or heavy pot over medium heat until the tip of the handle of a wooden spoon dipped in the oil gives off a steady sizzle (about 350°F). Using a rounded tablespoonful for each, carefully slip only as many fritters into the oil as will fit without crowding and cook, turning them as necessary, until deep golden brown on all sides and heated through, about 4 minutes; adjust the heat as necessary to keep the oil as close to 350°F as possible. Remove the fritters and drain on a paper-towel-lined plate. Repeat with the remaining fritters. Serve hot.

TIP: Freeze any leftover clam steaming liquid. You pay three bucks for one little bottle of that clam juice in the supermarket!

"O.S.S.M.": Old-School Stuffed Mussels

This is a traditional tapa that you can find in just about every old-school Spanish restaurant, like El Quijote, next door to the Hotel Chelsea in Manhattan. The mussel filling is creamy and loaded with bits of ham and mushroom. The crisp-golden crust is beautiful to look at and lovely to bite into. These require some last-minute attention to crisp them up in oil, but the filling can (and should) be done hours in advance.

MAKES ABOUT 40 STUFFED MUSSELS • PREP TIME: 30 MINUTES (PLUS CHILLING) • COOK TIME: 10 MINUTES

FOR THE BÉCHAMEL

3 tablespoons unsalted butter

3 tablespoons all-purpose flour

1 cup milk

FOR THE MUSSELS

1 pound small mussels (about 20; see Note, page 214), scrubbed and debearded

2 tablespoons olive oil

1/3 cup finely diced yellow onion

2 cloves garlic, minced

1 cup finely chopped white or cremini mushrooms

3 ounces sliced serrano ham or prosciutto (have it cut 1/8 inch thick), cut into tiny dice (about 1/3 cup)

2 tablespoons chopped fresh flat-leaf parsley

1 tablespoon dry sherry

Kosher or fine sea salt

1 egg

1 cup plain dry bread crumbs, plus more as needed

Canola oil, for frying

1. Make the béchamel: Melt the butter in a medium saucepan over medium-low heat. Whisk in the flour and cook until the roux is smooth and bubbly but hasn't taken on any color, about 3 minutes. Pour the milk into the roux, whisking constantly until smooth. Bring to a simmer and cook, whisking constantly, until the sauce is thickened and glossy, about 4 minutes. Remove from the heat and set aside.

2. Pour 1/2 inch of water into a wide skillet. Bring to a boil, add the mussels, and cover the pan. Steam, shaking the pan occasionally, just until the mussels open, 3 to 4 minutes. Drain the mussels and discard the cooking liquid. Pull the mussels out of the shells and twist each shell into 2 halves. Line up the shells on a baking sheet. Chop the mussels very coarsely, put them in a small bowl, and set aside.

3. Heat the olive oil in a small skillet over medium heat. Add the onion and garlic and cook, stirring, until the onion is softened but not browned, about 4 minutes. Add the mushrooms and cook, stirring, until any liquid they have given off is evaporated. Stir in the ham and parsley and cook for 1 minute. Pour the sherry into the pan and cook until it is evaporated. Scrape the onion mixture into the bowl with the mussels and season lightly with salt. Stir in 2 tablespoons of the béchamel sauce. The filling can be made up to a day in advance. Cover it and the remaining béchamel well and refrigerate.

4. Fill as many of the mussel shells as you can with the filling, making sure the filling goes from one end of the shell to the other and mounding it very slightly. Using the remaining béchamel and working with a small spoon, coat the filling in each shell with an even layer of béchamel just thick enough to completely mask the filling. Chill the mussels for at least 15 minutes, or up to a few hours, to firm up the béchamel.

5. Coat the mussels: Beat the egg well in a shallow bowl. Spread the bread crumbs on a plate. Holding each shell by the edges, dip only the béchamel-coated stuffing into the beaten egg, hold the mussel over the egg for a second or two to get rid of the excess, and then dip the eggy part into the bread crumbs to coat the filling completely. Return the mussels to the baking sheet, crumb side up, as you go. Once the mussels are breaded, they should be cooked within 30 minutes.

6. Heat ¾ inch of vegetable oil in a wide heavy skillet over medium heat until the tip of the handle of a wooden spoon dipped into the oil gives off a steady stream of bubbles (about 350°F). Add only as many of the mussels, crumb side down, to the oil as will fit comfortably, and fry until the crumbs are golden brown and the filling is warmed through, about 4 minutes. If the crumbs start to brown much before that, turn down the heat and wait a few minutes before frying the rest. Drain briefly on paper towels and fry the remaining mussels. Serve hot.

Rice Croquettes

Croquettes transform leftovers into little gems that can be enjoyed as a tapa, as an after-school snack, or even as a side dish to any saucy, stewy dish, like Multi-Culti Braised Oxtails (page 221) or Braised Chicken with Coconut Milk and Curry (page 139).

MAKES ABOUT 24 CROQUETTES • PREP TIME: 30 MINUTES (PLUS TIME FOR RICE TO COOL) • COOK TIME: 4 MINUTES PER BATCH

1 tablespoon vegetable oil (if starting with raw rice)

1 cup medium-grain (not long-grain!) rice or 2$\frac{1}{2}$ cups cooked and cooled medium-grain rice

3 extra-large eggs

1 cup coarsely shredded drunken goat cheese (see Note)

$\frac{1}{2}$ cup frozen peas, defrosted

1$\frac{1}{2}$ tablespoons chopped fresh chives

2 tablespoons all-purpose flour

2 cups fine dry bread crumbs (homemade, or store-bought plain or seasoned) or as needed

Canola oil, for frying

1. If you don't have cooked rice on hand, make the rice: Heat the oil in a heavy 2-quart saucepan over medium heat. Add the rice and stir until it turns chalky, about 2 minutes. Pour in enough water to cover the rice by 1 inch and bring to a boil. Cook until the level of the water meets the rice. Cover the pan, reduce the heat to very low, and cook until the rice is tender but still firm, about 20 minutes. Remove from the heat, fluff with a fork, and transfer to a bowl. Let cool to room temperature.

2. Beat 1 of the eggs well in a small bowl. Stir the egg, cheese, peas, chives, and flour into the rice until well blended. Chill until a little of the mixture holds its shape when pinched together, at least 1 hour. The mix can be made up to 2 hours before cooking and refrigerated.

3. Using a heaping tablespoon of the rice mixture for each, form smooth, round croquettes by rolling the mixture between your palms. Line the croquettes up on a baking sheet as you go.

4. Beat the remaining 2 eggs well in a shallow bowl. Spread the bread crumbs on a plate. Roll a croquette in the egg until coated, hold it over the bowl for a few seconds to let the excess egg drip back into the bowl, and then lay the croquette in the bread crumbs and shake the plate to coat the croquette on all sides. Pat the bread crumbs onto the croquette to help them stick, and shake off the excess crumbs. Repeat with the remaining croquettes, lining them up on a clean baking sheet as you go.

5. Fry the croquettes: Heat 2 inches of oil in a deep skillet or heavy pot over medium heat until the tip of the handle of a wooden spoon dipped in the oil gives off a steady sizzle (about 350°F). Slip only as many croquettes into the oil as will fit without crowding and cook, turning them as necessary, until deep golden brown on all sides and heated through, about 4 minutes; adjust the heat as necessary to keep the oil as close to 350°F as possible. Remove and drain on a paper-towel-lined plate. Repeat with the remaining croquettes.

NOTE: Drunken goat cheese is a Spanish semisoft goat cheese that has been soaked in red wine for 2 to 3 days. The result is a creamy and fairly mellow cheese with a little kick and a pale burgundy rind. It can be tricky to find, but any semisoft, assertively flavored cheese will do. Smoked Gouda is a good, though not very traditional, alternative.

Yuca Fritters ⋰ AREPITAS DE YUCA

MAKES ABOUT 18 FRITTERS • PREP TIME: 15 MINUTES • COOK TIME: 4 MINUTES PER BATCH

1 small yuca (about 1¼ pounds, or 2 cups frozen grated yuca; see Note, page 85)
2 tablespoons grated onion
2 large eggs, beaten
4 tablespoons unsalted butter, melted
2 teaspoons anisette or other anise-flavored liqueur

2 teaspoons baking powder
¼ teaspoon sugar
Kosher or fine sea salt and freshly ground pepper
1 tablespoon chopped fresh cilantro
Canola oil, for frying

1. Peel the yuca and grate enough to measure 2 cups. Put the grated yuca into a bowl and add the onion, then the eggs, and then the butter, mixing after each addition. Stir in the anisette, baking powder, and sugar. Season with salt and pepper. Stir in the cilantro.

2. Heat ½ inch of oil in a skillet over medium-high heat until the tip of the handle of a wooden spoon dipped in the oil gives off a slow, steady stream of tiny bubbles (about 340°F). Using a heaping tablespoon for each, carefully slip only as many fritters into the oil as will fit without crowding and fry until golden on the first side, about 2 minutes. Flip the fritters gently, to avoid splattering, and cook until the second side is golden, about 1 minute. Drain on paper towels. Repeat with the remaining batter. Serve hot.

Clam, Bacon, and Piquillo Pepper Coca

MAKES ABOUT 30 HORS D'OEUVRES OR 6 MAIN-COURSE SERVINGS
• PREP TIME: 30 MINUTES • COOK TIME: 20 MINUTES

3 dozen cherrystone or other small hard-shell clams, such as Manila, scrubbed
Olive oil
Coarse yellow cornmeal
1 pound store-bought pizza dough

¾ pound sliced bacon
Half a 10-ounce jar piquillo peppers (about 6), torn into rough 1-inch-or-so pieces
3 cloves garlic, thinly sliced
1 cup whole-milk ricotta cheese

1. Preheat the oven to 425°F.

2. Pour enough water into a large heavy pot to cover the bottom generously. Bring to a boil, add the clams, and cover the pot. Steam just until the clams open, 6 to 7 minutes. Drain the clams and reserve the juice for another use, if you like. As soon as the clams are cool enough to handle, discard the shells.

3. While the clams are cooling, grease a 13 × 18-inch half sheet pan (see Tip) or a jelly-roll pan with olive oil and sprinkle a generous amount of cornmeal over the oil. Roll the dough out on a lightly floured surface to a rectangle approximately 12 × 14 inches and lay it on the baking sheet. Poke the whole surface of the dough at ½-inch intervals with a fork.

4. Cook the bacon in a skillet or microwave until lightly browned and somewhat crisp; don't cook until all of the fat is rendered or the bacon is completely cooked—the remaining fat will flavor the dough and the bacon will finish crisping in the oven. Drain on paper towels, and cut crosswise into 1½-inch pieces.

5. Cover the top of the dough with the clams, bacon, and peppers, spacing them all more or less evenly and leaving a ½-inch border. Scatter the garlic over the toppings. Dot any open dough with rounded tablespoonfuls of ricotta. Bake until the dough is a deep golden brown around the edges and puffed and the bacon is crisp, about 15 minutes. Let cool for 5 minutes, then slide from the baking sheet onto a cutting board and cut into pieces.

TIP: Half sheet pans are a restaurant kitchen staple that come in incredibly handy in a home kitchen. They aren't very glamorous looking, but they are sturdy, inexpensive, and a little larger (13 × 18 inches) than even the largest housewares-store baking sheet. You may spot them in housewares stores, but you will almost certainly find them cheaper in restaurant supply houses.

Artichoke, Asparagus, and Goat Cheese Coca

MAKES ABOUT 30 HORS D'OEUVRES OR 6 MAIN-COURSE SERVINGS
• PREP TIME: 20 MINUTES • COOK TIME: 20 MINUTES

1 yellow onion, cut lengthwise in half, then into thin slivers (about 2 cups)

2 tablespoons olive oil, plus more for oiling the pan

One 9-ounce box frozen artichoke hearts, defrosted

1 tablespoon fennel seeds

1 teaspoon coarsely chopped fresh thyme

Kosher or fine sea salt and freshly ground pepper

1/2 pound asparagus (see Note)

Yellow cornmeal

1 pound store-bought pizza dough

1/4 pound plain goat cheese, cut into 1/2-inch slices

1. Put the onion, olive oil, and 1/4 cup water in a large deep skillet and bring to a boil over high heat. Cover the skillet and boil, stirring occasionally, until the onion is translucent and softened and the liquid is nearly evaporated, about 10 minutes. Uncover the skillet and cook until all the liquid is evaporated and the onion is beginning to brown, about 5 minutes. Reduce the heat to low and cook, stirring occasionally, until the onion is very tender and golden brown, about 10 minutes. Scrape into a mixing bowl and cool.

2. Squeeze the artichokes very dry and stir them into the onion along with the fennel seeds, thyme, and salt and pepper to taste.

3. Bring 1/2 inch of salted water to a boil in a wide skillet over high heat. Add the asparagus and cook, turning them a few times, until tender but still firm and bright green, about 2 minutes for very thin asparagus, up to 6 minutes for thick asparagus. Drain the asparagus in a colander, run them briefly under cold water, and drain on paper towels.

4. Preheat the oven to 400°F. Lightly grease a half sheet pan (see Tip, opposite) with olive oil and sprinkle it generously with cornmeal.

5. Roll out the dough on a lightly floured surface to a 12 × 14-inch rectangle and lay it on the prepared pan. Poke the dough at 1/2-inch intervals with a fork. Spread the onion mixture evenly over the dough, leaving a border of 1/2 inch or so around the edges. Arrange the asparagus evenly over the onion mixture—crisscrossing them, lining them up, or however you like, depending on how big they are and how they're cut. Dot the top of the vegetables with the goat cheese.

(continued)

6. Bake until the edges of the crust are a deep golden brown and the goat cheese is lightly browned, about 20 minutes. Let cool for 5 minutes, then slide from the baking sheet onto a cutting board and cut into pieces.

NOTE: The *coca* can be made with asparagus of any thickness. However, for the sake of neatness, cut any asparagus that are pinky-thickness or wider in half lengthwise. You can also cut whole spears crosswise into shorter pieces if you like.

Coca—Spain's Answer to the Pizza

If I were to count the number of *cocas* that I sampled in Barcelona, I might have to dedicate a whole chapter, or maybe even a book, to them alone. On the morning that we arrived in Barcelona, jet lagged and disoriented, we set out on the Paseo de Gracia in search of food. We found a tapas chain and ordered just about one of everything on the menu. We agreed that a *coca* with the stellar combination of tiny baby clams, bacon, and red piquillo peppers was the hands-down winner in our virgin journey into the world of tapas! The second *coca* here—topped with goat cheese, asparagus, and caramelized onion—is (loosely) based on another one of my favorites from Spain. The original featured only thin asparagus and fennel seed, but I thought the tang of goat cheese and melty-sweet onions would round out all the flavors. It certainly did that and more, and it proved that when it comes to *cocas*, the sky's the limit.

Clam, Bacon, and Piquillo Pepper Coca (page 200)

DINNER PARTIES

I t should come as no surprise that I love to entertain. When I was growing up, *Abuela* always had a house full of people. She loved the hustle and bustle and took immense pride in making the food she loved for other people. I couldn't wait to grow up and do the same. Of course, back then, it wasn't thought of as entertaining; we called it "life."

When we were first married, Jerry was doing his residency. His hours were long and we weren't exactly well-off, but we still managed to gather people together: new friends, old friends, and, always, family. When my mother and father moved to Florida, the holidays moved too—to our house. Sometimes it was just our growing family that gathered together, but more often, especially during the big holidays like Thanksgiving or special occasions like my sister's engagement party, I'd be feeding thirty or forty people! I got what I wished for as a little girl—a house full of people I loved, the same excitement, and, not least of all, the noise!

As I gained more experience in the kitchen and learned to appreciate the advantages of getting together with friends around our table, not a restaurant table, I started to host more dinner parties. Dinner parties are a lot calmer than big holiday get-togethers, but in some ways, they require more planning than a buffet for twenty-five. That is one of the things I like about them. For me, the anticipation is what a dinner party is all about. It isn't unusual for Jerry to come downstairs on the days leading up to one of these events and find me reading cookbooks or poring over my notes from my trips to get an idea of what I'd like to serve.

Some of these recipes may seem to make generous amounts for 6 people. In fact, all these recipes will most likely serve 8 if you plan to serve a first course, main course with a side dish or two, and dessert. Given my background, cooking for a big crowd is a hard habit to break and, truthfully, I've never really tried to. I like leftovers. What can I say?

Mussels with Corn and Tomatoes (page 214)

Salt Cod and Japanese Eggplant Napoleons

As unusual as it sounds, the pairing of salt cod and eggplant is a traditional one in the Caribbean. It is a wonderful marriage, full of flavor and very much alive. Even if you think you're a fan of neither, you may be won over by my take on the theme, featuring layers of well-seasoned salt cod sandwiched between thin slices of grilled (or panfried) Japanese eggplant.

MAKES 6 SERVINGS • PREP TIME: 10 MINUTES (PLUS A DAY FOR SOAKING THE SALT COD) • COOK TIME: 30 MINUTES

¾ pound salt cod fillets, soaked (see page 261)

2 tablespoons olive oil, plus more for brushing the eggplant

½ cup Sofrito (page 305)

¼ cup alcaparrado or coarsely chopped pimiento-stuffed olives

½ cup Spanish-style tomato sauce

½ teaspoon ground cumin

Kosher or fine sea salt and freshly ground pepper

3 medium Japanese eggplants (about 1 pound), cut on the bias into ½-inch slices (see Note)

1. Make the salt cod filling: Drain the soaked salt cod and put it in a large saucepan with enough fresh cold water to cover it generously. Bring the water to a boil, then adjust the heat so the water is simmering and cook until the cod flakes apart easily, 6 to 10 minutes, depending on the thickness of the fillets. Drain gently.

2. As soon as it is cool enough to handle, shred the cod coarsely: It will fall apart a little more as it cooks with the other ingredients, and you want to be sure there is some texture to the filling.

3. Heat the oil in a medium skillet over medium heat. Add the sofrito and alcaparrado and cook, stirring, until the liquid has evaporated and the sofrito starts to sizzle. Add the salt cod, tomato sauce, and cumin and bring to a boil. Taste and season with salt (if needed) and pepper. Set aside.

4. Preheat a gas grill to medium, if using.

5. Season the eggplant slices lightly with salt. Brush the slices with olive oil and grill them over medium heat, turning once, until well marked and tender, about 8 minutes. Or heat a large heavy skillet over medium heat and cook the eggplant slices, turning them once, until well

browned and tender, about 8 minutes. Both the eggplant and the filling can be prepared up to 2 hours in advance and kept at room temperature.

6. To serve, heat the salt cod filling to simmering. Lay an eggplant slice on a small serving plate and top with about 3 tablespoons of the cod filling. Repeat, and top with a third slice of eggplant to finish off the napoleon. Repeat with the remaining eggplant and filling. Serve right away.

NOTE: For 6 servings, you will need 6 slices from each eggplant. If the slices end up a little thicker or thinner, it is not a big deal.

Spicy Shredded Pork Tacos

This recipe makes more than you will need for a meal. Leftover *tinga,* which only gets better after a couple of days in the fridge, makes a main course (especially when enhanced with frozen peas and diced carrots), paired with Mexican Rice (page 158) or Cumin-Scented Fried Potatoes (page 153). If there's any leftover pork after *that,* use it to fill empanadas (see page 61) and freeze them.

MAKES ENOUGH TO FILL 18 TORTILLAS (6 AMPLE FIRST-COURSE SERVINGS), PLUS 6 MAIN-COURSE SERVINGS • PREP TIME: 10 MINUTES (PLUS 2 TO 24 HOURS MARINATING TIME) • COOK TIME: 2½ HOURS

FOR THE PORK *TINGA*

2 tablespoons dry adobo, homemade (page 307) or store-bought

One 4-pound boneless pork shoulder roast, cut into 5 or 6 pieces, each about 2 inches wide

Juice of 1 grapefruit

Juice of 2 lemons

2 tablespoons vegetable oil, plus more as needed

4 Mexican chorizos (about 1 pound), removed from casings

2 medium yellow onions, finely diced

4 cloves garlic, minced

1 teaspoon dried oregano

1 teaspoon ground cumin

1 teaspoon ground cinnamon

1 teaspoon ground allspice

¼ teaspoon ground cloves

2 bay leaves

One 28-ounce can crushed tomatoes

Kosher or fine sea salt and freshly ground pepper

18 corn tortillas

1. Marinate the pork: Rub the dry adobo into the slices of pork, seasoning all sides well. Put in a roasting pan or baking dish large enough to hold the pork in a single layer. Pour the citrus juices over the pork and turn to coat all sides. Refrigerate for at least 2 hours, or as long as overnight, turning the pork in the marinade occasionally.

2. Make the filling: Remove the pork from the marinade and pat dry; discard the marinade. Heat the vegetable oil in a Dutch oven or large casserole over medium-high heat. Lay only as many of the pork slices in the pot as will fit comfortably and cook, turning the pieces as necessary, until browned on all sides, being careful not to burn the bottom of the pot; lower the heat a little if necessary. Transfer the pork pieces to a plate as they brown and add the remaining pieces to the pan, replenishing the oil if necessary.

3. Add the chorizo to the pot and cook, stirring to break up any big pieces, until browned, about 5 minutes. Add the onions and garlic, stirring to pick up any brown bits from the bottom of

the pot. Add the oregano, cumin, cinnamon, allspice, and cloves and toss in the bay leaves. Stir in the canned tomatoes and season with salt and pepper to taste. Return the pork to the pot, turning it to coat with the sauce. Bring to a boil, then adjust the heat so the sauce is simmering, and cover the pot. Cook until the pork falls apart easily when poked with a fork, 1½ to 2 hours. Skim the fat off the top of the sauce occasionally as the pork cooks.

4. Remove the pork to a large plate. Coarsely shred the pork with 2 forks and stir back into the sauce. Check the seasoning and add salt and pepper if necessary. The pork can be prepared up to 2 days in advance. Let cool completely and refrigerate. Rewarm the pork over low heat, adding a small amount of water if necessary to make the sauce smooth.

5. To serve, wrap the tortillas in aluminum foil and place in a preheated 350°F oven until warmed through and softened, about 15 minutes. Place a heaping tablespoonful of the filling on each tortilla and roll up. Serve hot with your favorite salsa.

Gnocchi with Vegetables and Goat Cheese
✑ NOQUI NUEVO ANDINO

In Peru, the train we took to the ruins at Macchu Pichu made an overnight stop at a beautiful resort built into the side of the mountains. In Casa Andina, the resort's restaurant, Chef Teddy Bouroncle took very good care of us, including this fantastic pasta course among his offerings.

The blending of local ingredients—like the *ají amarillo* paste and lima beans found here—with non-traditional dishes like gnocchi reflects a trend I saw throughout my travels in Central and Latin America. Young Latin chefs are coming to the States or going to Europe to train and are gaining exposure to classic dishes and techniques. Back home, they incorporate this knowledge into the cuisine of the region, in much the same way that Douglas Rodriguez and other chefs revitalized Latin cooking in America. In Peru, Ecuador, and Chile, this style of cooking is known as *Nuevo Andino,* or New Andean.

MAKES 12 FIRST-COURSE OR 6 MAIN-COURSE SERVINGS (SEE A STITCH IN TIME) • PREP TIME: 1 HOUR • COOK TIME: 30 MINUTES

FOR THE SAUCE
2 tablespoons olive oil
2 cloves garlic, very thinly sliced
One 10-ounce package cremini mushrooms, thinly sliced (about 2 cups)
4 plum tomatoes, peeled, seeded (see page 38), and cut into $1/2$-inch dice (about 3 cups)
1 cup frozen baby lima beans
$1/4$ cup chopped fresh cilantro

FOR THE GNOCCHI
3 large Yukon gold potatoes (about 2 pounds), scrubbed

$1/4$ cup grated cotija cheese or Parmesan cheese
1 extra-large egg, beaten
1 tablespoon *ají amarillo* paste or Improvised *Ají Amarillo* Puree (see page 37)
1 teaspoon salt
$1/8$ teaspoon freshly grated or ground nutmeg
$1^3/4$ cups all-purpose flour, plus more as needed

1 cup crumbled goat cheese (about 4 ounces)

1. Make the sauce (if cooking the gnocchi immediately after forming them; if freezing the gnocchi, make the sauce up to a day before serving them): Heat the olive oil in a large skillet over medium heat. Add the garlic and shake the pan until the garlic is sizzling. Add the mushrooms and cook until lightly browned, about 4 minutes. Add the tomatoes and lima beans and toss until the tomatoes and mushrooms begin to give off their liquid. Raise the heat to high and bring the sauce to a boil. Cook until there is just enough liquid left to lightly coat the vegetables. The sauce can be made to this point and kept at room temperature for up to 2 hours, or refrigerated for as long as overnight. Reheat to simmering over low heat while you cook the gnocchi.

2. Make the gnocchi: Put the potatoes in a large pot with enough cold water to cover them generously. Bring to a rolling boil, then adjust the heat so the water is boiling gently and cook the potatoes until tender at the center when poked with a paring knife, about 35 minutes.

3. Drain the potatoes and, as soon as you can stand the heat, peel them. Cut the potatoes into quarters and pass them through a ricer or food mill fitted with the fine disk onto a baking sheet. Spread them out in an even layer so as much of the steam as possible is released. Let cool to room temperature.

4. Gather the potatoes gently into a mound. Make a well in the center and add the grated cheese, egg, pepper paste, salt, and nutmeg. Beat together to mix well, then blend the potatoes into the egg mixture just until more or less evenly distributed—the dough will get more thoroughly mixed when the flour is added. Add the flour and knead gently just until evenly blended. The dough should be soft but not at all sticky. If necessary, knead in more flour 1 tablespoon at a time until the dough is no longer sticky.

5. Cut the dough into 6 pieces. Roll each one out to a ½-inch-thick rope: Shape each piece of dough into a rough log first. Then, starting at the center of the log and working toward the ends, roll the dough back and forth under your palms and fingertips. Keep your fingertips pointing away from each other as you roll to help the dough in the right direction. Cut the ropes into ½-inch pieces. You can cook the gnocchi as is, or form them into little ridged dumplings: Sprinkle flour over the pieces of dough and roll each between your palms into a little ball. Hold a dinner fork at an angle to the work surface, impale a dough ball with the tip of your thumb, and drag it downward against the tines of the fork. The dough will curl around your thumb and the outer surface will pick up ridges from the tines of the fork. Transfer the gnocchi to a baking sheet as you form them. The gnocchi can be refrigerated for up to 20 minutes or frozen for up to several weeks. Freeze the gnocchi right on the baking sheet and, once frozen solid, transfer the gnocchi to resealable plastic bags.

6. Heat a very large pot (about 16 quarts) of salted water to a boil. If you don't have a pot that large, cook the gnocchi in batches. Slip as many of the gnocchi as you are going to cook into the water. Cook just until they rise to the top of the water and are tender but still firm, about 1 minute for freshly made gnocchi, up to 2 minutes for frozen. If the gnocchi will fit into the

pan with the sauce, lift them from the water with a spider (see page 154) or a slotted spoon and transfer them to the sauce. If they won't, drain them in a colander, return them to the pot, and add the sauce to the pot. In either case, add the goat cheese and cook over low heat until it is melted, stirring gently to blend it into the sauce. Stir in the chopped cilantro and serve in warm shallow bowls.

TIP: Stir the boiling water *before* you add the gnocchi to it. The swirling water—and continued gentle stirring—will help keep the gnocchi from sticking together. This works with pasta too.

A STITCH IN TIME: This recipe makes enough to serve 12 as a first course (twice the amount of most other recipes in this chapter). It really doesn't take all that much more time to make 12 servings of gnocchi than it does to make 6, so you may as well go for it. And because they freeze beautifully, you are much better off making a full batch, even if you'll be serving only a few people. The sauce freezes well too, so if you are freezing half the gnocchi, freeze half the sauce. Think of it—a completely effortless, impressive first course weeks down the line with virtually no effort. I love it!

Mexican Chicken-Lime Soup

There isn't much to this soup, and that is the beauty of it: stick to high-quality ingredients and don't take any shortcuts, and you'll be rewarded with a delicious, satisfying soup every time. This soup was part of a lunch we enjoyed at a *mezcal* distillery in Mexico (see page 11). Lunch was capped off with peaches poached in agave-spiked syrup flavored with cloves—another delicious triumph from the less-is-more school of cooking. If you haven't already discovered what a simple squeeze of lime can do for just about anything, let me be the first to pass you a lime wedge. It's not just for your Corona.

MAKES 8 TO 10 FIRST-COURSE SERVINGS • PREP TIME: 2 HOURS (MOSTLY UNATTENDED; OR 20 MINUTES IF STARTING WITH PREMADE BROTH) • COOK TIME: 30 MINUTES

Homemade Chicken Broth (page 303)

1 small celery root (about 8 ounces), peeled and cut into ½-inch dice (about 1½ cups)

2 ears corn, shucked, silk removed, and cut into 1½-inch rounds

2 large ripe tomatoes, cored and cut into ¼-inch dice (about 3 cups)

4 scallions, trimmed and thinly sliced (about ¼ cup)

Juice of 2 limes

1 to 2 chipotles in adobo, finely diced (see Note)

1. Make the broth.
2. When the broth has cooled, strain it, remove the chicken meat from the bones, and coarsely shred the meat back into the broth. The broth and chicken can be prepared in advance and refrigerated for up to 2 days or frozen for up to 2 months.
3. Add the celery root and corn and heat the broth to a boil over medium heat. Adjust the heat so the broth is simmering and cook until the celery root is fork-tender, about 10 minutes.
4. Stir in the tomatoes, scallions, and lime juice. Stir the chipotles into the soup if you know your crowd likes heat, or pass a small bowl of the chiles at the table.

NOTE: The smoky heat from the chipotles is easy to control by adding just as much or as little as you like. If chopped chiles seem too much, just spoon a little of the sauce the chipotles are packed in into the broth. That tomato sauce packs quite a bit of heat on its own.

Mussels with Corn and Tomato (see photo, page 204)

✑ CHOROS A LA CHALACA

On a family vacation to Peru, we spent a lot of time in Cuzco and considerably less time in Lima, which is a shame, but even so, our trip to Lima was memorable. After the family took a tour of the city (which included a sex museum—don't ask!), our guide made good on a promise to take us to an extraordinary restaurant: La Rosa Nautica, situated at the end of a pier that jutted out into the sea. The flavor of the mussels we sampled that night stuck with me, and now I can make them anytime I like.

MAKES 8 SERVINGS • PREP TIME: 25 MINUTES • COOK TIME: 10 MINUTES

3 pounds mussels (see Note), scrubbed and debearded

1 cup fresh or frozen corn kernels

2 large tomatoes (about 1 pound), cored and cut into small dice (about 3 cups)

1 small red onion, minced (about 1/2 cup)

1/2 yellow bell pepper, cored, seeded, and cut into small dice (about 1/2 cup)

1/4 cup chopped fresh cilantro

2 large cloves garlic, minced

1/2 serrano chile, minced

2 tablespoons olive oil

Juice of 1 lime

Kosher or fine sea salt and freshly ground pepper

1. Put the mussels, corn kernels, and 1/2 cup water in a wide deep skillet or Dutch oven, cover, and bring to a boil. Steam just until the mussels open, 3 to 5 minutes.
2. While the mussels are steaming, toss the tomatoes, red onion, bell pepper, cilantro, garlic, chile, olive oil, and lime juice together in a bowl. Season with salt and pepper to taste.
3. With a spider (see page 154) or a slotted spoon, scoop the mussels and corn out of the skillet into a large bowl. Pour the tomato mixture into the broth in the skillet. Shake the pan over low heat until the vegetables are warmed through. Pour over the mussels and toss gently to mix. Serve hot or at room temperature.

NOTE: There are a few things to keep in mind when buying mussels. They should have shiny black shells that are tightly closed. Or if they're open, they should close and stay closed when tapped on a counter. The mussels should smell sweet and briny. Whether they are "cultivated" or wild-caught, they may have a wiry little growth, called the beard, sticking out of the flat edge of the shell. Tug on the beards firmly to get rid of them before cooking the mussels.

Cream of Chestnut Soup with Posole

"Chestnuts? Latin? Is she kidding?" In Puerto Rico, chestnuts are known as *pan en grano,* which translates literally as "breadfruit in nut form," a reference to their earthy flavor. Chestnut lovers will flip for this soup.

MAKES 8 SERVINGS • PREP TIME: 15 MINUTES • COOK TIME: 35 MINUTES

3 tablespoons olive oil

2 small leeks, white parts only, cleaned and
    cut into $^1/_2$-inch slices

3 stalks celery, from the heart, chopped

4 cloves garlic, minced or pressed

2 sprigs fresh thyme

Kosher or fine sea salt and freshly ground
    pepper

10 ounces white mushrooms, thinly sliced

One 8.75-ounce package cooked chestnuts
    (1 heaping cup; see Note)

3 tablespoons sweet sherry

4 cups chicken broth, homemade (page 303)
    or store-bought

1 smoked ham hock

2 bay leaves

$1^1/_2$ cups heavy cream

One 29-ounce can posole, drained and rinsed

1. Heat the olive oil in a Dutch oven or other heavy 4-quart pot over medium heat. Add the leeks, celery, garlic, and thyme; season lightly with salt and pepper; and cook, stirring, until the leeks and celery are wilted, about 4 minutes. Stir in the mushrooms and chestnuts, raise the heat to high, and cook until the mushrooms start to release their liquid. Add the sherry, bring to a boil, and cook until the sherry is almost entirely evaporated.

2. Pour in 3 cups of the chicken broth, add the ham hock and bay leaves, and bring to a boil. Adjust the heat so the broth is simmering and cook, covered, for 20 minutes.

3. Discard the bay leaves. Reserve the ham hock for another use, such as the "refried" beans on page 162. With a slotted spoon, transfer the vegetables and chestnuts to the work bowl of a food processor. Pour in the remaining 1 cup broth. (If the work bowl is not large enough to hold all the solids comfortably, work in batches.) Process until smooth, stopping once or twice to scrape down the sides of the work bowl. Return the puree to the Dutch oven. The soup can be made ahead to this point up to 2 days in advance.

4. Gently bring the soup back to a simmer. Stir in the cream and bring to a simmer. Stir the posole into the soup and simmer until heated through. Season with salt and pepper to taste.

NOTE: Vacuum-sealed chestnuts are available at Chinese, Italian, and specialty grocers. All the dog work—roasting and peeling—is done for you, so they are a tremendous time-saver.

Cuzco Roast Pork Loin with Onion and Pepper Stir-Fry ✍ LOMO SALTADO

MAKES 8 SERVINGS • PREP TIME: 30 MINUTES (PLUS 2 TO 24 HOURS MARINATING TIME) • COOK TIME: 1½ HOURS

One 4-pound boneless center-cut pork loin roast

1 tablespoon dry adobo, homemade (page 307) or store-bought

1 teaspoon liquid smoke

2 cups beef broth, homemade or store-bought

2 tablespoons grapeseed oil

1 each red, yellow, and orange bell pepper, cored, seeded, and cut into strips

1 large Spanish onion, cut lengthwise in half, then into ¼-inch-wide strips

1½ tablespoons all-purpose flour

Kosher or fine sea salt and freshly ground pepper

Chopped fresh cilantro, for garnish

1. Rub the entire surface of the loin with the adobo and liquid smoke. Tie with kitchen twine at 2-inch intervals. Place the roast fat side down on a rack in a roasting pan and refrigerate for at least 2 hours, or up to 1 day. Bring to room temperature before continuing.

2. Preheat the oven to 400°F.

3. Roast the pork fat side down for 30 minutes. Turn over and cook until an instant-read thermometer registers 150°F when inserted into the thickest part of the roast, about 30 minutes longer. Transfer the roast to a carving board, tent with aluminum foil, and set aside to rest.

4. Pour the beef broth into the roasting pan and, with a wooden spoon, scrape up the brown bits that are stuck to the bottom of the pan. If the brown bits are stubborn, set the roasting pan over low heat and continue stirring. Strain the pan juices and set aside.

5. Heat the oil in a large skillet over medium-high heat until just starting to smoke. Add the vegetables and cook, stirring, until crisp-tender, about 3 minutes. Sprinkle with the flour and stir for a few minutes. Stir in the strained pan juices, adjust the heat so the liquid is simmering, and season with salt and pepper to taste. Simmer for 1 to 2 minutes. Remove from the heat.

6. Cut the roast into ½-inch slices and arrange overlapping on a platter. Spoon some of the onion-pepper sauce over the pork and sprinkle a little chopped cilantro over the peppers.

Sweet Peppers Stuffed with Rice and Cheese

My grandmother made the best stuffed peppers. (I know everyone says that, but I happen to be sure!) She had a neat little trick that I'm passing on to you: instead of covering the filling with the tops of the peppers, she soaked slices of bread in seasoned egg and used those to top them. Not only do the slices brown beautifully, they make a little bonus—a savory mini bread pudding to eat along with the peppers.

Charring and peeling the peppers may seem like a lot of work if you're used to stuffing raw peppers, but if you take care to char the peppers thoroughly over high heat, the burnt skin will slip right off. And it is hard to overemphasize what it does for the flavor and texture of the finished dish. The sauce penetrates the peppers better, and the roasty-toasty flavor of the pepper permeates the rice. It is my mission to have everyone in America make stuffed peppers this way!

MAKES 6 SERVINGS, WITH (MAYBE) LEFTOVERS

• PREP TIME: 45 MINUTES • COOK TIME: 35 MINUTES (UNATTENDED)

10 large yellow, orange, or red bell
    peppers, or a mix of all three

FOR THE FILLING

1 small zucchini

2 tablespoons olive oil

1 small yellow onion, finely diced (about
    1 cup)

1/2 pound cremini mushrooms, thinly sliced
    (about 2 cups)

1 1/4 cups long-grain white rice

1 tablespoon salt

6 ounces smoked Gouda, shredded (about
    1 3/4 cups)

5 extra-large eggs

1/2 teaspoon onion powder

Kosher or fine sea salt and freshly ground
    pepper

5 slices white bread

1 1/2 cups tomato juice

1. Roast the peppers until well blackened on all sides (see page 274). Wrap each one in a double thickness of damp paper towels as it is done. Let the peppers stand until cool.

2. Make the filling: Trim the ends from the zucchini and cut the zuke lengthwise into quarters. Scoop out the seeds and coarsely grate the zucchini.

3. Heat the olive oil in a medium saucepan over medium-high heat. Add the onion and mushrooms and cook, stirring, until softened, about 4 minutes.

4. Pour the rice into the saucepan, stirring to coat with oil, then add the salt. Pour in enough water to cover the rice by about 1 inch (about 2 cups) and bring to a boil. Cook until the

water reaches the level of the rice. Stir the rice once, cover the pan, and lower the heat to very low. Cook, without uncovering the pan or stirring, until the rice is tender but not mushy and the water is absorbed, about 20 minutes. Fluff with a fork and set aside to cool a bit.

5. Preheat the oven to 350°F.

6. Stir the zucchini and Gouda into the warm rice.

7. Slide the paper towels from the peppers, removing as much of the blackened skin as you can with them. Wipe off the rest of the blackened skin with the paper towels. Cut a circle around the stems and remove the stems and cores from the peppers. If you feel like being meticulous, use a spoon to scoop out any remaining seeds. Place the peppers in a 13 × 9 × 2-inch baking pan (or any baking pan that fits the peppers snugly) and, using a tablespoon, fill the peppers with the rice mixture, leaving about ½ inch of headroom. Set aside.

8. Beat the eggs, onion powder, and a generous amount of salt and pepper together in a large bowl until smooth. Cut the bread slices in half and add them to the beaten egg. Soak, turning them gently occasionally, until well saturated.

9. Cover the filling in each pepper with a piece of the sliced bread, folding and tucking it in as necessary to completely cover the filling. Pour the tomato juice around the peppers. Cover with aluminum foil and bake for 20 minutes. Uncover and bake until the bread lids are golden brown, about 10 minutes. Serve, spooning some of the baking juices around each pepper.

TIP: High heat for roasting the peppers is important. It will blacken the skins completely while leaving the pepper shells firm enough for stuffing.

Multi-Culti Braised Oxtails

I love dishes, like this one, that pinch a little bit from each of my many influences. We ate oxtails when I was a little girl, but believe me, never like this! In this very classic braise (that's The French Culinary Institute at work!), I fortify the hearty flavor of oxtails with malbec from Argentina and a very subtle kick from Mexican chipotles. The oxtails are sturdy enough to stand up to both. The best thing about this as a dinner party dish is that it is even better if made ahead. A simple reheating just before dinner, and you're in business.

Make this dish for people you love and who are comfortable getting a little messy. No matter how you work a plateful of oxtails with a knife and fork—and Jerry's pretty good at it—you're going to end up picking up the bones and going to town to finish the job. Extra napkins help.

MAKES 6 SERVINGS • PREP TIME: 20 MINUTES • COOK TIME: 5 HOURS (MOSTLY UNATTENDED)

12 large pieces oxtail (about 4½ pounds; see Note)

Kosher or fine sea salt and freshly ground pepper

Olive oil, for cooking the oxtails

2 tablespoons all-purpose flour, plus more for dredging the oxtails

1 large yellow onion, coarsely chopped

5 stalks celery, coarsely chopped

3 carrots, peeled and coarsely chopped

3 cloves garlic, chopped

1 tablespoon tomato paste

2 cups malbec or other hearty dry red wine

2 cups beef broth, homemade or store-bought

½ teaspoon whole cloves

1 tablespoon pureed chipotles in adobo

1. Pat the oxtails dry with paper towels. Season them generously on all sides with salt and pepper. Heat ½ inch of oil in a large Dutch oven or heavy casserole over medium heat. Dredge as many of the oxtails as will fit in the pot in flour to coat evenly, and tap off any excess flour. Add the oxtails to the pot and cook, turning as necessary, until well browned on all sides, about 8 minutes; remove them to a plate as they brown. Dredge more oxtails in flour and brown them as space becomes available in the pot, until all the pieces are browned. Adjust the heat during cooking so the brown bits that stick to the pot don't burn, and replenish the oil if necessary.

2. Pour off all but about 3 tablespoons of fat from the pot. Add the onion, celery, carrots, and garlic and cook over medium-high heat, stirring, until the vegetables have softened and picked up all the delicious brown bits from the bottom of the pot, about 5 minutes. Add the tomato

paste and stir until it coats the vegetables. Sprinkle the 2 tablespoons flour over the vegetables and cook until it disappears, just a minute or two. Pour in the wine, bring to a boil, and cook, stirring, until reduced by about half.

3. Return the oxtails to the pot, pour in the beef broth, and add the cloves and chipotles. Bring to a boil, then adjust the heat so the liquid is simmering, cover, and cook until the meat is ready to fall off the bone, about 4 hours. Turn the pieces in the liquid a few times as they simmer so they cook evenly.

4. Remove the oxtails to a plate and strain the cooking liquid into a bowl. Discard the vegetables and return the oxtails to the pot. Skim the fat from the surface of the strained cooking liquid and pour it back over the oxtails. The oxtails can be reheated gently and served right away, but they are best prepared ahead and then reheated. Let cool completely, then refrigerate for up to 2 days. Whatever fat you missed when skimming the cooking liquid will rise to the top and solidify, making it very easy to remove.

5. To serve, heat the oxtails over low heat until heated through.

NOTE: Ideally, for this dish, you would start with 12 nice big pieces (about 4 inches across) from the larger ends of oxtails. However, your butcher (or supermarket) would like to sell you a whole tail, which contains pieces as small as ½ inch across. If you have no luck wheedling the pieces you need from the person behind the counter, try this: Buy 3 whole oxtails and braise them all. Pick the 12 largest pieces to serve at dinner (throw in a few extra pieces if the portions look a little skimpy) and set the smaller pieces aside. After dinner, shred the meat from the reserved smaller pieces back into any leftover sauce, which will be terrific over pasta, mashed potatoes, or Quinoa Polenta (page 229).

Multi-Culti Braised Oxtails and Spicy Collard Greens (page 230)

Oven-Roasted Halibut
with Black Olive Tapenade

Pair this recipe with the Yellow "Rice" with Serrano Ham on page 230, and you've got a showstopping main event. The colors—yellow-orange orzo, brilliant red peppers, jet-black tapenade, and pearly white fish fillets—are only the beginning of the story. The happy ending is the way the sweet, salty, earthy, briny flavors come together so beautifully.

MAKES 6 SERVINGS • PREP TIME: 20 MINUTES • COOK TIME: 10 MINUTES

FOR THE TAPENADE
1½ cups Gaeta olives, pitted

1½ cups Sicilian or Greek oil-cured black olives, pitted

2 anchovy fillets

½ teaspoon ground cumin

3 tablespoons capers, preferably "nonpareil," drained

¼ cup chopped fresh flat-leaf parsley

FOR THE HALIBUT
Six 7- to 8-ounce halibut fillets, with skin

Kosher or fine sea salt and freshly ground pepper

2 tablespoons canola oil

3 large red bell peppers, roasted, peeled, and seeded (see page 274) or 3 cups sliced (¼-inch-wide strips) bottled roasted red peppers (be sure the label says "roasted" or "fire-roasted")

1. Put all of the tapenade ingredients into the work bowl of a food processor. Pulse, stopping occasionally to scrape down the sides of the work bowl, until smooth. Scrape the tapenade into a bowl, cover with plastic wrap, and refrigerate. The tapenade can be made up to 3 days in advance.

2. Preheat the oven to 375°F.

3. Pat the halibut fillets dry with paper towels. Season generously with salt and pepper. Heat the canola oil in a large ovenproof skillet (no plastic handles!) over medium-high heat until hot but not smoking. Slip the halibut fillets skin side down into the pan and cook until the skin is browned and blistered and the edges of the fish are starting to look opaque, about 3 minutes. Flip the fish over and place in the oven for 4 to 5 minutes, or until the fillets are just opaque in the center.

4. While the fish is cooking, warm the red peppers in a skillet over low heat.

Oven-Roasted Halibut with Black Olive Tapenade and Yellow "Rice" with Serrano Ham (page 230)

5. To serve, place a small mound of red peppers on each plate and place the halibut next to the peppers. Using 2 teaspoons, form a quenelle (egg shape) of tapenade and set atop each fillet.

NOTE: The tapenade recipe makes more than you will need for this dish, but it keeps for a good long time in the refrigerator. You can use it to top just about any fish or chicken off the grill, to enhance a salad dressing, or as a sandwich spread.

Pan-Seared Cod
with Lentils and Chorizo (see photo, page 125)

Pork and seafood may seem like an odd couple, but there are happy marriages between the two all around the globe, from New England's seafood chowders speckled with rendered salt pork to Italy's calamari stuffed with fennel sausage. The spicy, rich bits of chorizo that stud these homey lentils play very well against the sweet-lean cod fillets. You've got everything you need for dinner right here. Well, a loaf of crusty bread and a salad wouldn't hurt.

MAKES 6 SERVINGS • PREP TIME: 20 MINUTES • COOK TIME: 40 MINUTES

FOR THE LENTILS

1 pound brown lentils

1 Spanish onion, unpeeled, quartered through the root

2 stalks celery, snapped in half

2 carrots, peeled and cut in half

2 bay leaves

1 teaspoon freshly ground pepper

6 cups beef broth, homemade or store-bought

FOR THE CHORIZO

2 tablespoons olive oil

2 shallots, finely chopped

2 links Mexican chorizo (about 7 ounces), removed from casings

2 stalks celery, finely diced (about 1 cup)

2 carrots, peeled and coarsely shredded (about 1/2 cup; the coarse side of a box grater works well)

2 sprigs fresh thyme

Kosher or fine sea salt and freshly ground pepper

6 thick cod or other firm white fillets, such as Chilean sea bass or halibut (about 1 1/2 inches thick and 8 ounces each)

All-purpose flour, for dredging

Olive oil

1. Cook the lentils: Pick over and rinse the lentils in a sieve under cold water. Drain them well. Put them in a pot large enough to hold them and the vegetables comfortably. Add the vegetables (see Tip), bay leaves, and pepper and pour in the beef broth. Bring to a boil, then adjust the heat so the liquid is simmering and cook until the lentils are tender, about 25 minutes.

2. Meanwhile, cook the chorizo: Heat the olive oil in a Dutch oven or wide casserole over medium heat. Add the shallots and cook, stirring, until softened, about 3 minutes. Add the chorizo and cook, breaking up the clumps of meat with a spoon, until it has lost its raw look,

about 4 minutes. Add the celery, carrots, and thyme and cook, stirring, until the vegetables are softened and the chorizo is lightly browned, about 10 minutes. Remove from the heat.

3. Remove the vegetables and bay leaves from the lentils. Transfer the lentils with a slotted spoon to the pot with the chorizo and stir gently to mix well. Reserve the cooking liquid. Season the lentils with salt and pepper to taste if necessary. The lentils can be prepared up to an hour in advance and kept in a warm place.

4. Preheat the oven to 400°F.

5. Choose a heavy ovenproof skillet large enough to hold all the cod fillets. (If you don't have one, sear the cod in batches and transfer the fillets to a baking sheet.) Pat the fillets dry with paper towels and season all sides generously with salt and pepper. Dredge the fillets in flour to coat them lightly, and tap off the excess flour. Pour ¼ inch of oil into the skillet and heat over medium-high heat. Add the fillets to the pan, without crowding, and cook until the undersides are a deep golden brown, about 4 minutes. Flip and repeat. Put the pan in the oven and bake just until the fillets are opaque throughout, about 5 minutes.

6. While the cod is in the oven, reheat the lentil-chorizo mixture over low heat, adding a little of the reserved lentil cooking liquid if needed to make the lentils glisten.

7. Spoon some of the lentil mixture onto each serving plate and rest a cod fillet on the lentils. Or prepare a platter and serve from the platter at the table. Pass any remaining lentils at the table.

TIP: If you have some cheesecloth, cut off a square large enough to hold all the vegetables. Put the vegetables in the center of the square, add the bay leaves, tie up the corners securely, and add the vegetable bundle to the pot. Then simply remove and discard the whole bundle at the end of cooking.

Risotto with Pigeon Peas

I enjoyed a delightfully delicious risotto with fava beans in Buenos Aires, and it occurred to me that a not-quite-so-delicate legume—like my beloved pigeon peas—might make an interesting variation. Back in my kitchen, I put the idea to the test with out-of-the-ballpark results! The serrano ham lends a smoky saltiness to the earthy note of the pigeon peas, and the wine in the rice adds a light acidic note that balances the starch and creaminess of the risotto. It's like my "Soupy Rice" with Pigeon Peas (page 148) dressed up for the opera!

MAKES 6 SERVINGS • PREP TIME: 15 MINUTES • COOK TIME: 30 MINUTES

2 tablespoons olive oil

2 small yellow onions, cut into $1/2$-inch dice (about 2 cups)

$1/4$ pound serrano ham or prosciutto in one thick slice, cut into $1/4$-inch dice

One 14-ounce bag frozen pigeon peas

2 cups Arborio rice

Kosher or fine sea salt and freshly ground pepper

$1/4$ teaspoon ground saffron

2 to 3 cups dry white wine

2 bay leaves

$3^1/2$ to $4^1/2$ cups chicken broth, homemade (page 303) or store-bought, or as needed

$1/2$ cup heavy cream

$1/2$ cup freshly grated Parmesan cheese

1. Heat the olive oil in a 3- to 4-quart wide heavy saucepan or Dutch oven over medium heat. Add the onions and cook, stirring, until they just begin to soften, about 2 minutes. Stir in the ham and cook, stirring, until the onions are softened but not browned, about 4 minutes. Stir in the peas, then stir in the rice and saffron and cook, stirring, until the rice turns chalky, 2 to 3 minutes.

2. Season the rice lightly with salt and pepper. Pour in the wine—2 cups for a mellower wine flavor, 3 cups for a more robust wine flavor. Toss in the bay leaves and cook, stirring constantly, until the wine is absorbed and you can see the bottom of the pan when you stir. Pour 2 cups of the broth into the pan and cook, stirring, until it is absorbed. Pour in another addition of broth—$1^1/2$ cups if you used 3 cups of wine, $2^1/2$ cups if you used the lesser amount of wine—and repeat as above.

3. When the rice has absorbed most of the last addition of broth, it should be tender but with a little bite and suspended in a creamy sauce. If it is not quite tender, add a little more broth, about $1/2$ cup, and keep stirring.

4. Remove the pan from the heat, remove the bay leaves, and stir in the heavy cream and grated cheese. Season with salt and pepper to taste and serve right away.

Quinoa Polenta

This, like the gnocchi on page 210, is a recipe in the *Nuevo Andino* style that we sampled at the restaurant Casa Andina. The earthy but subtle flavor of quinoa and the creamy texture of the finished polenta make it a perfect pairing with anything juicy and full-flavored, like the oxtails on page 221 or Barbecued Beef Short Ribs (page 88).

MAKES 6 SERVINGS • COOK TIME: 10 MINUTES

2 teaspoons kosher or fine sea salt
1 cup quinoa flour (available in some
    supermarkets and health food stores)

2 cups half-and-half
Pinch of cayenne pepper

Bring 2 cups water and the salt to a boil in a 2-quart saucepan over medium-high heat. Whisk in the quinoa flour, half-and-half, and cayenne and bring back to a boil. Adjust the heat so the liquid is simmering and cook, whisking constantly, paying special attention to the corners of the pan, until the polenta burbles and thickens, about 4 minutes. Serve hot.

VARIATIONS

MUSHROOM QUINOA POLENTA: Soak ½ cup dried mushrooms, such as porcini or a dried mushroom blend, in 2 cups hot water until the mushrooms are softened. Lift the mushrooms from the soaking liquid and reserve the liquid. Slice the mushrooms very thin. Strain the soaking liquid through a sieve lined with cheesecloth or a coffee filter. Add enough water to the soaking liquid to measure 2 cups, stir in the mushrooms, and use that in place of the water called for above.

CHEESY QUINOA POLENTA: Reduce the salt to 1 teaspoon and proceed as above. Stir ½ cup freshly grated Parmesan cheese into the finished polenta.

BREAKFAST QUINOA POLENTA: Reduce the salt to ½ teaspoon and add a cinnamon stick to the water before bringing it to a boil. Remove the pan from the heat and let steep for 10 minutes. Remove the cinnamon stick and proceed as above. Drizzle maple syrup or agave nectar over the polenta.

Spicy Collard Greens (see photo, page 223)

You have probably heard legends of southern cooks who boil their collards for hours, adding a little sugar and bacon fat or oil from the chicken-frying pan as the greens simmer away on the stove. The results are delicious. Not long ago, on a whim, I thought I would try just the opposite—giving collards a quick bath in some chile-spiked butter. The results are surprising, not to mention addictive.

MAKES 4 SERVINGS • PREP TIME: 15 MINUTES • COOK TIME: 5 MINUTES

2 pounds collard greens

4 tablespoons unsalted butter or ¼ cup vegetable oil

1 teaspoon crushed red pepper flakes

Kosher or fine sea salt

1. Trim the thick stems and any wilted or yellow leaves from the collards. Cut the leaves cross-wise into ½-inch-wide strips (see Tip, page 135). Wash them in plenty of cold water and drain them well. You will have about 12 cups shredded leaves.
2. Heat the butter in a large deep skillet over medium-high heat until foaming. Add the red pepper flakes and stir until fragrant. Add the greens and cook, tossing and stirring, until they are coated with butter and have wilted but maintain their vibrant color, about 4 minutes. Season with salt and serve.

Yellow "Rice" with Serrano Ham (see photo, page 225)

The perfect recipe for a person who may still be intimidated by making rice (despite my foolproof recipe!). The inspiration came from *fideuá,* the Spanish dish that blends seafood and thin egg noodles with a minimum of water to make a kind of noodle paella with a wonderful creamy texture. I use clam juice in this recipe, but you can substitute vegetable broth, mussel juice, or any other matrix that will complement the accompanying dish. The risotto technique that I use here, adding small amounts of liquid at a time and waiting for the pasta to soak it up, slowly draws the starch out of the pasta. Just like risotto, this has limitless possibilities for variation, such as the addition of mushrooms or shrimp or fava beans or . . .

MAKES 6 SERVINGS • PREP TIME: 10 MINUTES • COOK TIME: 15 MINUTES

Three 8-ounce bottles clam juice

3 tablespoons Achiote Oil (page 306)

4 cloves garlic, thinly sliced

1/3 cup finely diced serrano ham or prosciutto

1 pound orzo

Kosher or fine sea salt and freshly ground pepper

Chopped fresh flat-leaf parsley, for garnish

1. Pour the clam juice into a small saucepan and heat to simmering. Keep hot over very low heat.

2. Heat the achiote oil in a medium saucepan over medium-high heat. Add the garlic and cook, stirring, until lightly golden, about 2 minutes. Stir in the ham and cook until fragrant, 1 to 2 minutes. Add the orzo and stir until lightly toasted, about 2 minutes.

3. Pour enough hot clam juice into the skillet to cover the orzo by about 1/2 inch. Bring to a boil, then adjust the heat so the liquid is at a lively simmer and cook, adding small amounts of the hot clam juice as necessary to keep the orzo covered, until the pasta is tender but still firm, 6 to 8 minutes. The pasta should have a creamy consistency, but there should be little, if any, liquid left by the end of cooking. If it is a bit soupy, let stand for a minute or so; if it is a little dry, add a little bit of hot clam juice or hot water. Season with salt and pepper to taste. Transfer to a serving dish and garnish with the chopped parsley.

Asparagus with Brown Butter and Pecans (see photo, page vi)

In Spain, this would be made with big fat asparagus and, most likely, hazelnuts. In Peru, you would see something like it made with white asparagus. I make it with pecans because I like them better (and so does my Angela). Another example of a dish that is extremely simple and totally dependent on great ingredients.

MAKES 6 SERVINGS • PREP TIME: 10 MINUTES • COOK TIME: 10 MINUTES

1 1/2 pounds medium asparagus (see Note)

Kosher or fine sea salt

6 tablespoons unsalted butter

3/4 cup pecan halves

1. Prep the asparagus: Grasp the tip of each stalk and bend the stalk end with the other hand. The tough end of the stalk will break off, leaving the tender part of the stalk and tip.
2. Pour ½ inch of water into a large skillet and season well with salt. Add the asparagus and bring to a boil over high heat. Cook until tender but not mushy, 2 to 5 minutes, depending on the thickness. Rotate the stalks from top to bottom once or twice as they cook.
3. Drain the asparagus thoroughly and put it on a warm platter. Wipe out the skillet.
4. Add the butter and pecans to the skillet and cook over medium-low heat until the butter has stopped foaming and turned a light nut brown and the pecans are lightly toasted, about 4 minutes. Stir the pecans as they cook so they toast evenly. Immediately pour the pecan butter over the asparagus. Serve hot.

NOTE: Thin or very thick asparagus can be used for this as well. If the asparagus is thicker than your pinky, peel the base of the stalks after snapping them to be sure the thick ends and the tips will cook in the same amount of time.

Eggplant in Coconut Milk

This recipe, my version of a dish that is found in one guise or another all over the Caribbean, came to me from Doña Corina Castro, who runs Villa Shantal in the Dominican Republic. Doña Corina cooks her eggplant—and a lot of other things—over a *fogón,* a fire built inside a ring of rocks. The hot rocks double as a support for the bottom of a big round pan that she used for both this dish and one very similar to the Goat Braised in Coconut Milk on page 267. Doña Corina swears the flavor of the wood smoke permeates anything she cooks over the *fogón* and lends her dishes a special flavor.

This can easily stand in as an entrée in a meatless meal and often does in Puerto Rico, especially during Holy Week, when the meaty texture of the eggplant is welcome on "lean" days. A little white rice, a nice green vegetable, and you'd be all set.

MAKES 6 SERVINGS • PREP TIME: 30 MINUTES (INCLUDES FRYING TIME) • COOK TIME: 25 MINUTES

FOR THE EGGPLANT

Batter from Baby Banana Beignets
   (page 83)
2 large eggplants (about 1³/₄ pounds)
Kosher or fine sea salt and freshly ground
   pepper
Vegetable oil, for frying

FOR THE COCONUT SAUCE

2 tablespoons olive oil
1 cup Sofrito (page 305)

1 tablespoon tomato paste
¹/₂ teaspoon ground cumin
1 bay leaf
Two 13¹/₂-ounce cans unsweetened
   coconut milk

1. Make the batter and let it stand while you prep the eggplant.

2. Trim the ends of the eggplants but leave the skins on. Cut the eggplants lengthwise into ¹/₂-inch slices. Salt and pepper both sides of the slices.

3. Pour 1 inch of oil into a large wide skillet. Heat over medium heat until the tip of the handle of a wooden spoon dipped in the oil gives off a steady lively sizzle (about 360°F). Working with only as many of the eggplant slices as will fit in the skillet, dip each one in the batter to coat both sides, then hold over the bowl of batter to let the excess batter drip back into the bowl. Carefully lay the slice in the hot oil. Cook, turning once, until both sides are golden brown, about 5 minutes. Drain the slices on a paper-towel-lined baking sheet and repeat with the remaining eggplant and batter.

4. When all the slices are fried, arrange them in a baking dish large enough to hold them in one overlapping layer (about 11 × 15 inches). The eggplant can be fried up to 2 hours in advance and kept at room temperature.

5. Preheat the oven to 375°F.

6. Make the coconut sauce: Heat the oil in a medium saucepan over medium heat. Add the sofrito and cook until the liquid has evaporated and the sofrito is sizzling. Stir in the tomato paste, cumin, and bay leaf and stir until the tomato paste starts to change color. Pour in the coconut milk and bring to a boil, stirring. Adjust the heat so the liquid is simmering and cook until the sauce is slightly thickened, about 10 minutes. Remove from the heat. The sauce can be made up to 2 hours in advance and kept at room temperature. Bring to a simmer before continuing.

7. Remove the bay leaf and pour the sauce over the eggplant. Bake until the sauce around the edges of the dish is bubbling and the eggplant is piping hot, about 20 minutes. Serve hot or at room temperature.

Fava Beans with Serrano Ham and Cream

Spain—that's where one bite of this takes me. My trip to Spain was the awakening of my love for all things fava, which started after sampling this dish in Madrid at a New Year's Eve dinner. Coupled with those miraculous Spanish mushrooms (I wax poetic every time I talk about them!) and salty serrano ham, the delicate sweetness of the favas is highlighted by the touch of cream that binds the whole thing together.

MAKES 6 SERVINGS • PREP TIME: 45 MINUTES • COOK TIME: 15 MINUTES

5 pounds fava beans in the shell (see Tip)

2 tablespoons unsalted butter

3 large shallots, minced (about $^1/_4$ cup)

One $^1/_4$-inch-thick slice serrano ham or prosciutto (about 2 ounces), cut into $^1/_4$-inch dice (about $^1/_3$ cup)

$^1/_2$ cup heavy cream

3 sprigs fresh thyme, plus more, for garnish

Kosher or fine sea salt and freshly ground pepper

1. Shell, blanch, and peel the favas (see Note, page 109). You will have about 3 cups.
2. Heat the butter in a large skillet over medium heat until foaming. Add the shallots and cook, stirring, until wilted, about 2 minutes. Add the ham and stir until you smell it, then add the beans and stir gently to coat with butter. Pour in the cream, add the thyme, and bring to a boil. Reduce the heat to very low, cover the pan, and cook until the favas are tender and the cream is almost absorbed, about 5 minutes. Add a pinch of salt if necessary (the ham is salty) and season with pepper to taste. Garnish with thyme sprigs.

TIP: It is helpful if you can sneak a peek inside a couple of fava bean pods while at the store. If the beans inside the pods are very tiny, you may need a pound or so more for 6 servings. If they are very large, you might be able to make do with 4 pounds.

"Sweet Earth" (Chocolate Mousse with Chocolate Cookie Crumbles) ∽ TIERRITA DULCE

These adorable desserts, which look like little potted plants, are all the rage now in Puerto Rico. The "earth" is a rich chocolate mousse topped with dark chocolate cookie crumbs, and an edible fresh flower (or a sugar flower from a specialty baking store) poking out of the soil completes the illusion.

MAKES 6 TO 8 SERVINGS (DEPENDING ON THE SIZE OF THE POTS)
• PREP TIME: 45 MINUTES (PLUS 2 TO 24 HOURS CHILLING TIME)

One 12-ounce bag bittersweet chocolate chips

2 tablespoons dark rum

1½ tablespoons instant espresso powder

1 teaspoon vanilla extract

Pinch of salt

3 extra-large eggs, separated

¾ cup sugar

1 cup heavy cream, well chilled

2 packages Oreo Thin Crisps chocolate cookies or 1½ cups crushed Famous Chocolate Wafers

6 to 8 edible flowers, with stems if possible, or candy flowers (from a bakery supply shop)

1. Mix the chocolate chips, rum, espresso powder, vanilla, salt, and ½ cup water in a large heat-proof bowl. Set over a pot of simmering water and whisk until the chocolate is melted. Set aside.

2. Using a hand mixer, beat the egg yolks with ½ cup of the sugar in a medium bowl until they are pale yellow and fluffy and you can see the bottom of the bowl as you beat, about 2 minutes. Fold about one-third of the chocolate mixture into the yolks with a rubber spatula, then fold the yolk mixture into the chocolate remaining in the bowl. Set aside.

3. Wash the beaters and bowl thoroughly and dry them. Beat the egg whites with the remaining ¼ cup sugar in a medium bowl until they hold soft peaks when the beaters are lifted. Fold one-third of the whites into the chocolate mixture with a rubber spatula. Once they are incorporated, fold in the remaining whites.

4. Beat the cream in a clean bowl until it holds firm peaks. Using a rubber spatula, fold the cream into the chocolate mixture one-third at a time. Divide the mousse among 6 to 8 food-safe flowerpots (see Note) or dessert cups. Chill for at least 2 hours or up to 1 day.

5. Put the cookies in a heavy resealable plastic bag. Whack them with a rolling pin into coarse pieces, then roll until fine crumbs. Top each dish of mousse with crumbled chocolate cookies to resemble soil. Finish with the edible flowers, standing them straight up by inserting the stems into the mousse.

NOTE: Food-safe flowerpots are available in specialty bakeware shops, or feel free to use ramekins.

Cleriquot

Cleriquot is the Argentinean cousin of white sangria. I can tell you that my white sangria recipe in my previous book is a killer, and I am crazy proud of it. But after tasting a particularly delicious pitcher of cleriquot at the Pizzeria Meriole in Buenos Aires, I came home inspired enough to venture away from my standard recipe, and I think you'll agree that this is almost too delicious! I like to have the ingredients well chilled, so I don't dilute it with ice. You can, of course, add a few cubes if you like. It makes a great ice breaker at a dinner party where some of the guests don't know each other.

MAKES 8 SERVINGS • PREP TIME: 10 MINUTES

$^1/_4$ cup superfine sugar

One 750-ml bottle sparkling brut rosé, chilled

1 cup Absolut peach vodka, chilled

$1^1/_2$ cups sparkling water, chilled

1 mango, peeled, pitted, and cut into $^1/_2$-inch dice

1 peach, peeled, pitted, and cut into $^1/_2$-inch dice

1 cup raspberries

Juice of 1 lime

1. Dissolve the superfine sugar in $^1/_4$ cup water and refrigerate until thoroughly chilled.
2. Pour the sugar syrup into a large pitcher and add the rosé, vodka, and sparkling water. Toss the fruit with the lime juice and add to the pitcher. Serve chilled in wineglasses, and toast me!

Coconut Panna Cotta with Tropical Fruit

Mami is a lover of all things coconut, whether sweet dishes like the Coconut Kisses on page 169 or savory ones like the Eggplant in Coconut Milk on page 232. She loves coconut so much, in fact, that when she visits, I always make sure to have a special coconutty something for her arrival. This is the perfect recipe for such an occasion, because I can make it the night before. I set a pot of lentil soup on the stove to simmer before I pick her up at the airport, and then after she enjoys her lunch, I pull out my coconut surprise, all ready to go! The fruit helps her feel less guilty about the dessert.

MAKES 6 SERVINGS • PREP TIME: 30 MINUTES (PLUS 4 HOURS OR MORE CHILLING TIME)

1 tablespoon powdered gelatin
One 15-ounce can cream of coconut (preferably Coco López)
One 13½-ounce can unsweetened coconut milk
2 cups heavy cream, well chilled

¼ cup confectioners' sugar
Assorted tropical fruits, such as kiwi, mango, and papaya, peeled and cut into ½-inch dice (about 1½ cups total), for garnish

1. Sprinkle the gelatin evenly over 3 tablespoons of cool water in a small bowl. Set aside for about 10 minutes to soften.
2. Heat the coconut cream and coconut milk in a medium saucepan over medium heat until the edges begin to bubble. Lower the heat and whisk in the softened gelatin, stirring to make sure it is completely dissolved. Remove from the heat.
3. Fill a large bowl halfway with cold water. Strain the coconut mixture into a metal or heatproof bowl that will fit easily into the bowl of water and leave to cool, stirring every few minutes with a rubber spatula until the mixture starts to thicken. Remove the coconut mixture from the bowl of water.
4. Stir the heavy cream and confectioners' sugar together in a bowl until the sugar is dissolved. Stir into the coconut mixture. Divide the coconut mixture evenly among six 7- to 8-ounce custard cups or ramekins. Chill until firm, at least 4 hours or up to overnight.
5. To serve, run a knife around the edges of the molds and invert each panna cotta onto a serving plate. Spoon some of the diced fruit over each, allowing the fruit to spill onto the plate.

Guava Shells Filled with Cream Cheese Mousse

Here is another take on the classic Latin guava-cheese partnership (see the Guava–Cream Cheese Turnovers on page 168). In this case, guava shells are filled with a mousse made with sweetened cream cheese lightened with whipped cream. It is a beautiful and economical dessert—the sauce for decorating the plate is made from the delicious syrup from the canned guavas.

MAKES 6 SERVINGS • PREP TIME: 25 MINUTES (PLUS 2 TO 8 HOURS CHILLING TIME)

1 envelope unflavored gelatin

One 8-ounce container whipped cream cheese

⅓ cup sugar

1 teaspoon vanilla extract

1 teaspoon almond extract

¾ cup heavy cream, well chilled

One 17-ounce can guava shells (about 24)

1. Pour ½ cup cool water into a small saucepan, sprinkle the gelatin over the water, and let it stand until softened, about 10 minutes. Warm the gelatin mixture over low heat just until the gelatin is dissolved. Set aside.

2. Scrape the cream cheese into a medium mixing bowl. Add the sugar and vanilla and almond extracts and beat until fluffy. Beat in the gelatin mixture.

3. Whip the cream in a separate bowl until it forms soft peaks. With a rubber spatula, fold the whipped cream into the cream cheese mix. Refrigerate until set, at least 2 hours, or up to overnight.

4. Drain the guava shells, treating them gently and reserving the liquid. Arrange the shells smooth side down on a small baking sheet lined with paper towels. Spoon the mousse into the shells, mounding it high. (Or if you like, spoon the mousse into a pastry bag fitted with a large star tip and pipe the filling into the shells.)

5. Add any broken shells or small pieces of guava to the drained liquid. Transfer to a blender and blend until smooth. Set aside the sauce. The shells can be drained and filled and the sauce prepared up to several hours before serving. Keep refrigerated.

6. To serve, arrange 3 shells on each serving plate. Drizzle some of the sauce over and around each serving.

Banana and Dulce de Leche Strudel

My friend Paula's sister, Maria *Grande* (to distinguish her from her gorgeous daughter, Maria *Chiquita*), made arrangements for us to eat at a restaurant called Social Paraiso in Buenos Aires. The dessert was called *delicia tibia de banana,* and it resembled a phyllo "cigar" with a warm banana center and a drizzle of dulce de leche.

MAKES 12 SERVINGS • PREP TIME: 30 MINUTES • COOK TIME: 30 MINUTES

6 ripe bananas

Juice of 1 lemon

1¼ cups sugar

½ cup plus 2 tablespoons heavy cream

4 tablespoons unsalted butter

¼ teaspoon ground cinnamon

1 cup coarsely chopped pecans

16 sheets phyllo dough (see page 312)

6 tablespoons unsalted butter, melted

1 cup finely crumbled dry-textured almond cookies (such as Stella D'oro), amaretti, or anise toasts

1. Slice the bananas lengthwise into quarters, then cut them crosswise into ½-inch-or-so pieces. Toss them in a bowl with the lemon juice and set aside.

2. Using the sugar and ¼ cup water, make a caramel (see Caramelicious, page 124). As soon as the caramel is done, remove the pan from the heat and (carefully!) pour the cream into the pan. It will bubble up, then die down. As soon as it is safe, whisk the caramel until smooth and creamy. Return the skillet to low heat and whisk in the butter 1 tablespoon at a time. Whisk in the cinnamon and set aside to cool briefly.

3. Add the caramel and pecans to the bananas and stir well but gently. Set aside.

4. Preheat the oven to 375°F. Line a baking sheet with parchment paper.

5. Lay the phyllo sheets out on a work surface and cover them with a damp kitchen towel (see the tips on working with phyllo on page 312). Remove 2 sheets of phyllo, set them on a dry clean towel, and brush the top sheet with melted butter. Sprinkle about 2 tablespoons of the crumbled cookies over the butter. Repeat 3 more times to make 4 layers of phyllo, butter, and cookies. Spoon half of the banana mixture over the center of the top sheet of phyllo, leaving at least 1 inch on both of the short ends and about 2 inches on the long sides. Using the towel, fold the long sides of the phyllo over the filling, then pinch the ends together to seal. Flip the log onto the prepared baking sheet and tuck the ends under the log. Repeat the process to make another strudel.

6. Brush the strudels with butter and bake until golden and crispy on top, 25 to 30 minutes. Serve warm or at room temperature, cut crosswise into slices.

BUFFETS

Everybody loves a party! And nobody more than me, so the last thing I want to do when a house-ful of people is getting down to it, is to hang by myself in the kitchen. Don't get me wrong—I want my people to eat and drink to their hearts' content; I just want to have most of my work done before they start. I don't want to miss out on a single glass-clinking moment! Over the years, I have gradually developed a strategy for putting on a buffet. It's pretty simple and nothing revolution-ary, but it works for me. And it certainly works for my guests.

First of all, invite only the number of people that you're comfortable cooking for. True, a buffet doesn't involve the careful timing and attention to detail that a sit-down dinner does, but main courses and side dishes have to be prepared, the bar has to be stocked, the house has to be cleaned. Pace yourself. The nice thing about buffets is that they offer a feeling of abundance that doesn't necessarily mean slaving over twelve dishes to serve ten people but does mean a feeling of plenty: colorful bowls brimming with salads and vegetables, casseroles full of bubbly goodness, a carving board with the most fragrant and most gorgeous roast pork you've ever laid eyes on.

I get the whole thing off to a super-simple start by laying out an assortment of foods that require no effort from me (except a trip to the store). As it happens, most of these are from Spain and fea-tured on virtually every tapas menu in the country. And these hams, cheeses, olives, and more (see The No-Cook Tapas Table, page 244) are better at room temperature, which means they share one wonderful quality: they can all be arranged and laid out before the first guests ring the bell. Friends who show up at my house for a buffet find themselves with drinks in hand and a little nosh practically before my kids have coaxed their coats from them. And that's how I like it.

This approach is why you won't find any "appetizer" recipes in this chapter. If you like, you can pinch any number of recipes from the Cocktail Parties chapter (page 170) and use them here. Or pick either (or both) of the tortillas that start the recipe section on page 248 and cut them into appetizer-size squares, perfect for picking up and eating out of hand. Like all tortillas, these two are delicious at room temperature, which means they can be made and set out before the party.

As for the main event, this chapter includes dishes that can be almost completely finished before the buffet starts. Many of them feature components that can be made a day (or days) ahead of the party. Some can be popped into the oven when the first guests arrive and left to bake while guests mix and mingle. Others can be served at room temperature or just slid back into the oven for a few minutes before serving. All the details are in the recipes, and you'll find a few suggested buffet menus with helpful schedules on pages 301 and 302.

Having said that, I don't mind serving one or two dishes that need a finishing touch. When I sense that the "cocktail hour" is drawing to a close, I slip into the kitchen to collect my thoughts and pull the main-course dishes together. If there's carving to be done, as for the Turkey Breast *"Pavochon"* (page 269) or the *Pernil* (page 268), I hand Jerry the knife and let him do his thing right at the buffet table. With a couple of exceptions, the rest of the recipes in this chapter are "dig in and help yourself" kinds of dishes. Where people may need a little help serving themselves, as with the *Pastelón* (page 255) or Vegetable Potpie (page 251), I am always there to lend a hand. With the two of us working the table, guests balancing glasses and plates don't have to struggle and Jerry and I can be sure that everyone is taken care of, even the occasional shy guest.

And last, a word about the serving sizes for the recipes in this chapter. They are based on the assumption that you'll be serving two entrées and three side dishes. If you're serving only one main course along with two sides, obviously they'll serve a few less people. The more you add to the lineup, the more these dishes will serve.

The No-Cook Tapas Table

Here are a few of my favorite no-muss, no-fuss, store-bought tapas. I rely on this team to kick off any party centered around a buffet, from the most casual to the spiffiest. Serve as many or as few as you like, giving each item its own plate or platter. Arrange them in a group on a table or distribute them around the room. Make sure there is the right serving piece for each—a fork for slices of ham, a knife for cheese, a spoon for olives—and a basket of crusty bread torn or cut into pieces.

When people think of blue-veined cheese from Spain, what usually comes to mind is **CABRALES,** which does make a fine addition to a no-cook tapas table. But if it's available, try **VALDEÓN,** a blue cheese from Spain that is made from a mix of goat's and cow's milk, instead. The flavor is intense, with a little bite (which I love), and the texture is creamy. The wheels are wrapped in leaves (some say oak, some say chestnut, some say sycamore; I say, "Who cares, let's unwrap it and dig in!"), which add an earthy note to the flavor.

MANCHEGO CHEESE has gained enough popularity in the States that it can be found in just about any well-stocked supermarket cheese section. It is a sheep's-milk cheese that can vary from mild when young (about 60 days aging or so) to quite sharp when it reaches the 1- to 2-year mark. Look for a grayish basket-weave pattern on the rind—the distinguishing mark of a true Manchego—and an even distribution of tiny holes throughout the cheese.

The No-Cook Tapas Table (clockwise from top left): sliced crusty bread, Valdeón cheese, serrano ham, walnut bread, olives (at center), bottled piquillo peppers, white anchovies, and pickled artichoke hearts

TETILLA is a buttery, mild, fresh-tasting cow's-milk cheese in a shape that resembles an overgrown Hershey's Kiss. It is delicious on its own or used to top casseroles, as it melts well.

There are many types of **BOTTLED ROASTED PEPPERS** that, simply drained, patted dry, and cut into bite-size pieces, make a tasty tapa. Or take an extra step and drizzle them with olive oil, scatter a good amount of fresh herbs (oregano, basil, or rosemary is nice) over them, and let them steep at room temperature for an hour or so. Keep an eye out for bottled or canned roasted **PIQUILLO PEPPERS.** They are sweet with a little kick and are delicious on their own, but their small (1- to 2-inch) triangular shape makes them perfect vehicles for stuffing: think seafood (sweet lump crabmeat with a simple lemon and oil dressing) or cheese (soft goat cheese beaten with olive oil and the fresh herb of your choice). If you have any toasted bread crumbs (see page 73) on hand, dip the exposed part of the stuffing in them just before serving. The crunch plays nicely off the velvety texture of the pepper.

WHITE ANCHOVIES, sometimes known as **BOQUERONES,** are (generally speaking) milder, less salty, and meatier than "regular" anchovies. They are brined in vinegar and salt, which gives them a clean, fresh taste. Drain them well and serve them as is or drizzled with the best olive oil you have. Thinly sliced crusty bread, for guests to make little canapés if they like, is a good idea.

If you shop in a supermarket with a decent prepared-food section or have a favorite prepared-food shop, try their **MARINATED ARTICHOKE HEARTS.** They can be an incredible time-saver. Marinated artichoke hearts with a length of stem attached lend an elegant look to the tapas table. They're usually available in vacuum-sealed containers in supermarkets or specialty food stores. Place a stack of little plates and salad forks and a basket of good bread for mopping nearby.

It isn't just Italy and France that have raised dry-cured hams to the level of art—Spain has two of its own that are irresistible: **SERRANO AND IBÉRICO HAMS.** Serrano is a generic name (meaning "from the mountains") for hams that have been dry-cured for at least 12 months (the best are cured for up to 18 months) according to very specific guidelines. The best comparison is a really mellow prosciutto di Parma. Ibérico, on the other hand, is the name given to hams made from a special breed of black-footed pigs, fed on a diet of acorns, grains, and/or wild and foraged food, and then cured and aged with exceptional care. The meat is fragrant, buttery, mellow, and assertive at the same time—and incredibly good. Ibérico is expensive, but it's worth every penny! Either type of ham should be served thinly sliced and without embellishment.

Other **CHARCUTERIE,** such as Spanish chorizo (see page 312), **SALCHICHON** (see Note, page 285), and **LOMO**—a dry-cured, lean, intensely flavored loin of pork—are always welcome. Slice chorizo—hot or sweet—and salchichon by hand, but to fully appreciate its texture and flavor, have the *lomo* sliced very thin by the butcher.

Ibérico Ham

Several years ago, during a family trip to Spain, we made a point of eating in as many tapas bars as we were able to fit into our schedule. And every single time we sat down, the first thing we ordered was a plate of *jamón ibérico*. Made according to very strict guidelines from black-footed pigs that are raised on a special diet, Ibérico is ethereal, delicate, and unlike anything we had tasted before. We ate it for breakfast, we ate it for lunch, we ate it for dinner. Heck, I think Angela once ate it for dessert!

At La Taberna del Cura in Barcelona—where the chefs worked away in an open kitchen and hard cider was drawn from an enormous cask embedded in the restaurant's wall—the Ibérico came on a plate flanked by two other masterpieces of Spanish charcuterie: thin slices of chorizo and *lomo*, a dry-cured loin of pork (see opposite). As delicious as those two were, the Ibérico, as always, was the first thing to be devoured. At De Tapa Madre, another little gem of a restaurant in Barcelona run by two sisters, row after row of the beautiful hams hung from the ceilings for the customers' viewing (and drooling!) pleasure! Marc was so inspired during one of many meals we enjoyed at De Tapa Madre that he went over to where the hams were hanging and pretended to hang by his wrists alongside the fragrant beauties—his little, if somewhat kooky, tribute to the ham we had all come to love.

Serving Ibérico was always a very dramatic to-do no matter where we dined. Servers wheeled a cart bearing the ham tableside and carved it expertly while we did our best to control ourselves in anticipation of the first buttery sliver. I'm afraid it came to me to tell little Angela that there was no way to take one of the luscious hams home, as we would never be able to get it through customs. I can't say she took the news well.

Not long ago, I was thrilled to find out that *jamón ibérico* is now available in the United States. I was so happy that I immediately bought a whole ham (it was a luxury, I know, but did I mention that my family loves it!). Now I can watch Angela's eyes dance when I'm the one who presents and carves the *jamón* for her tableside.

(above) The family gets ready to enjoy a feast at De Tapa Madre.

(right) Marc, the biggest jamón of all!

Salt Cod Tortilla

This is absolute heaven and the perfect opportunity to use the less-than-pretty trimmings from a piece of salt cod that you may have left over from another recipe. Most often, the aromatic vegetables in a tortilla are cooked first, to soften them up a bit, but I like the bite of onion and pepper in this particular tortilla, so I just add the vegetables along with the eggs.

MAKES 8 MAIN-COURSE BUFFET SERVINGS OR AT LEAST 12 APPETIZER SERVINGS
• PREP TIME: 15 MINUTES (PLUS A DAY FOR SOAKING THE SALT COD) • COOK TIME: 15 MINUTES

2 cups soaked, cooked, and shredded salt cod (see page 261)

1 red bell pepper, cored, seeded, and cut into $1/4$-inch dice (about $1^1/3$ cups)

1 medium Spanish onion, cut into $1/4$-inch dice (about $1^1/4$ cups)

$1/4$ cup minced fresh flat-leaf parsley

8 extra-large eggs, beaten

2 tablespoons unsalted butter, softened

1. Set the rack about 6 inches from the broiler and preheat the broiler.
2. Toss the salt cod, bell pepper, onion, and parsley together in a bowl. Pour the beaten eggs over the cod-veggie mix and stir to combine.
3. Spread the butter evenly over the bottom and sides of a 10-inch ovenproof skillet (cast iron is ideal) and place over medium-high heat until the butter is bubbling but not browned. Tilt the pan to make sure the bottom and sides are well coated. Pour the egg mixture into the pan. Stir with a wooden spoon or heatproof spatula while shaking the pan. Lift the edges of the tortilla as they set, letting the raw eggs run into the empty spaces. When the eggs are about half set, stop stirring, reduce the heat to low, and cook until the bottom of the tortilla is set (lift an edge gently to peek).
4. Place the pan on the broiler rack and broil until the top of the tortilla is lightly browned and the center is set, about 4 minutes. The tortilla can be made up to 4 hours in advance. Serve at room temperature or rewarm in a 250°F oven for 10 minutes or so.

TIP: Tortillas can be cut into wedges and served right from the pan, but for a buffet, it is a nice touch to invert the tortilla onto a cutting board and cut it into thin wedges or smallish squares. (When cooled, the tortilla will be firm enough to pick up and eat with your fingers.) Hold a cutting board over the cooled tortilla in the pan and, with a quick flip, invert the tortilla onto the board. Or try this method: Wiggle a thin metal or rubber spatula around the edges of the tortilla to make sure they're free. Hold the skillet at a 45-degree angle, place a flat plate next to the lip of the skillet, and coax the tortilla out onto the plate with the spatula. Cut and serve the tortilla from the plate, or slide it onto a cutting board and serve it from there.

Tortillas

Let me clear up a little confusion about the word "tortilla." In Mexico, tortillas are round, very thin flatbreads made with wheat or corn flour, but in Spain they are slow-cooked thick omelets, very similar, in fact, to the Italian frittata. You will find them in every tapas bar in Spain, from the very simple *tortilla española* made with potatoes and onion to complex creations containing everything from piquillo peppers and crab to clams and bacon.

Tortillas are perfect buffet food. They are delicious served at room temperature, so they can be made before your first guest shows up. Any tortilla can be cut into small squares and served along with an array of appetizers (see pages 244 through 246) or cut into larger pieces to join the parade of main courses.

Tortillas are also ideal everyday food. Make one for dinner during the week to serve with a salad. Regardless of the ingredients, the procedure stays pretty much the same, so they are perfect for cleaning odds and ends out of the vegetable drawer and the rest of the refrigerator. Those who make it to dinner on time are treated to a warm tortilla; those who straggle in later can enjoy it at room temperature, when it is equally delicious (some think better!) with a salad or wedged between two slices of hearty bread.

The best pan for making a tortilla is a well-seasoned cast-iron skillet. First, it is heavy, which means slow, steady, even heat—just what you want for making tortillas. The seasoned surface means no sticking and the all-metal construction makes it ideal for finishing the tortillas under the broiler or in the oven. If you don't own a cast-iron skillet, learning to make tortillas is the perfect excuse to go out and buy one. The new generation of cast-iron skillets (notably the "Logic" line manufactured by Lodge) are sold preseasoned—a lazy cook's dream.

Artichoke, Potato, and Serrano Ham Tortilla

This exotic-sounding tortilla is nothing more than the classic *española* taken to the next level with the addition of briny artichokes and the richness of serrano ham. If you have a good relationship with the store where you buy your serrano ham, they may save you the bone from the ham (if you ask nicely). What one of those bones will do for a pot of soup or beans, I can't even begin to tell you.

MAKES 8 MAIN-COURSE BUFFET SERVINGS OR AT LEAST 12 APPETIZER SERVINGS • PREP TIME: 15 MINUTES • COOK TIME: 15 MINUTES

1 large Idaho (baking) potato (about 12 ounces), peeled and cut into ½-inch dice (about 2 cups)

2 tablespoons olive oil

One 9-ounce box frozen artichoke hearts, defrosted

2 shallots, minced

½ teaspoon chopped fresh thyme

¼ pound thinly sliced serrano ham or prosciutto, cut crosswise into ¼-inch-wide ribbons

3 bottled piquillo peppers, cut into ½-inch-wide strips

2 tablespoons unsalted butter

12 extra-large eggs, beaten

Kosher or fine sea salt and freshly ground pepper

1 cup shredded tetilla cheese (see page 246) or Gouda

1. Put the diced potato in a saucepan with enough cold salted water to cover and bring to a boil over high heat. As soon as the water boils, drain the potato thoroughly and spread the cubes out on a baking sheet to air-dry.

2. Set the rack about 6 inches from the broiler and preheat the broiler.

3. Heat the olive oil in a 10-inch ovenproof skillet (cast iron is ideal) over medium-high heat. Add the artichoke hearts and cook, tossing, until they are lightly browned, about 5 minutes. Add the potatoes, then add the shallots and thyme, adjust the heat to low, and cook until the thyme smells delicious and the shallots have softened, about 2 minutes; the potatoes should not brown. Stir in the serrano ham and toss for another minute, just until it frizzles. Scrape the vegetable-ham mix and the piquillo peppers into a bowl and wipe the pan clean with a wad of paper towels.

4. Heat the butter in the pan over medium-high heat until it stops foaming. Tilt the pan to make sure the bottom and sides are well coated, then pour in the eggs. Shake the pan while stirring the eggs with a wooden spoon or heat-resistant spatula. Lift the edges of the tortilla as they set, letting the raw eggs run into the empty spaces. When the eggs are no longer runny, spread the vegetables and ham evenly over the top of the tortilla and season with salt and pepper. Lower the heat, sprinkle with the cheese, and cook until the edges of the tortilla are firm, about 5 minutes.

5. Put the tortilla under the broiler until golden brown and bubbly, 3 to 4 minutes. Slide the tortilla out of the skillet (see Tip, page 249). Serve hot or at room temperature.

Vegetable Potpie

On a recent trip to the Dominican Republic, my friend Walewska Estevez Christine invited me to the home of her family, where I was introduced to her dad, Dr. Uvaldo; her mom, "Mignon"; and the rest of her lovely family. Walewska's sister Ninoschtka is an enthusiastic cook who went all out to throw a dinner party for us. The centerpiece was this outstanding vegetable potpie. Now, I love potpie, but I tend to think of beef or chicken, even seafood, as the main ingredient. Add to that the fact that vegetarian dishes in general are not something you see a lot of in the Caribbean, so this was a real surprise. Ninoschtka's vegetable potpie is perfect for a buffet: the filling and pastry can be made up to a day ahead, and the whole pie can be put together and popped into the oven well before your guests arrive. By the time they ring the bell, your house will smell like a million bucks and you'll be out of your apron and into something festive.

MAKES 12 BUFFET SERVINGS • PREP TIME: 40 MINUTES (PLUS CHILLING TIME FOR THE DOUGH) • COOK TIME: 1 HOUR AND 40 MINUTES (MOSTLY UNATTENDED)

FOR THE DOUGH

4 cups all-purpose flour

1 tablespoon baking powder

1 tablespoon sugar

1 teaspoon salt

2 extra-large egg yolks

1/2 cup milk

12 tablespoons (1 1/2 sticks) very cold unsalted butter, cut into 12 pieces

1/4 cup cold vegetable shortening

4 tablespoons unsalted butter

2 medium Spanish onions (about 1 pound), finely diced (about 3 cups)

1 large or 2 medium cubanelle peppers, cored, seeded, and finely chopped (about 1 1/2 cups)

1 stalk celery, minced (about 1/3 cup)

1 small green cabbage (about 2 1/2 pounds), cored and chopped (about 1/2-inch pieces; see Tips)

2 medium carrots, peeled and grated (about 1/2 cup)

1 cup frozen corn kernels

One 10 3/4-ounce can condensed cheddar cheese soup

1 cup heavy cream

Kosher or fine sea salt and freshly ground pepper

FOR THE GLAZE

1 extra-large egg yolk

1 teaspoon sugar

1. Make the dough: Sift the flour, baking powder, sugar, and salt together into a large bowl. Pour into the work bowl of a food processor. Beat the egg yolks and milk together in a small bowl. Add the chilled butter to the flour mixture and pulse several times, until the mixture is the consistency of cornmeal. Add the shortening and repeat. Add the milk mixture and pulse once or twice, just until the mixture forms a rough dough. Scrape the dough out onto a lightly floured surface and knead a few times, just to gather it together. Wrap the dough in waxed paper and then in aluminum foil. Chill for at least 30 minutes, or for up to a day.

2. Make the filling: Heat the butter in a large Dutch oven or heavy casserole over medium heat. Add the onions, peppers, and celery and cook, stirring occasionally, until wilted, about 5 minutes. Add the cabbage and carrots and continue stirring until the cabbage is wilted and softened, about 10 minutes. Stir in the corn, then add the cheese soup and cream and stir until thoroughly blended. Season with salt and pepper to taste. Let cool to room temperature before using. The filling can be prepared up to a day in advance.

3. Preheat the oven to 350°F. Set out a 13 × 11-inch glass baking dish (see Tips).

4. Assemble the potpie: Sprinkle the work surface with flour. Cut off slightly more than one-third of the dough and set that piece aside. Roll the larger piece out to a 17 × 15-inch rectangle, flouring the surface and rolling pin as necessary to keep the dough from sticking. Don't worry if the dough tears or if the rectangle isn't perfect; it can be patched up later. Roll the dough up around the rolling pin. Unroll the dough so it is more or less centered over the baking dish. Gently edge the dough into the dish, making sure to nudge it into the corners and leaving

about ½ inch of overhanging dough all the way around the lip of the baking dish. Most likely there will be tears in the dough and it will overhang the dish more in some places than in others. Mend the tears by pressing them together; cut off sections of dough that overhang the dish by more than ½ inch and use them to fix sections of the dough that don't quite overhang the dish.

5. Scrape the cooled filling into the dough and spread it into an even layer. Roll the smaller piece of dough out to a 13 × 11-inch rectangle. Roll it up around the rolling pin, then unroll it over the filling. Fold the overhanging dough over the top piece of dough and crimp the edges to seal them (or use the tines of a fork to seal the two pieces of dough together).

6. Glaze the potpie: Beat the egg yolk, sugar, and 1 tablespoon water together in a small bowl until thoroughly blended. Brush the glaze over the top of the pie, including the crimped edges. Make 2 slits in the top piece of dough, about 3 inches long and about 3 inches apart.

7. Bake until the top and bottom crusts are golden brown and you can see the filling bubbling through the slits in the top crust, 50 minutes to 1 hour. Let stand for 10 minutes before serving. The filling is fairly firm, so the pie can be cut and served easily with a serving spatula.

TIPS: To subdue a whole head of cabbage and turn it into manageable ½-inch pieces, try this method: First, strip off any yellow or sad-looking leaves from the outside of the head. Next, cut the cabbage into quarters through the core. Cut the core out of each piece, then slice the cabbage lengthwise into ½-inch-wide strips. Cut those strips crosswise into ½-inch pieces. If some are larger than others, no worries: it will all even out in the cooking. The 2½-pound cabbage called for in this recipe will yield about 12 cups chopped.

A glass baking dish that holds 3 quarts and measures 13 × 11 inches (check the bottom of the dish—both measurements should be listed) is the perfect vessel for this potpie. Not only will the crust and filling fit perfectly, but the glass conducts heat very well and browns the underside of the crust as well as the top—not an easy thing to do with a potpie!

Pastelón ∾ PLANTAIN AND PICADILLO CASSEROLE

This is sometimes called Puerto Rican lasagna, but I think that's a misnomer. It is really more like an over-the-top Spanish tortilla, the slow-cooked Spanish classic omelet (page 249). You will find versions of *pastelón* all over Puerto Rico and the Dominican Republic. It is a real party dish that is at home at an evening buffet or an early afternoon brunch.

This is a very traditional version of *pastelón*. There are easier versions that use cooked and mashed plantains in place of the sliced and browned plantains, but I figure that if you're going to go, you may as well go all the way. There is one little shortcut I found that doesn't compromise the quality: baking the slices to a golden brown rather than panfrying them, which is usually how it's done. While the plantains are baking, you're free to put the picadillo filling together and let it cool. Even so, *pastelón* is still an undertaking, make no mistake about it. And it isn't exactly light. But, then again, this isn't everyday food—it's a dish for very special occasions.

One final note: Because of the sweetness of the plantains, the picadillo should be very well seasoned.

MAKES 12 BUFFET SERVINGS • PREP TIME: 2 HOURS • COOK TIME: 1 HOUR

Vegetable oil cooking spray
9 fully ripe plantains (see Note)

FOR THE PICADILLO (MAKES 4 CUPS)
1 1/2 pounds ground beef, pork, or turkey
1 cup Sofrito (page 305)
1/4 cup alcaparrado or coarsely chopped pimiento-stuffed olives
2 tablespoons tomato paste
1 teaspoon ground cumin

Pinch of ground cloves (if using beef or pork)
Kosher or fine sea salt and freshly ground pepper
2 tablespoons all-purpose flour
1/2 cup raisins (optional)

1 tablespoon unsalted butter, softened
1 tablespoon vegetable oil
12 extra-large eggs, well beaten

1. Preheat the oven to 375°F. Line 2 baking sheets with parchment paper and spray the paper with cooking spray.
2. Peel the plantains and cut them on a sharp diagonal into 1/2-inch slices. The slices should be about 3 inches long (they'll be shorter near the ends). Line up as many of the plantain slices as will fit in a single layer side by side on the prepared baking sheets and spray the tops with cooking spray. Bake until well browned on the bottom, about 20 minutes. Pile the plantain slices up on a plate to cool. Repeat as necessary with the remaining plantains.

(continued on page 257)

255

BUFFETS

Make a layer of overlapping baked plantains to cover the bottom of the greased skillet.

Spoon the picadillo over the bottom layer of the plantains.

Cover the picadillo with a second layer of plantains.

The assembled *pastelón,* ready for cooking.

3. While the plantains are baking, make the picadillo: Spray a large deep skillet with cooking spray and set over high heat. Crumble the ground beef into it and cook, stirring, until all traces of pink are gone, about 4 minutes. Add the sofrito and cook, stirring, until the liquid from the meat and sofrito has evaporated and the mixture is sizzling, about 6 minutes. Add the alcaparrado, tomato paste, cumin, cloves, and salt and pepper to taste. Lower the heat so the tomato paste doesn't stick to the pan and burn, and cook, stirring, until the tomato paste changes color, a minute or two.

4. If necessary, spoon off all but 1 tablespoon of the fat from the pan. Add the flour and cook, stirring, for 2 minutes. Add ¼ cup water, raise the heat to medium, and bring to a boil. Stir in the raisins if using, and add salt and pepper if you think they're needed. Remember, you want a well-seasoned picadillo to balance the sweetness of the plantains. Set aside to cool.

5. Assemble the *pastelón:* Grease the bottom and sides of a 12-inch cast-iron skillet with the butter, then pour the oil over the butter. Using half the plantains, cover the bottom of the pan with concentric circles of overlapping plantain slices (see photos, opposite). Spoon the picadillo over the plantains and smooth into an even layer. Using the remaining plantains, cover the picadillo (as you covered the bottom of the pan) with concentric circles of overlapping plantain slices. The *pastelón* can be assembled up to an hour in advance and kept at room temperature covered with a damp kitchen towel or several thicknesses of damp paper towels.

6. Heat the skillet over medium-low heat just until you can hear sizzling. Reduce the heat to low and very slowly pour the beaten eggs around the edges of the pan and over the top of the *pastelón*—pour in as much of the eggs as you can without overfilling the pan. Run a heat-resistant spatula around the edges of the pan, separating the plantains and picadillo from the sides of the pan and letting the eggs from the top seep in, making room for more eggs. Add the remaining eggs while continuing to run the spatula around the edges of the pan until the *pastelón* has "drunk up" the rest of the eggs.

7. Set the skillet in the oven and bake until the *pastelón* is bubbling around the edges and the center is set, about 25 minutes. Let cool for 15 minutes before serving. If left in the pan, the *pastelón* will stay warm enough to serve for up to an hour. Unmold it just before serving.

8. To serve, run a thin knife around the edges of the pan to make sure the *pastelón* isn't sticking to the pan. The *pastelón* can be served directly from the pan, which is easiest to do with an offset spatula. Or for a more dramatic presentation, invert the *pastelón* onto a serving platter: Choose a large round serving platter—if it has a rim, the "well" of the plate should be at least an inch or two wider than the pan. Put the platter upside down over the *pastelón*. With pot holders or oven mitts, grasp the pan handle with one hand and use the other hand

to clamp the platter in place over the *pastelón*. Invert the pan and the platter—be brave, and use one quick motion. Leave the pan in place for a few minutes, then gently lift it off. If any of the plantains have stuck to the pan, simply scrape them off and replace them on top of the *pastelón*. Cut into wedges using a very sharp knife and a gentle sawing motion.

NOTE: The ideal plantains for this version of *pastelón* are completely black but not at all mushy. If you were to fry the plantain slices (as is done traditionally) instead of baking them, slightly less ripe plantains would be ideal, since frying will soften up plantains much more than baking. If there's any question about whether your plantains are ripe enough to make *pastelón*, it is better to err on the side of riper rather than "greener" plantains. The sweet flavor of ripe plantains is a key part of this dish.

VARIATIONS
- Add a little heat to the picadillo by seasoning it to taste with chile powder or crushed red pepper flakes.
- Spike the filling by soaking the raisins, if using, in rum or brandy for an hour or so; drain them before adding them to the picadillo.
- Substitute ground chicken or turkey for the ground beef.
- For an earthy note, soak a handful of dried mushrooms in hot water to cover. Drain and rinse them well, then coarsely chop them. Add along with the sofrito.

Crab Filling for Pastelón

I don't remember the very first time I ever tasted *pastelón,* but I do remember that all of the *pastelones* that I ate growing up were filled with traditional picadillo, like the one above. That combination of salty and sweet was enough to make me want to break into a mambo! It wasn't until I tasted a crab *salmorejo* (very similar to this filling) in Puerto Rico that I decided to try my hand at the plantain-crabmeat combination. I drew on the inspiration from my grandmother's crab *alcapurrias* (yuca fritters), and the result is a cozy, family-friendly recipe dressed up in its Sunday finest for family and friends. The filling on its own is delicious with white rice and fried sweet plantains.

MAKES 2½ CUPS, ENOUGH FOR A 10-INCH *PASTELÓN* • PREP TIME: 15 MINUTES • COOK TIME: 5 MINUTES

2 tablespoons olive oil
½ cup Sofrito (page 305)
½ cup canned Spanish-style tomato sauce
½ teaspoon crushed red pepper flakes, or
   to taste

½ cup alcaparrado or coarsely chopped
   pimiento-stuffed olives
1 pound lump crabmeat, picked over for
   shells and cartilage

1. Heat the olive oil in a large skillet over medium heat. Add the sofrito and cook until the liquid has evaporated and the sofrito is sizzling. Stir in the tomato sauce, red pepper flakes, and alcaparrado and heat to simmering. Stir in the crab gently, to keep the lumps from breaking up, and cook just until the crab is coated with the sauce. Let cool before using.

2. Assemble and cook the *pastelón* as described on pages 255 through 258, with the following modifications:
   • Reduce the number of plantains to 8.
   • Reduce the number of eggs to 9.
   • Use a 10-inch cast-iron skillet.

TIPS: Save the ends of the plantains, which aren't neat little slices, to plug up odd little spots in the top and bottom layers of the *pastelón.*

A well-seasoned cast-iron skillet is really the best pan for this. It will cook the underside of the *pastelón* evenly and gently, and the seasoned finish reduces the chances of the *pastelón* sticking when it comes time to invert it.

Yellow Rice with Bacalao and Peas

Nothing says Lent in Puerto Rico like this satisfying dish of salt cod, bright green peas, and yellow rice. I grew up eating this and I've never stopped.

MAKES 8 GENEROUS BUFFET SERVINGS • PREP TIME: 15 MINUTES (PLUS A DAY FOR SOAKING THE SALT COD) • COOK TIME: 45 MINUTES (INCLUDES COOKING THE SALT COD)

½ cup Achiote Oil (page 306)

1 cup Sofrito (page 305)

¼ cup alcaparrado or coarsely chopped pimiento-stuffed olives

2 tablespoons kosher or fine sea salt, or to taste

1 teaspoon freshly ground pepper

1 teaspoon ground cumin

2 bay leaves

3 cups long-grain white rice

2 cups soaked, cooked, and flaked salt cod (see opposite)

Five 8-ounce bottles clam juice, or as needed

2 cups frozen peas, defrosted

Bottled roasted red peppers, cut into thin strips, for garnish

1. Heat the achiote oil in a Dutch oven or a large deep skillet with a tight-fitting lid over medium-high heat. Stir in the sofrito, then add the alcaparrado and cook until the liquid has evaporated and the sofrito is sizzling. Season with the salt, pepper, and cumin, and toss in the bay leaves.

2. Stir in the rice, raise the heat to high, add the flaked salt cod, and stir until the rice and fish are coated with the sofrito mixture. When the rice grains begin to turn chalky, pour enough clam juice into the pan to cover the rice by 1 inch. Bring the liquid to a boil and cook until the level of the liquid meets the top of the rice.

3. Add the peas, lower the heat to very low, stir the rice thoroughly, and cover the pan. Cook until the rice is tender but with a little bit of bite and the liquid is absorbed, about 20 minutes. The rice can be made up to 45 minutes in advance. Keep covered in a warm place until ready to serve. Fluff the rice with a fork and remove the bay leaves before serving. Garnish with strips of roasted red peppers.

TIP: If you find yourself making recipes from this book (or your own personal favorites) that call for a fair amount of clam broth, as this one does, you may discover that the cost of those little bottles of clam juice adds up pretty quickly. It's worth it to search out large (usually 48-ounce) cans of clam broth on your next trip to a big-box store.

Soaking and Cooking Salt Cod

It has become increasingly difficult to find top-quality salt cod fillets or whole "sides" of bone-in salt cod. Avoid, whenever possible, relatives of the cod, like hake or pollock, that have been salted and come in 1- to 2-pound packages. They are thinner and lack the true flavor of well-salted cod. Search out the thick fillets of salt cod sold loose (not packaged) in Italian, Latin, or Greek markets. The surface should feel grainy and the fillets should feel firm but still somewhat pliable.

Start soaking the salt cod a day before cooking it. Clear space in the refrigerator for a bowl or container large enough to hold the salt cod and plenty of water. Rinse the salt cod well under cold running water, then put it in the bowl. Cover with plenty of cold water and refrigerate for anywhere from 12 to 24 hours, depending on the thickness and saltiness of the cod. (The thicker and saltier the salt cod, the longer it will need to soak.) Change the water a few times as the cod soaks. This low-tech trick is the only way I can tell when the salt cod is ready for cooking: pull off a little piece of the cod and taste it. It should be pleasantly, not overly, salty. Remember, the salt cod will lose a little more salt when poached.

To cook the salt cod, put it in a pot large enough to hold it comfortably. (Cut the cod in half crosswise if necessary.) Pour in enough cold water to cover and bring to a boil over medium heat, then immediately adjust the heat so the water is simmering. Cook just until the cod flakes easily with a fork, about 8 minutes for a 1-inch-thick fillet. Drain the cod carefully and let cool it completely. It is now ready to use in any recipe.

Grilled Octopus Salad

Small octopus—sometimes weighing as little as 4 ounces—prepared in all sorts of ways can be found in tapas bars all over Spain. Larger specimens, like the one I use here, have a very different texture. And they are, frankly, a pain in the neck to peel, so I don't peel them until after they're cooked. Then the purplish skin slips right off. Like calamari, octopus is best if cooked either very briefly—a few minutes—or at a very slow simmer for an hour or two, or even longer depending on the size. Anything in between will result in a chewy, tough texture. In Puerto Rico, we like our octopus salad nice and juicy, so there is plenty of dressing for this salad. There is also a good amount of celery, which complements the rich flavor of octopus and adds a nice crunch.

MAKES 8 BUFFET SERVINGS (CAN BE EASILY HALVED) • PREP TIME: 20 MINUTES (PLUS COOLING AND MARINATING) • COOK TIME: 2½ HOURS (MOSTLY UNATTENDED)

¼ cup kosher or fine sea salt, plus more as needed

2 bay leaves

1 tablespoon black peppercorns

One 7-pound octopus, cleaned (see Note)

½ cup plus 2 tablespoons lemon olive oil, homemade (page 155) or store-bought, or extra-virgin olive oil

¼ cup white wine vinegar

Finely grated zest of 2 lemons

4 large stalks celery, trimmed, cut into thirds lengthwise, then crosswise into ½-inch pieces

4 large scallions, trimmed and cut into ½-inch pieces

½ cup chopped fresh flat-leaf parsley

Juice of 1 lemon

Freshly ground pepper

1. Bring 4 quarts water, the salt, bay leaves, and peppercorns to a boil in a large nonaluminum pot. Slip the octopus into the water and return to a boil. Adjust the heat so the liquid is barely simmering and cook until the octopus is tender, but not mealy or mushy, when poked with a paring knife, 2 to 2½ hours. You can tell when the octopus is close to being done because the purple skin at the thick base of the arms will start to peel back, exposing the white flesh. Drain the octopus in a colander and let sit until cool enough to handle. The octopus can be cooked up to 2 hours before grilling. Keep at room temperature; do not refrigerate.

2. While the octopus is cooling, whisk the ½ cup of the lemon olive oil (or olive oil), the vinegar, and lemon zest in a large bowl until blended. Add the celery, scallions, and parsley and toss well.

(continued on page 264)

3. When the octopus has cooled, cut between the arms to separate them from the head and from each other. Discard the head. (Some people eat the head, but I don't care for it.) Wipe off the purple skin from the arms, being careful around the suckers—you want to keep those intact. The easiest way to do it is to hold the thick end of an arm and swipe with your fingers along the whole length of the side of the arm opposite the suckers. Discard all the skin and place the cleaned arms in a shallow baking dish. Drizzle the 2 tablespoons lemon olive oil (or olive oil) and the lemon juice over them. Season liberally with salt and pepper. Let the octopus marinate at room temperature for up to 2 hours, occasionally turning the arms gently in the marinade.

4. Heat a gas grill to high or build a hot charcoal fire.

5. Grill the octopus, turning once, until well browned, even charred in spots, on both sides, about 8 minutes. While they are still warm, cut the octopus arms crosswise into ½-inch-or-so pieces. Add them, while still warm, to the dressed vegetables and toss. Serve immediately, or let stand for up to 30 minutes, tossing occasionally.

VARIATIONS: The flavorings can be taken from traditional to vibrant by replacing some or all of the parsley with cilantro and replacing the lemon zest with orange zest.

For an absolutely delicious and more substantial salad, prepare the Butter Beans *en Escabeche* (page 164) and stir the beans together with the prepared octopus salad. Give the salad 30 minutes for the flavors to mingle, and serve at room temperature.

NOTE: Octopus is available at many (especially ethnic—Greek, Italian, or Latin) seafood markets. If your market doesn't carry it regularly, you will most likely be able to order it. If the octopus is frozen, put it in a bowl and defrost overnight in the refrigerator. Most octopus is sold cleaned, that is, with the eyes and viscera removed. Ask to be sure. Most likely, the hard, marble-size "beak" will have been left intact. To remove it, before cooking the octopus, turn it upside down and force the beak through the opening at the center of the arms. Cut out the beak with kitchen shears or a paring knife.

Shellfish Cannelloni

These cannelloni, which have a very old-school Italian restaurant feel, were inspired by a visit to what many people consider the best Italian restaurant in Buenos Aires (and that's saying something!), Tomo Uno.

MAKES 12 BUFFET SERVINGS • PREP TIME: 1 HOUR (INCLUDES MAKING SAUCE AND FILLING, AND USING STORE-BOUGHT CREPES) • COOK TIME: 40 MINUTES (UNATTENDED)

FOR THE SAUCE

12 tablespoons (1 1/2 sticks) unsalted butter

1 1/4 cups all-purpose flour

6 cups hot milk

Kosher or fine sea salt

Pinch of cayenne pepper

Pinch of freshly grated nutmeg

4 medium vine-ripened tomatoes (about 1 3/4 pounds), peeled, seeded (see page 38), and cut into 1/4-inch dice

1/4 cup finely chopped fresh flat-leaf parsley

FOR THE FILLING

4 tablespoons unsalted butter

1/4 cup minced shallots

1/4 cup dry sherry

2 sprigs fresh thyme (leaves only)

2 pounds medium shrimp (30 to 40 per pound), peeled and deveined

1 pound jumbo lump crabmeat, picked over for shells and cartilage

Finely grated zest of 1 lemon

Kosher or fine sea salt and freshly ground pepper (preferably white)

12 large (7- to 8-inch) crepes or 18 medium (6-inch) crepes, homemade (page 28) or store-bought, or 20 manicotti wrappers (see Note)

About 1 cup shredded mozzarella cheese

1/2 cup grated Manchego cheese

1. Make the sauce: Melt the butter in a large saucepan over medium-low heat. Whisk in the flour and cook until bubbling and fragrant, about 3 minutes; keep the heat low enough to avoid browning the roux at all. Gradually pour in the hot milk, whisking constantly, until smooth and glossy. Lower the heat and continue to whisk gently, making sure to get in the corners of the saucepan with the whisk. Season with salt to taste, and stir in the cayenne and nutmeg.

2. Scrape the sauce into a bowl and stir in the diced tomatoes and chopped parsley. Cover the sauce with plastic wrap, pressing the plastic onto the surface of the sauce to keep a skin from forming. Set aside.

(continued)

3. Make the filling: Heat the butter in a large skillet over medium heat until foaming. Add the shallots and cook until softened and fragrant but not browned, about 3 minutes. Stir in the sherry, bring to a boil, and cook until almost evaporated. Stir in the thyme, raise the heat to high, and add the shrimp. Toss until the shrimp turn pink but are not cooked through, about 1 minute. Remove from the heat and fold in the crabmeat gently, to keep the pieces as large as possible. Add 2 cups of the sauce and stir gently until mixed. Stir in the lemon zest and season with salt and pepper to taste.

4. Preheat the oven to 375°F.

5. Assemble the cannelloni: Pour enough of the remaining sauce into a 13 × 11 × 2-inch baking dish (or any 2-inch-deep baking dish that holds 16 cups) to cover the bottom. Use a scant ½ cup filling for larger crepes, ⅓ cup filling for smaller crepes or store-bought manicotti wrappers. Center the filling over the bottom half of a crepe/wrapper. Sprinkle a heaping teaspoon of the mozzarella over the filling. Fold the top half of the crepe/wrapper over the filling, then fold the sides over the filling. Roll up snugly and place in the baking dish, seam side down. Repeat with the remaining crepes, filling, and mozzarella. Pour the remaining sauce over the cannelloni, wiggle the baking dish to settle the sauce between the cannelloni, and smooth the sauce on top into an even layer. Sprinkle the grated Manchego cheese over the sauce. Cover the baking dish with foil. The cannelloni can be prepared to this point up to a few hours before being cooked. Refrigerate, and bring to room temperature while the oven is heating.

6. Bake until the sauce is bubbly around the edges, 20 to 25 minutes. Uncover the baking dish, switch the oven setting to broil, and broil until the top of the cannelloni is bubbly and brown.

NOTE: Manicotti wrappers are squares of fresh pasta, approximately 6 inches per side. They are available in Italian markets and some supermarkets. If they are unavailable, look for large sheets of fresh pasta that can be cut to size, or make the cannelloni using crepes. The wrappers do not need to be cooked before forming these cannelloni.

A STITCH IN TIME: If you are using crepes and you have a little extra time, make a double batch of crepes. Wrap the crepes you don't use for the cannelloni securely in plastic wrap and then aluminum foil and freeze for up to 3 months, ready for your next round of cannelloni or a super-quick dessert like the Crepe and Dulce de Leche Stack on page 291.

Goat Braised in Coconut Milk

Here is another dish I picked up on my trip to the Dominican Republic. My friend Ninoschtka knew two women in the town of San Cristóbal who ran a catering operation, Villa Shantal, with great outdoor party venues, one of which boasted grounds filled with four hundred different types of orchids! Doña Corina Castro, the owner of Villa Shantal, asked her three chefs to prepare a feast for us. The menu included this slow-cooked goat, rice with *gandules* (pigeon peas—you can't get much more Dominican than that!), and a delicious avocado salad. This goat with coconut milk is a terrific special-occasion and buffet dish because it is easy to make in a large quantity and tastes even better when reheated the next day.

MAKES 12 BUFFET SERVINGS • PREP TIME: 30 MINUTES (INCLUDES MAKING THE SOFRITO) • COOK TIME: 2½ HOURS (MOSTLY UNATTENDED)

4 pounds bone-in goat (preferably shoulder), cut by your butcher into large (2-inch-or-so) pieces
Kosher or fine sea salt and freshly ground pepper
2 tablespoons olive oil

1 cup Sofrito (page 305)
¼ cup alcaparrado or coarsely chopped pimiento-stuffed olives
1 teaspoon ground cumin
One 13½-ounce can unsweetened coconut milk

1. Pat the pieces of goat dry with paper towels. Season them generously with salt and pepper. Heat the oil in a large Dutch oven or heavy casserole over medium-high heat. Add only as many pieces of goat as will fit in a single layer and cook, turning as necessary, until well browned on all sides, about 10 minutes. Adjust the heat as the goat browns so the little bits that stick to the pot don't burn. Transfer the goat to a plate and repeat with the remaining pieces.

2. Pour off most of the fat from the pot. Add the sofrito, alcaparrado, and cumin and cook until the liquid has evaporated and the sofrito is sizzling. Pour in the coconut milk, scrape to free up the little brown bits stuck to the pot, and bring to a boil. Return the goat to the pot, season the sauce lightly with salt and pepper, and adjust the heat so the liquid is simmering. Cover and cook until the goat is tender, about 2 hours. The stew can be prepared up to a day in advance. Let cool, then refrigerate; bring to a simmer before continuing.

3. Transfer the goat to a serving bowl or platter with tongs or a slotted spoon, leaving the sauce in the pot. Spoon off as much fat from the sauce as possible and taste the sauce. Add salt and pepper if necessary and spoon the sauce over the goat. Serve hot.

Pernil ✑ PUERTO RICAN ROAST PORK SHOULDER

Nothing, and I mean *nothing,* says holiday party like a beautiful, fragrant, juicy *pernil.* Whatever you're celebrating, try to get the pork marinating at least 2 days before the big event. That will not only flavor the roast completely, it will get the main-course prep out of the way well in advance.

MAKES 12 BUFFET SERVINGS, PLUS LEFTOVERS • PREP TIME: 30 MINUTES (PLUS 1
TO 3 DAYS MARINATING TIME) • COOK TIME: 3 HOURS (UNATTENDED)

One 6-pound skin-on, bone-in pork
  shoulder roast (aka "fresh ham")
Wet Adobo Rub (page 307)

1. Marinate the roast up to 3 days before you plan to cook it: Make several slits about 2 inches apart and 1½ inches long through the skin of the roast and into the meat, going about half-way through the roast (unless you hit the bone). Wiggle your finger in the slits to make them easier to fill. (Although the adobo isn't spicy, you may find that a pair of latex gloves comes in handy for this.) Fill each slit with adobo, coaxing as much as you can into each with the help of an espresso spoon or small teaspoon. Turn the roast, and do the same on all sides. If you have adobo left over, rub it all over the outside of the roast. Refrigerate, covered, for at least 1 day, or up to 3 days.

2. Preheat the oven to 450°F.

3. Set the roast skin side up on a rack in a roasting pan. Roast for 1 hour. Turn the heat down to 400°F and roast until the skin is deep golden brown and crackly and there is no trace of pink near the bone, about 2 hours. An instant-read thermometer inserted into the thickest part of the roast should register 150°F; to be sure, check the roast in a few spots. Let the roast rest for at least 15 minutes before carving.

4. To serve, remove the crispy skin. It will pull right off in nice big pieces. Cut them into smaller pieces—kitchen shears work well for this—and pile them up in the center of the serving platter. Carve the meat parallel to the bone all the way down to the bone. (It will get trickier to carve neat slices as you get near the bone; don't let that bother you.)

Turkey Breast "Pavochon"

Pavochon is a Puerto Rican word used to describe a turkey *(pavo)* seasoned and roasted like a suckling pig *(lechón)*. This is how we season a whole roast turkey for the holidays in our house. It occurred to me that a double boneless breast of turkey seasoned in the same way would make a perfect buffet item—so much easier to carve than a whole turkey. (Jerry can take the night off!) The *jibaritos* or *cubanos* (page 80) that are made from the leftovers are killer and the perfect easy dinner a night (or two) after the big buffet.

MAKES 12 BUFFET SERVINGS PLUS LEFTOVERS • PREP TIME: 15 MINUTES (PLUS 3 TO 24 HOURS MARINATING TIME) • COOK TIME: ABOUT 2 HOURS

> A double boneless turkey breast (about
> 5 pounds; from a whole 6- to 8-pound
> turkey breast), skin left on
> ¹/₂ cup Wet Adobo Rub (page 307)

1. Working from the top (i.e., rounded, not pointed, end) of the turkey breast, gently separate the skin from the meat by wiggling your fingers between the skin and the turkey, leaving the skin attached along the sides of the breast. Be careful not to tear the skin. Rub a generous amount of adobo under the skin, massaging it into the meat (you might want to wear latex gloves for this). Flip the breast over and rub the remaining adobo into the skinless side of the turkey.

2. Cut several 14-inch lengths of kitchen twine. Roll the breast up, tucking in any scraggly edges to make a tight, smooth roll. Tie the turkey breast securely with the twine at 1¹/₂-inch intervals. Wrap the turkey well in plastic wrap and refrigerate for at least 3 hours, or as long as overnight.

3. Place an oven rack in the lowest position and preheat the oven to 400°F. Place the turkey skin side up on a rack in a roasting pan and let it come to room temperature while the oven is heating.

4. Roast the turkey for 45 minutes. Lower the oven temperature to 375°F and continue roasting until an instant-read thermometer inserted into the thickest part of the turkey breast registers 150°F, about 1 hour and 15 minutes. (The temperature will continue to rise after the turkey is removed from the oven; a final internal temperature of 160°F is the goal.) Remove the roasting pan from the oven and tent the turkey loosely with aluminum foil. Let stand for 20 to 30 minutes before carving.

5. To carve, cut the turkey breast at a slight angle into ¹/₄-inch slices.

Arroz con Pollo ∽ CHICKEN WITH RICE

When I was growing up, chicken with rice was not something that was taken lightly—it was something my mother made over the weekend for company. Preparation started on Saturday with a trip to the live-poultry market, and finished with a house filled with a beautiful aroma on Sunday afternoon. Sunday dinner was a special occasion, so not just any dessert would do—one of the *tías* would stop on the way to our house to pick up a box of fresh Dunkin' Donuts. None of those packaged supermarket doughnuts for us!

I had always thought of *arroz con pollo* as "our" Sunday dinner, so I was really surprised to find that it is the unofficial national Sunday dinner dish of the Dominican Republic.

MAKES 6 BUFFET SERVINGS • PREP TIME: 30 MINUTES • COOK TIME: 45 MINUTES

¼ cup Achiote Oil (page 306)

2 small (3-pound or slightly less) chickens, cut into 10 pieces each (see Note, page 304; see Tip)

Kosher or fine sea salt and freshly ground pepper

½ cup Sofrito (page 305)

¼ cup alcaparrado or coarsely chopped pimiento-stuffed olives

1 teaspoon ground cumin

Pinch of ground cloves

4 cups long-grain white rice

6 cups chicken broth, homemade (page 303) or store-bought, or as needed

2 large bottled roasted red peppers, cut into ¼-inch-wide strips (about 1½ cups)

1. Heat the achiote oil in a paella pan or wide shallow pan with a tight-fitting lid over medium-high heat until the oil is rippling. Season the chicken with salt and pepper and add as many pieces to the pan, skin side down, as will fit without touching. Cook, turning as necessary, until well browned on all sides, about 10 minutes. Remove the pieces as they are done and set aside. Adjust the heat under the pan, especially after you start removing the chicken, so the chicken browns without the oil darkening. Add the remaining chicken, in batches if necessary, and brown as above.

2. When all the chicken has been removed from the pan, add the sofrito and alcaparrado. Season lightly with salt and pepper, raise the heat to medium-high, and cook until the liquid has evaporated and the sofrito is sizzling.

3. Stir in the cumin and cloves, then stir in the rice until it is coated with oil. Return the chicken to the pan, pour in enough broth to cover the rice by 1 inch, and bring to a boil. Cook over

high heat until the level of liquid reaches the top of the rice. Stir gently and reduce the heat to low. Cover the pan and cook until the liquid is absorbed, the chicken is cooked through, and the rice is tender but firm, about 20 minutes. Fluff the rice with a fork.

4. The *arroz con pollo* can be brought to the table right in the pan or transferred to a large serving platter. Either way, garnish with the roasted red peppers before serving.

TIP: If you make your own chicken broth, the cooked chicken from the strained broth can be used in place of the cut-up chicken called for above. Proceed as above, but brown the chicken very lightly to keep the overall cooking time to a minimum and so prevent the chicken from overcooking.

VARIATION: Add 1½ cups frozen corn kernels or baby peas just before covering the pan.

Chicken Braised in Peruvian Yellow Pepper Puree ∽ AJÍ DE GALLINA

Think of this as the national dish of Peru. It is made with a type of pepper, the *ají amarillo*, that is found all over Peru. My family, especially David, was so taken with the dish that I knew I had to re-create it once we got back home. *Ají amarillo* paste is available bottled in some Latin markets, but I think my mixture of yellow bell peppers, jalapeño, and lime juice comes closer to the bright flavor and tinge of heat that I loved in Peru.

MAKES 8 BUFFET SERVINGS • PREP TIME: 30 MINUTES (LESS IF STARTING WITH COOKED CHICKEN) • COOK TIME: 45 MINUTES (LESS IF STARTING WITH COOKED CHICKEN)

FOR THE BÉCHAMEL
2 tablespoons unsalted butter
2½ tablespoons all-purpose flour
1½ cups milk
½ cup grated Spanish onion
Kosher or fine sea salt
Pinch of cayenne pepper, or to taste

5 cups shredded cooked chicken, preferably thigh meat (see page 276)
⅔ cup *ají amarillo* paste or Improvised *Ají Amarillo* Puree (page 37)
Black olives
Sliced hard-boiled eggs
Basic White Rice (page 159)

1. Make the béchamel: Melt the butter in a medium saucepan over medium-low heat. Whisk in the flour and cook until the roux is smooth and bubbly but not taking on any color, about 3 minutes. Pour in the milk, whisking constantly until smooth. Bring to a simmer, whisking, and stir in the onion. Cook, whisking constantly, making sure to get into the corners of the pan, until the sauce is thickened and glossy, about 4 minutes. Season the béchamel with salt and cayenne to taste.

2. Fold the chicken and then the yellow pepper paste into the sauce. Check the seasonings again, adding salt and/or cayenne if you like. Heat over low heat, stirring gently, until heated through and bubbly.

3. Transfer the chicken to a platter and top with the black olives and hard-boiled eggs. Set a serving bowl of the rice alongside.

Chicken Braised in Peruvian Yellow Pepper Puree and Basic White Rice (page 159)

Roasting Peppers

Roasted peppers should be firm, sweet, and slightly smoky. The idea is to char the peppers over very high heat so the skins turn black as quickly as possible, to impart that smoky flavor without overcooking the peppers. Start with square-sided peppers without a lot of nooks and crannies. Imported peppers, sometimes labeled Holland peppers, usually have the right boxy shape and thick flesh, which make them ideal for roasting. This is a wonderful addition to a Sunday task list (see Sundays in the Kitchen with Daisy, page 127).

TO ROAST THE PEPPERS OVER THE BURNER OF A GAS STOVE: Turn a burner to high. (Use more burners if you're roasting more than 2 peppers and are comfortable juggling that many peppers.) Balance the peppers on the grate(s) over the flame. With a pair of long tongs, turn the peppers as necessary until all sides are black and blistered. If the occasional crevice remains unroasted, let it go—it's better than overcooking the rest of the pepper.

TO ROAST THE PEPPERS UNDER THE BROILER: Set the oven rack 5 to 6 inches from the broiler and preheat the broiler (to high, if that's an option). Broil the peppers, turning as necessary, until blackened as described above.

Wrap each pepper in a double thickness of damp paper towels and let cool to room temperature.

Unwrap each pepper, stand it on its stem end, and pull the pepper apart into strips (it will tear naturally at the indentations). Get rid of the stem and seeds and scrape off the blackened skin with a wad of paper towels or the back of a knife. Layer the roasted peppers in a small bowl (seasoning them with dried oregano if you like) and top them off with a little olive oil. They will keep for a week in the refrigerator. The pepper oil is delicious in a vinaigrette or brushed onto meat, fish, or poultry as it grills.

A STITCH IN TIME: In most of these recipes, feel free to substitute bottled roasted peppers for homemade. Be sure it says "fire-roasted" on the label. Little flecks of black on bottled peppers is a good sign that they will have the char-roasted flavor you're looking for.

Chicken Braised in Peruvian Yellow Pepper Puree, String Beans with Rosemary (page 155), and Tuna *"Chilindron"* with Penne (page 133)

Cooked and Shredded Chicken (with Bonus Broth)

Here's how I make the cooked and shredded chicken called for in several recipes in this book, including the Chicken Enchiladas (opposite) and Chicken Braised in Peruvian Yellow Pepper Puree (page 273) in this chapter. This is a good idea to put into rotation on your "prep day" (see Sundays in the Kitchen with Daisy, page 127). The bonus—about 8 cups of delicious chicken broth—is suitable for any recipe in this book.

MAKES 5 CUPS CHICKEN, PLUS BROTH • PREP TIME: 15 MINUTES • COOK TIME: 40 MINUTES

1 stalk celery, cut in half

1 carrot, peeled

1 yellow onion, unpeeled, cut into quarters through the root

1 red bell pepper, cored, seeded, and cut in half

1/2 bunch cilantro

2 bay leaves

3 cloves garlic

8 cups good-quality chicken broth

3 1/2 pounds boneless, skinless chicken thighs

1. Put the celery, carrot, onion, bell pepper, cilantro, bay leaves, and garlic in a 4- to 5-quart pot and pour in the broth. Bring to a boil, then adjust the heat so the liquid is simmering and cook for 10 minutes.

2. Slip the chicken pieces into the liquid and simmer until the chicken is cooked through, about 25 minutes.

3. Strain the broth. Set the chicken aside and discard the other solids.

4. When the chicken is cool enough to handle, coarsely shred it, getting rid of any fat as you go. You now have the makings of a meal as well as a bonus batch of enriched broth.

Chicken Enchiladas

On a trip through Mexico, my family enjoyed enchiladas (who doesn't?) everywhere we went. They were mostly of the beefy persuasion, which is fine with me, but in my never-ending crusade to bring authentic Latin flavors to the table in a somewhat more healthful package, I came up with this version of chicken enchiladas, which still boasts bold flavors in spite of the streamlined fat content.

I have a friendly rivalry going with my son Erik when it comes to enchiladas. He loves to play around with the sauces, using traditional Mexican ingredients like chipotle chiles and bittersweet chocolate. My approach is a little more user friendly, and the chicken thighs make it both economical and a great make-ahead dish. In fact, I always make a double recipe, freeze half of the enchiladas as well as the sauce, and then pull it out on a busy night when I'm running late.

MAKES 8 BUFFET SERVINGS • PREP TIME: 1 HOUR (INCLUDES COOKING AND SHREDDING CHICKEN) • COOK TIME: 30 MINUTES

FOR THE FILLING
2 tablespoons olive oil
1 cup Sofrito (page 305)
¼ cup pureed chipotles in adobo
1 teaspoon ground cumin
½ teaspoon cayenne pepper
Pinch of ground cinnamon
5 cups shredded cooked chicken, preferably thigh meat (see opposite)
Kosher or fine sea salt and freshly ground pepper

FOR THE SAUCE
2 tablespoons olive oil
2 tablespoons grated Spanish onion
1 clove garlic, minced
1¼ teaspoons chile powder
½ teaspoon ground cumin
½ teaspoon dried oregano
Two 8-ounce cans Spanish-style tomato sauce
1½ cups chicken broth, homemade (page 303), left over from cooking the chicken for this recipe, or store-bought

Vegetable oil cooking spray
16 corn tortillas
1 cup shredded Monterey Jack cheese

1. Make the filling: Heat the olive oil in a large skillet over medium-high heat. Add the sofrito and cook, stirring, until the liquid has evaporated and the sofrito is sizzling. Stir in the chipotle puree, cumin, cayenne, and cinnamon and cook, stirring, until your kitchen smells great. (It won't take more than a minute!) Stir in the chicken until it is coated with the seasoning. Remove from the heat, season with salt and pepper to taste, and set aside.

(continued)

2. Make the sauce: Heat the olive oil in a medium saucepan over medium-high heat. Stir in the onion, garlic, chile powder, cumin, and oregano and cook for a minute or so, until fragrant. Pour in the tomato sauce, followed by the chicken broth, and bring to a boil, then adjust the heat so the sauce is simmering. Cook until the sauce is slightly thickened, about 10 minutes. Remove from the heat.

3. Preheat the oven to 350°F.

4. Spray a 13 × 11 × 2-inch baking dish (or any other 2-inch-deep baking dish that holds 16 cups) with cooking spray. Cover the bottom with a thin layer of sauce. Set aside.

5. Spray a large pan or griddle with cooking spray and heat over medium heat. Add only as many tortillas as will fit without overlapping (possibly only 1 in a skillet, or up to 4 on a large griddle). Heat, turning once, until softened, about a minute per side. As each tortilla softens, remove it from the pan and add another in its place. Fill each warmed tortilla with 2 heaping tablespoons of the chicken filling spooned across the center, roll up the tortilla, and place it seam side down in the prepared baking dish. Repeat until all the tortillas are softened and filled.

6. Spoon half of the remaining sauce over the enchiladas, spreading it evenly. Sprinkle the cheese over the enchiladas and cover with aluminum foil. The enchiladas can be prepared up to this point several hours in advance and refrigerated.

7. Bake until heated through and bubbly, about 30 minutes. (Allow 35 to 40 minutes for refrigerated enchiladas.) Let stand for 5 minutes before serving.

8. Meanwhile, warm the remaining sauce in a saucepan over low heat, and pour it into a gravy boat or pitcher for guests to help themselves at the buffet.

SIDE DISHES

Creamed Spinach

The kids and I decided to dedicate the better part of a day in Buenos Aires to touring La Recoleta, the famous (and almost 200-year-old) cemetery. Of course, we couldn't do all that walking on empty stomachs, so we made our first stop of the day at Café Biela, the oldest café in Buenos Aires. Breakfast in Argentina is a serious affair. On that morning, mine included this delicious version of creamed spinach and a dish of soft-scrambled eggs with sweet baby shrimp (page 18). The trip through La Recoleta was amazing. The grounds were laid out like a small town, with wide avenues, beautiful sculptures, and gorgeous landscaping. It is the final resting place for many well-known names in the arts, sciences, and politics—most notably, Eva Perón. If you ever visit the city, you should make La Recoleta a part of your itinerary. And don't leave out the stop at Café Biela beforehand.

MAKES 8 BUFFET SERVINGS (CAN BE DOUBLED EASILY)
• PREP TIME: 15 MINUTES • COOK TIME: 10 MINUTES

1½ pounds baby spinach
2 tablespoons unsalted butter
2 tablespoons all-purpose flour
1 cup milk

Pinch of cayenne pepper
Pinch of freshly grated or ground nutmeg
Kosher or fine sea salt and freshly ground
    pepper

1. Bring a large pot of salted water to a boil. Set a colander in the sink and a large bowl of ice water near the sink. Stir the spinach into the boiling water and cook, stirring constantly, until it is bright green and tender, about 1½ minutes. Immediately drain the spinach and set the colander into the bowl of ice water. Drain again, then press as much water out of the spinach as you can with your hands. To get the spinach really dry (important for this dish), wrap it in a clean kitchen towel and squeeze out as much of the remaining water as you can. Coarsely chop the spinach and set aside.

2. Melt the butter in a medium saucepan over medium heat. Whisk in the flour and cook until bubbling and fragrant, about 3 minutes; keep the heat low enough that the roux doesn't brown at all. Gradually whisk in the milk and cook, whisking constantly—don't miss the corners of the pan—until the sauce is thickened and glossy, about 5 minutes.

(continued)

3. Stir the spinach into the pan and mix well until any little clumps of spinach are broken up and the spinach is completely coated with the sauce. Stir in the cayenne and nutmeg, then season with salt and pepper to taste. The creamed spinach can be made up to a day in advance and refrigerated. Reheat gently over low heat, thinning it with a little additional milk if needed. Check the seasoning before serving.

VARIATIONS
- Add a clove or two of chopped garlic or 2 minced shallots to the saucepan along with the butter.
- Substitute ground cloves for the nutmeg.
- Stir in a handful of raisins or toasted pine nuts along with the spinach.

Spicy Kale with Turkey Sausage

One of my favorite antidotes for a chilly day is the Portuguese *caldo verde,* a chunky soup of linguiça sausage, kale, and potatoes that is as hearty as it is delicious. One day while shopping for groceries, I picked up some kale with *caldo verde* in mind, after hearing a weather broadcast calling for snow the next day. When I got home, I realized that I had not picked anything up for a veggie side for that evening's dinner. Put together with some turkey sausage that I had in the freezer, this dish was enough to give me my *caldo verde* "fix" and give me a new twist on the kale and sausage combo. After his second helping, David said, "Mom, this would be delicious with pasta!" I told him he should leave the menu planning to me, but I made a mental note of his suggestion, and guess what? He was right!

MAKES 12 BUFFET SERVINGS • PREP TIME: 20 MINUTES • COOK TIME: 30 MINUTES

2 bunches (about 3 pounds) kale, thick stems removed, leaves cut into ¹/₂-inch-wide ribbons (see Tip, page 135)

2 tablespoons olive oil, plus extra for finishing

6 turkey sausages (about 1¹/₂ pounds), spicy if you like

4 cloves garlic, thinly sliced

¹/₂ medium Spanish onion, finely diced (about ³/₄ cup)

2 tomatoes, cored and finely diced (about 1¹/₂ cups)

¹/₄ teaspoon crushed red pepper flakes

One 15¹/₂-ounce can chickpeas, drained and rinsed

Kosher or fine sea salt and freshly ground pepper

1. Bring a large pot of salted water to a boil. Set a colander in the sink and a large bowl of ice water near the sink. Stir the kale into the boiling water and cook until it turns bright green, about 3 minutes. Drain the kale and set the colander into the bowl of ice water. Drain again, and press as much water out of the kale as you can with your hands, then set the kale aside.

2. Heat the olive oil in a large skillet over medium heat until hot but not smoking. Add the turkey sausages and cook, turning as necessary, until well browned on all sides and cooked through, about 10 minutes. Remove the sausages from the pan and set aside.

3. Lower the heat to medium-low, add the garlic to the pan, and stir until golden and fragrant. Add the onion and cook for 2 minutes, then stir in the tomatoes, crushed red pepper, and chickpeas, and salt and pepper to taste. Stir the kale into the pan until it is coated with sauce.

4. Cut the sausages into ½-inch slices and return them to the pan. Cook, partially covered, until the sausages are heated through and the kale is tender but retains its color and bite, about 5 minutes. Drizzle with olive oil to give the dish some shine right before serving.

VARIATIONS
- This recipe is also delicious with Mexican chorizo in place of the turkey sausages.
- The kale and sausages make a wonderful one-pot meal if you cook 1 pound of pasta—shells, rotini, or penne, for example—and mix it into the finished dish. Save some of the pasta cooking water and add it just before serving if the dish looks a little dry.
- For a delicious vegetarian version (with or without pasta), simply leave out the sausages.

Roasted Cauliflower with Anchovies and Garlic

If anyone had ever told me when I was a young girl that the day would come when I would literally be salivating over a dish that included cauliflower, anchovies, and roasted garlic, I'd have told them they were one enchilada short of a combination plate! The day of enlightenment came while I was dining in a little tapas bar in Barcelona and a small plate of this seemingly humble dish was placed in front of me. I ended up ordering two more portions—and wrote it off to research. (I swore that I would re-create the dish at home.) It's a cinch, especially with store-bought roasted garlic, as once the ingredients are tossed, there's nothing more than an occasional peek or stir with a spoon.

MAKES 10 TO 12 BUFFET SERVINGS • PREP TIME: 15 MINUTES (WITH PREMADE OR STORE-BOUGHT ROASTED GARLIC) • COOK TIME: 1¼ HOURS (LARGELY UNATTENDED)

2 medium heads cauliflower (about 2 pounds each)

⅓ cup olive oil

2 tablespoons unsalted butter

One 2-ounce can anchovy fillets, drained

⅓ cup mashed roasted garlic, homemade (page 309) or store-bought

Kosher or fine sea salt and freshly ground pepper

1. Preheat the oven to 400°F.
2. Cut the heads of cauliflower in half, then break or cut them into about 1½-inch florets. (Remember, this is for a buffet, so the florets should be easy to handle even if eaten while guests are standing.) Put the cauliflower in a large bowl.
3. Heat the oil and butter in a small skillet over medium-low heat until the butter is bubbling. Add the anchovies and roasted garlic and cook, breaking up the anchovies with a fork, until the anchovies are dissolved.
4. Pour the anchovy-garlic mixture over the cauliflower and toss well. Season lightly with salt and pepper. Turn the coated cauliflower into a 4-quart baking dish or any dish that the cauliflower fits in comfortably. Pour ½ cup water into the bowl, swish it around, and pour over the cauliflower. Cover the baking dish tightly with aluminum foil. The cauliflower can be prepared to this point up to a day in advance and refrigerated.
5. Bake until the cauliflower is tender but with a little bit of bite, about 45 minutes (slightly longer if the cauliflower went straight from the refrigerator to the oven.)

6. Uncover the baking dish and stir the cauliflower gently. Taste and add salt and pepper if you think it needs it. Continue roasting until most of the liquid is evaporated and the top of the cauliflower is browned, about 25 minutes. Stir the cauliflower gently one more time to coat it one more time with the sauce. Serve hot or at room temperature.

A STITCH IN TIME: Double the amount of anchovy-garlic sauce and reserve half for a quick sauce for pasta for two. It will keep in the refrigerator for up to 4 days.

Artichoke and Sweet Bell Pepper Sauté

This dish, with its combination of earthy artichokes and lightly cooked sweet, jewel-bright peppers, always evokes visions of fabulous summer dining alfresco. Maybe it is because this is my one "go-to" dish when I visit friends hosting barbecues. Whatever the reason, it is as delicious as it is colorful, and it combines the beautiful flavors of Spain with a minimum of fuss and strain on the purse strings. Any leftovers are excellent in a tortilla (see page 249) for lunch the next day.

MAKES 10 TO 12 BUFFET SERVINGS • PREP TIME: 15 MINUTES • COOK TIME: 15 MINUTES

2 tablespoons extra-virgin olive oil
Two 9-ounce boxes frozen artichoke hearts, defrosted and drained
2 large yellow bell peppers, cored, seeded, and cut into ¹/₂-inch-wide strips

2 large red bell peppers, cored, seeded, and cut into ¹/₂-inch-wide strips
3 cloves garlic, minced
Kosher or fine sea salt and freshly ground pepper

1. Heat the olive oil in a large deep skillet over medium heat. Add the artichoke hearts and cook, stirring, until the little bit of liquid left in the artichokes is evaporated and the artichokes just start to take on a little color, about 5 minutes.
2. Stir the yellow and red peppers and garlic into the artichokes and cook, stirring and tossing, until the peppers are wilted, about 3 minutes. Season lightly with salt and pepper, cover the skillet, and cook until the peppers are crisp-tender, about 3 minutes. Taste, and add more salt and pepper if necessary. Serve hot or at room temperature.

Red Beans with Salchichon and Potato

My *tía* Maria used to make the most unbelievably delicious red beans. The fact that I preferred *Tía's* beans to my mother's drove my poor mother crazy. It wasn't until I was a grown woman that I tried to decipher the secret to my aunt's beans, and I spent an afternoon watching her closely. Salchichon, which I like to call "Puerto Rican pepperoni," gives the beans a delicious smoky, peppery note, and the slow-cooked potato releases a bit of starch to make the broth sinfully silky. These beans are so good that I'm happy to eat them without the benefit of rice! *Tía* left some pretty big shoes to fill, and I like to think of this as my own little personal homage to her.

**MAKES 10 TO 12 BUFFET SERVINGS • PREP TIME: 15 MINUTES •
COOK TIME: 2 TO 2½ HOURS (LARGELY UNATTENDED)**

1 pound dried red kidney beans, picked over and rinsed

2 bay leaves

2 tablespoons olive oil

½ pound salchichon or pepperoni (see Note), cut in half lengthwise, then crosswise into ¼-inch slices

½ teaspoon ground cumin

1 teaspoon smoked paprika

¼ teaspoon ground cloves

One 8-ounce can Spanish-style tomato sauce

2 cups chicken broth, homemade (page 303) or store-bought

1 large Idaho (baking) potato (about 12 ounces), peeled and cut into 1-inch cubes (about 2 cups)

1. Put the beans in a heavy 3- to 4-quart pot. Pour in enough cold water to cover by 2 inches, add the bay leaves, and bring to a boil over high heat. Adjust the heat so the liquid is simmering and cook, skimming the foam that rises to the top, until the beans are tender, about 2 hours. Check occasionally and make sure the level of water never dips below the top of the beans; if it gets close, simply top up with a little water. Remove from the heat. The beans can be cooked up to 3 hours in advance and kept at room temperature; in fact, I like all beans better that way.

2. Heat the olive oil in a large skillet over medium heat. Add the salchichon and cook, stirring, just until fragrant and lightly browned, about 4 minutes. Add the cumin, smoked paprika, and cloves and stir well. Pour in the tomato sauce and broth and bring to a boil.

3. Scrape the sausage mixture into the pot of beans. Add the potato, bring to a boil, and cook until the potato is tender, about 10 minutes. Remove the bay leaves. The beans can be prepared up to 2 days before serving. They're even creamier and more delicious if they are made ahead. Reheat them over gentle heat, adding a small amount of water if necessary to return them to their original silkiness.

NOTE: Salchichon can mean different things to different people. The type of salchichon I like to use for this recipe is about the size and shape of a plump supermarket stick of pepperoni. The texture is similar to Genoa salami and the flavor is somewhere between Genoa and good pepperoni. Salchichon is available in Latin markets and through online sources. If you cannot find salchichon, substitute good-quality Italian pepperoni.

Candied Squash Pastries

Time to raid the vegetable garden for dessert again! Like the Sweet Tomato "Conserva" on page 38, this turns a traditionally savory ingredient into a surprise dessert. We enjoyed these first on a trip to Barcelona, where we saw them, along with *brazo gitano* ("gypsy's arm," a jelly roll filled with various fruits), in almost every pastry shop. In Barcelona, these pastries took the shape of hollow tubes of puff pastry (like cannoli), or *canutillos* ("little horns"), filled with candied squash and dusted with powdered sugar. When I was back home in my kitchen, I was surprised at how easy they were to re-create, especially in this simplified rectangular shape. Brush with a confectioners' sugar glaze (see page 168) or drizzle store-bought or homemade dulce de leche (see page 242) over the pastries before serving if you like, instead of dusting with confectioners' sugar.

MAKES 12 PASTRIES • PREP TIME: 1½ HOURS (INCLUDES SQUASH COOKING TIME) • COOK TIME: 25 MINUTES (UNATTENDED)

1 small spaghetti squash (about 3 pounds)
5 cups sugar
3 cinnamon sticks
1 teaspoon whole cloves
2 tablespoons unsalted butter, melted

One 17.3-ounce package frozen puff
    pastry, defrosted (see page 169)
1 extra-large egg, well beaten with
    1 tablespoon water
Confectioners' sugar

1. Cut the squash in half and scrape out the seeds and fibers. Put the squash halves into a heavy pot that will hold them comfortably. Pour in 10 cups water and add the sugar, cinnamon, and cloves. Bring to a boil, then adjust the heat so the sugar syrup is boiling gently and cook, partially covered, until the squash is very tender and looks translucent, about 45 minutes. Lift the squash from the pot with a slotted spoon and let cool on a baking sheet. Discard the syrup.

2. When the squash is cool enough to handle, pick out the cloves and cinnamon and scrape the candied "spaghetti" from the squash shells by raking across the strands with a fork. Put the strands into a sieve and drain thoroughly. You will have about 4 cups.

3. Preheat the oven to 400°F. Line 2 baking sheets with parchment paper.

4. When the squash is thoroughly drained but still warm, transfer it to a bowl, add the butter, and toss to coat. Set aside while you roll out the pastry.

5. Roll 1 sheet of the puff pastry out on a lightly floured board to a rectangle measuring about 10 × 15 inches. Cut the rectangle in half lengthwise and then crosswise into 3 strips to make six 5-inch squares. Mound 2 heaping tablespoonfuls of the candied squash on one side of a square. Moisten the edges of the square with a little of the beaten egg. Fold the other side over the filling to make a neat rectangle shape and press the edges to seal completely. Transfer the pastry to a prepared baking sheet. Repeat with the remaining pastry squares and then the second sheet of pastry. Brush the tops of the pastries with the beaten egg. Snip several slits in the top of each pastry with a pair of kitchen shears.

6. Bake until the pastries are puffed and golden brown, about 25 minutes. Serve warm or at room temperature, sprinkled with confectioners' sugar.

Guava Flan

The inspiration for this dish came from Mario Santiago, executive chef of the oh-so-fabulous May Street Café in Chicago. I was in town for an event and my dear friend Art Smith took me there for an art exhibit/cocktail party. I don't have to be sold on guava anything, but this flan is so floral and delicate that you will be hooked after one bite, even if you have never tasted guava before. I make this flan in a large rectangular baking dish (it serves more people), but if you'd prefer to use a round pan, I'm sure the flan police won't break down your door! Just cut the ingredients in half and use a deep (about 1½ inches) 9-inch glass pie plate. The caramel is super easy too. A note: Mario uses sour cream. I'm sticking with my first choice, *media crema,* for a nice smooth texture.

MAKES 12 BUFFET SERVINGS • PREP TIME: 25 MINUTES • COOK TIME: 50 MINUTES (PLUS 4 TO 24 HOURS CHILLING TIME)

2 cups sugar

Two 12-ounce cans evaporated milk

Two 14-ounce cans sweetened condensed milk

Two 7.6-ounce cans Nestlé's *media crema* (see Notes)

8 extra-large eggs

Two 14-ounce packages frozen guava puree, defrosted and strained (see Notes)

2 teaspoons vanilla extract

1. Set a rack in the center of the oven and preheat the oven to 325°F.

2. Have ready an 11 × 13-inch glass baking dish and a pair of thick pot holders or oven mitts. Make a caramel using the sugar and ½ cup water (see Caramelicious, page 124), and use the hot caramel to line the bottom and halfway up the sides of the dish.

3. Pour the evaporated milk, condensed milk, and *media crema* into a blender and blend on low speed until completely mixed. Add the eggs and blend on low speed until smooth. Add the guava puree and vanilla and blend just until incorporated. (Do this in 2 batches if your blender won't hold all the ingredients.)

4. Place the prepared baking dish (don't pour the custard into the dish yet!) in a roasting pan or other baking dish large enough to hold it comfortably. Set the pan on the oven rack and pour the guava mixture into the baking dish. Pour enough very warm water into the roasting pan to come halfway up the sides of the baking dish. Bake until the edges of the custard are set but the center is still jiggly when you wiggle the baking dish, 45 to 50 minutes; a paring knife poked into the center should come out clean. Let the flan cool to room temperature, then chill for at least 4 hours, or up to a day, before serving.

5. To serve, choose a rectangular platter large enough to hold the flan. Cover the flan with the platter and clamp the baking dish to the platter with your hands. With one quick motion, flip the flan onto the platter; it will release easily from the baking dish. Let it stand for a minute or two, then scrape any remaining liquid caramel from the dish over the top.

NOTES:

- *Media crema,* found in many supermarkets, adds a tart, buttermilky tang and smooth texture to flans without the grittiness sometimes found in flans made with sour cream.
- Frozen guava puree is available in most Latin groceries and many supermarkets. It is also available online from www.perfectpuree.com. Defrost the puree overnight in the refrigerator or in a large bowl of warm water. A very smooth puree makes this flan truly special: Work the puree through a very fine sieve, scraping the puree with the back of a large spoon to extract as much of the puree as possible while leaving the grit of the guava behind.

Pumpkin Flan

Panchito, a cousin on my father's side who lives in Puerto Rico, is the go-to dessert guy for any special event—birthdays, christenings, you name it. His claim to fame is *cazuela de calabaza,* a pumpkin-flavored pudding-y dessert, baked in a banana leaf, that is out of this world. It got me thinking of other ways to use pumpkin in traditional Latin desserts, and here is one I am particularly proud of. Try this flan instead of pumpkin pie for Thanksgiving, and play around with it a little to make it yours. Maybe a little freshly grated ginger and/or a pinch of allspice?

MAKES 12 BUFFET SERVINGS • PREP TIME: 20 MINUTES • COOK TIME: 50 MINUTES (PLUS 4 TO 24 HOURS CHILLING TIME)

2¼ cups sugar

One 12-ounce can evaporated milk

One 14-ounce can sweetened condensed milk

5 extra-large eggs

½ teaspoon ground cinnamon

¼ teaspoon ground cloves

¼ teaspoon ground ginger

1 teaspoon vanilla extract

One 15-ounce can pureed pumpkin

1. Place a rack in the center of the oven and preheat the oven 350°F.
2. Have ready a 10-inch deep-dish pie plate and a pair of thick pot holders or oven mitts. Make a caramel using 1¼ cups of the sugar and ¼ cup water (see Caramelicious, page 124). Use the caramel to coat the bottom and sides of the dish.
3. Put the remaining 1 cup sugar and the remaining ingredients in a blender jar and blend on low speed just until smooth.
4. Place the prepared pie plate (don't pour the custard into the dish yet!) in a roasting pan or other baking dish large enough to hold it comfortably. Set the pan on the oven rack and pour the pumpkin mixture into the pie plate. Pour enough very warm water into the roasting pan to come halfway up the sides of the pie plate. Bake until the custard is set around the edges but the center still jiggles when you wiggle the pan, 45 to 50 minutes; a paring knife poked into the center should come out clean. Let the flan cool to room temperature, then chill for at least 4 hours, or up to a day, before serving.
5. To serve, choose a round platter large enough to hold the flan. Cover the flan with the platter and clamp the pie plate to the platter with your hands. With one quick motion, flip the pie plate onto the platter; the flan will release easily from the pie plate. Let it stand for a minute or two, then scrape any remaining liquid caramel from the pie plate over the top.

Crepe and Dulce de Leche Stack

A tall, somewhat gooey but still elegant dessert like this is just the thing at a buffet. The ultrasweetness of the dulce de leche is tempered by the crepes, and the little bit of toasted pecans sprinkled between the layers adds a nutty crunch that goes nicely with the dulce.

As for the dulce de leche: This is the way home cooks have been making it forever, but the people who make sweetened condensed milk won't go on record as endorsing this method for one very simple reason: if you let the water in the pot boil off so the can (or cans) of condensed milk rests on the bottom of the empty pan, it can heat to the point where the can explodes. Imagine the mess, not to mention the danger! So while you don't have to sit and stare at the pot the whole time the condensed milk is cooking, you do have to be sure to start with a large pot, use plenty of water, and check every 20 minutes or so to make sure the cans are still covered by water. Don't say you haven't been warned!

**MAKES 12 BUFFET SERVINGS • PREP TIME: 15 MINUTES
(WITH STORE-BOUGHT CREPES, MORE FOR HOMEMADE CREPES; PLUS 5 HOURS,
LARGELY UNATTENDED, IF MAKING—AND COOLING—THE DULCE DE LECHE)**

Two 14-ounce cans sweetened condensed milk or 1½ cups store-bought dulce de leche

Twelve 7- to 8-inch crepes, homemade (page 28) or store-bought

⅔ cup coarsely chopped toasted pecans, plus pecan halves, for garnish

Confectioners' sugar

1. If starting with condensed milk, make the dulce de leche: Remove as much of the label from the cans as you can. (This won't affect the finished dulce de leche; it just makes things a little neater.) Put the cans in a large (at least 6-quart) pot and pour in enough water to almost fill the pot. Bring to a boil over medium heat, then adjust the heat so the water is simmering. Cook for exactly 3 hours from the time the water comes to a boil; check often, and top up the water every 20 to 30 minutes. THE LEVEL OF THE WATER MUST NEVER DIP BELOW THE TOPS OF THE CANS! After 3 hours, turn off the heat and let the cans stand in the water for 1 hour.

2. Remove the cans from the water and let cool to room temperature. Do not attempt to open the cans while they are still hot.

3. Open the cans and scrape the dulce de leche into a bowl. Whisk it well to loosen up the texture a little.

(continued)

Begin spreading the dulce de leche over a crepe.

Continue spreading to make a thin, even layer.

Scatter chopped pecans over the dulce de leche; repeat the layering

4. Line a flat plate large enough to hold a crepe with a circle of parchment or waxed paper. Lay a crepe on top of it and spread the crepe with a thin, even layer of dulce de leche (about 2 tablespoons). Scatter a tablespoon of the chopped pecans over the dulce. Repeat with the remaining crepes, dulce, and pecans, but top the stack with a plain crepe. You most likely will not use all the dulce de leche. Refrigerate the stack for at least 1 hour to firm up. The stack can be refrigerated for up to 1 day.

5. Remove the stack from the refrigerator about 30 minutes before serving. Just before serving, sprinkle the top with confectioners' sugar and garnish with pecan halves. Cut the stack into wedges using a serrated knife and a gentle sawing motion. The wedges will be a little sloppy—that's the nature of the beast.

VARIATIONS:

- Dust the top of the stack with cinnamon sugar instead of confectioners' sugar.
- Add a small amount of grated chocolate to each layer, along with or instead of the pecans. Dust the top with sweetened cocoa powder.
- Alternate layers of dulce de leche and very thinly sliced bananas between the crepes.
- Make the stack with jam instead of dulce de leche or, even more fabulously, with alternating layers of dulce de leche and jam.

A STITCH IN TIME: Make 1 or 2 extra cans of dulce de leche. It keeps for weeks in the refrigerator and is a great emergency dessert sauce, cake frosting, dip for apples, and so on.

Mini Almond-Apple Cakes ✎ MANTECADAS

In the Caribbean, the word *mantecado* can mean "ice cream" or a crumbly shortbread cookie that melts in the mouth. In Spain, however, *mantecada* refers to a little muffin that is served with café con leche. On our first morning in Barcelona, we dragged our jet-lagged selves to a little café off Paseo de Gracia that served coffee and the thickest, richest hot chocolate I had ever tasted, along with croissants, doughnuts, and *mantecadas*. That revived us enough to make a lengthy stroll along the Paseo de Gracia possible, complete with snack stops, of course. I can still smell the coffee and hot chocolate we enjoyed with our cinnamon *mantecadas* that beautiful brisk morning in Barcelona.

MAKES 24 MINI CAKES • PREP TIME: 15 MINUTES • COOK TIME: 15 MINUTES

Vegetable oil cooking spray

1¼ cups all-purpose flour

¼ cup finely ground Marcona almonds
   or almond flour

¼ cup sugar

2 teaspoons baking powder

¼ teaspoon salt

¼ teaspoon ground cinnamon

½ cup applesauce

4 tablespoons unsalted butter, melted

1 extra-large egg

1. Preheat the oven to 350°F. Spray a 24-cup mini muffin tin (or two 12-cup tins) with cooking spray.

2. Stir the flour, almonds, sugar, baking powder, salt, and cinnamon together in a mixing bowl. Beat the applesauce, melted butter, and egg together in a separate bowl until well blended. Pour the liquid ingredients into the dry ingredients and fold together with a rubber spatula just until the dry ingredients are evenly moistened.

3. Divide the mixture among the muffin cups, filling each cup almost all the way. Bake until the cakes are light golden brown and spring back when poked gently, about 15 minutes. Serve warm or at room temperature. The cakes, once cooled, can be stored tightly covered for up to 2 days. Rewarm them in a 300°F oven (or split and broil them) before serving.

MENUS

Brunch Menus

MENU 1

Caribbean Breeze (page 32)
Potato "Jelly Roll" with Tuna Salad Filling (page 35)
Puerto Rican Shortbread Cookies (page 41)

UP TO 3 DAYS BEFORE: Make the cookies and keep them in an airtight container.

UP TO 2 DAYS BEFORE: Make the tuna filling and refrigerate.

THE DAY BEFORE: Assemble the "jelly roll" and chill. • Prepare and chill the fruit beverage. • Make the avocado sauce.

SERVES 12

MENU 2

Shrimp Ceviche *"Xni Pec"* (page 69)
Creamed Spinach Crepes with Mushroom-Tomato Sauce (page 27)
Basic Crepes (page 28), if using
Sweet Tomato "Conserva" with Salty Cheese (page 38)

UP TO A WEEK BEFORE: Make the crepes; refrigerate them for up to 2 days, or freeze them for up to a week.

UP TO 2 DAYS BEFORE: Make the creamed spinach and mushroom-tomato sauce.

THE DAY BEFORE: Make the tomato "conserva" and chill. • Grate the cheese for the crepes. • Squeeze the citrus juice for the ceviche.

THREE HOURS BEFORE: Make and chill the ceviche.

TWO HOURS BEFORE: Make the *xni pec* salsa. • Stuff the crepes and assemble the casserole.

WHEN GUESTS ARRIVE: Finish the ceviche. • Pop the crepes into the oven. • Remove the cheese for the dessert from the refrigerator.

SERVES 6

MENU 3

UP TO SEVERAL DAYS BEFORE: Make the *vinagre* or cilantro pesto.

THE DAY BEFORE: Hollow out the tomatoes and refrigerate them. • Make the tomato sauce, but do not add the asparagus and peas. • Make the Coconut Kisses.

ONE HOUR BEFORE GUESTS ARRIVE: Set up the tomatoes on their rack and line them with the ham.

JUST BEFORE GUESTS ARRIVE: Make the plantain fritter batter.

WHEN GUESTS ARRIVE: Fry the fritters (preferably with your guests, drinks in hand, to keep you company!).

AS PEOPLE ARE MUNCHING ON THE FRITTERS: Crack the eggs into the tomatoes and pop the tomatoes into the oven. • Add the asparagus and peas to the tomato sauce and keep warm.

AT THE TABLE FOR DESSERT: As people pass the Coconut Kisses around, make the *cafecito*.

SERVES 6

Barbecue Menus

MENU 1

PARRILLADA BLOWOUT!
Spicy Gazpacho Shooters (page 179)

Barbecued Beef Short Ribs (page 88) with Cilantro Pesto (page 104)

Provoletta (page 105)

Grill-Roasted Boneless Pork Shoulder (page 97)

Classic Argentinean Rice Salad (page 111)

Potato-Egg Salad (page 107)

Napa Cabbage Slaw (page 113)

Store-bought ice cream and cones

UP TO 2 DAYS BEFORE: Marinate and tie the pork roast. • Make the cilantro pesto.

THE DAY BEFORE: Make the gazpacho shooters and chill. • Cut the vegetables for the rice salad and Napa slaw; store in the refrigerator.

THREE HOURS BEFORE: Marinate the beef and refrigerate it. • Make the rice and potato salads. • Start the pork roasting.

ONE HOUR BEFORE: Dress the slaw.

WHILE THE PARRILLADA IS UNDER WAY: Mix and serve the gazpacho shooters. • Grill the short ribs. • While the short ribs are resting, make the provoletta (a portable burner set alongside the grill so you won't have to leave your guests is nice).

SERVES 12

MENU 2

ON THE LIGHTER SIDE
Daisy's Grilled Chicken Express (page 92)

Shrimp Without Chorizo Skewers (page 95)

"Boricua Slaw" (page 112) / Red Beet and Green Apple Salad (page 108)

Borinquen Sunset (page 118)

THE DAY BEFORE: Make the dessert and sauce. • Marinate the chicken.

FOUR HOURS BEFORE: Assemble the shrimp skewers. • Make the slaw. • Cook the beets for the salad.

ONE HOUR BEFORE: Microwave the chicken. • Assemble the beet salad.

WHILE THE BARBECUE IS UNDER WAY: Finish the chicken on the grill and grill the shrimp skewers. • Unmold and serve the dessert.

SERVES 12

Weeknight Dinner Menus ALL MENUS SERVE 6

MENU 1

Braised Chicken with Coconut Milk and Curry (page 139)

Spinach Rice (page 159)

PREP-AT-A-GLANCE: Make the sofrito for the chicken if you don't have it on hand. • Brown the chicken. • Meanwhile, prepare the rice to the point where the water is added. • Continue with the chicken up to the point where the chicken is added to the sauce. • Finish cooking the chicken and rice; they should be ready at about the same time. If one finishes first, just pull it from the heat and keep it covered.

MENU 2

Simple Salad with Spanish Blue Cheese Dressing (page 130)

Work-Night Chicken Breasts (page 137)

String Beans with Rosemary (page 155)

PREP-AT-A-GLANCE: Marinate the chicken breasts and bring a pot of water to a boil. • Meanwhile, make the lemon oil (if not using store-bought), prep the lettuce, and make the dressing. • Prepare the chicken and pop it into the oven. • While the chicken is baking, trim and blanch the beans and make the rosemary-garlic oil. • When the chicken is done, let it rest while you warm the beans in the oil.

MENU 3

Pigeon Peas in Coconut Milk (page 163)

Basic White Rice (page 159)

Guava–Cream Cheese Turnovers (page 168)

PREP-AT-A-GLANCE: Make the sofrito for the pigeon peas if you don't have it on hand. • Make the rice up to the point where the pot is covered. • While the rice liquid is boiling down, start the pigeon peas. • While the rice and pigeon peas are cooking, make the turnovers. (I hope you remembered to move the frozen dough from the freezer to the refrigerator in the morning!) • The rice and the peas should be ready at about the same time. If one finishes first, just pull it from the heat and keep it covered. • Pop the turnovers into the oven just before serving the rice and peas.

MENU 4

Avocado Stuffed with Crab-Mango Salad (page 129)

Calabaza and White Bean Soup (page 131)

PREP-AT-A-GLANCE: Prepare the doctored broth for the soup if you don't have it on hand. • Make the soup. • Meanwhile, make the crab salad and prep the avocados. Serve as soon as they are ready; the soup can bubble away as you enjoy the salad. • Serve the soup (if the pasta is tender before you are ready to serve the soup, simply take the pot off the heat and serve when you are ready).

MENU 5

Shrimp Tacos with Tomato-Avo Salsa (page 145)

New-Style "Refried" Beans (page 162)

Basic Yellow Rice (page 157)

PREP-AT-A-GLANCE: Start the black beans. While the broth is cooking, make the salsa and the chile sauce. Rub the shrimp. • Make the yellow rice up to the point where the pot is covered. • While the rice is cooking, puree the beans; keep them warm over low heat. • When the rice has about 5 minutes left to cook, grill the shrimp and warm the tortillas. • Serve the beans and rice right from their pots, pile the shrimp and tortillas on a platter, and pass the sauce separately.

MENU 6

Pork *milanesa* (page 142; topped with a mixed green salad)

Cumin-Scented Fried Potatoes (page 153)

PREP-AT-A-GLANCE: Fry the potatoes for the first time. • While the potatoes are soaking up the seasoning, clean the greens and make the dressing of your choice (or use a store-bought dressing). • Bread the cutlets and start to panfry them. Reheat the potato oil. • Dress the salad and plate up the cutlets (don't top the cutlets yet!). • Fry the potatoes. While the potatoes are draining, top the cutlets with salad. • Pile the potatoes on a platter and pass them separately.

Dinner Party Menus ALL MENUS SERVE 6

MENU 1

THE BOSS IS COMING! THE BOSS IS COMING!

Salt Cod and Japanese Eggplant Napoleons (page 206)

Gnocchi with Vegetables and Goat Cheese (page 210)

Guava Shells Filled with Cream Cheese Mousse (page 240)

UP TO A WEEK BEFORE: Make and freeze the gnocchi.

TWO DAYS BEFORE: Start soaking the salt cod.

THE DAY BEFORE: Make the salt cod filling for the napoleons. • Make the cream cheese mousse. • Make the vegetable sauce for the gnocchi.

UP TO 4 HOURS BEFORE: Drain the guava shells and make the guava sauce. • Fill the shells with the mousse. • Season the eggplant.

TWO HOURS BEFORE: Cook the eggplant.

THIRTY MINUTES BEFORE: Bring a large pot of salted water to a boil.

JUST BEFORE SITTING DOWN FOR THE FIRST COURSE: Warm the eggplant slices and the salt cod filling.

JUST BEFORE THE SECOND COURSE: Reheat the gnocchi sauce. • Cook and sauce the gnocchi.

MENU 2

A TOUR OF LATIN AMERICA

Mussels with Corn and Tomato (page 214)

Linguine with Artichoke–Serrano Ham "Bolognese" (page 136)

"Sweet Earth" (page 236)

TWO DAYS BEFORE: Make the pasta sauce.

THE DAY BEFORE: Make the mousse (but don't decorate).

UP TO 4 HOURS BEFORE: Prep all the ingredients for the mussels; clean the mussels. • Decorate the mousse.

JUST BEFORE SITTING DOWN FOR THE FIRST COURSE: Steam the mussels. • Put on a pot of water to boil.

JUST BEFORE THE SECOND COURSE: Cook and sauce the pasta.

Sweet Peppers Stuffed
with Rice and Cheese

MENU 3

AN AUTUMN SUNDAY DINNER
Mexican Chicken-Lime Soup (page 213)
Sweet Peppers Stuffed with Rice and Cheese (page 219)
Spicy Collard Greens (page 230)
Banana and Dulce de Leche Strudel (page 242)

UP TO 2 WEEKS BEFORE: Make the dulce de leche.

UP TO 2 DAYS BEFORE: Make the chicken broth and shred the chicken back into it.

THE DAY BEFORE: Roast the peppers and make the filling (keep them separate). • Clean the collards.

TWO TO 3 HOURS BEFORE: Assemble and bake the strudels. • Stuff the peppers and sauce them. Leave them at room temperature until baking.

THIRTY MINUTES BEFORE: Start baking the peppers. • Bring the broth to a simmer and add the celery root and corn.

JUST BEFORE SITTING DOWN FOR THE FIRST COURSE: Stir the scallions and lime juice into the soup.

JUST BEFORE THE SECOND COURSE: Cook the collards.

Buffet Menus

MENU I

INFORMAL GET-TOGETHER FOR TWELVE FRIENDS

No-cook tapas (optional; see page 244)

Artichoke, Potato, and Serrano Ham Tortilla (page 250)

Turkey Breast *"Pavochon"* (page 269)

Roasted Cauliflower with Anchovies and Garlic (page 282)

Red Beans with Salchichon and Potato (page 284)/Basic White Rice (page 159)

Crepe and Dulce de Leche Stack (page 291) and store-bought ice cream

TWO DAYS BEFORE: Marinate the turkey breast. • Roast the garlic for the cauliflower (if not using store-bought). • Make the crepes and dulce de leche (if not using store-bought).

THE DAY BEFORE: Make the red beans and refrigerate. • Prep the cauliflower and store in a plastic bag in the refrigerator.

FOUR HOURS BEFORE: Roast the cauliflower and cool. • Assemble the dulce de leche stack.

TWO HOURS BEFORE: Start roasting the turkey breast. • Make the tortilla. • Lay out the tapas, if serving.

ONE HOUR BEFORE: Make the rice.

TWENTY MINUTES BEFORE SERVING: Remove the turkey from the oven and let it rest. • Reheat the cauliflower and beans.

(continued)

MENU 2

CELEBRATION FOR SIXTEEN
No-cook tapas (optional; see page 244)

Pastelón with Crab Filling (page 255)

Goat Braised in Coconut Milk (page 267)

Basic Yellow Rice (page 157)

Creamed Spinach (page 279)

Artichoke and Sweet Bell Pepper Sauté (page 283)

Guava Flan (page 287)

TWO DAYS BEFORE: Make the braised goat.

THE DAY BEFORE: Make the crab filling. • Make the creamed spinach. • Make the guava flan.

ABOUT 3 HOURS BEFORE: Bake the plantains and assemble the *pastelón*.

ABOUT 1 HOUR BEFORE: Complete the *pastelón*. • When it goes in the oven, start the yellow rice, then put out the tapas, if serving.

JUST BEFORE SERVING (WHILE THE *PASTELÓN* IS RESTING): Rewarm the creamed spinach. • Sauté the artichokes and peppers.

MENU 3

CHRISTMAS BUFFET FOR TWELVE
No-cook tapas (optional; see page 244)

Pernil (page 268)

Yellow Rice with Pigeon Peas (page 158)

Daisy's Favorite Salad (page 56)

"Fatback from the Heavens" (page 123)

Puerto Rican Shortbread Cookies (page 41)

THREE DAYS BEFORE: Marinate the pork. • Make the shortbread cookies. • Make the sofrito and achiote oil for the rice.

THE DAY BEFORE: Make the flan. • Clean and prep all the salad ingredients and make the dressing.

FOUR HOURS BEFORE: Start roasting the pork.

ABOUT 1 HOUR BEFORE: Lay out the tapas, if serving. • Start the rice. • Remove the pork when it is finished and tent with aluminum foil to keep warm.

JUST BEFORE SERVING: Toss the salad. • Unmold the flan.

BASICS

In my first book, *Daisy Cooks! Latin Flavors That Will Rock Your World,* I waved a big banner that read "SOFRITO!" I was so very excited to let the world know about a secret weapon in the Latin kitchen that takes 10 minutes to make, keeps for weeks in the freezer, and dramatically improves the flavor of any dish it is added to. My sofrito recipe is still important and still gets a lot of use in this book—believe me, it's never going anywhere—but working on the recipes for this collection reinforced for me the importance of another kitchen staple: good homemade broths. They are vital not only for fantastic soups and stews, but also for cooking things like rice and couscous that don't have a lot of flavor on their own: the broth is what gives the dish depth of flavor. If you start out with flat broth, your dish will be one-dimensional. Last time around, I asked you to make sofrito just once, knowing you'd be hooked. And judging from the e-mails, you did! This time I'm asking you to take a few minutes to put together a pot of homemade chicken broth, just like *Mami* and *Abuela*'s.

Recipes like the Homemade Chicken Broth, Sofrito (of course!), Achiote Oil, and *Vinagre* are all very personal, handed down from generation to generation. I don't think that I could cook without them. Well, maybe I could, but nothing would taste anything like *Mami* and *Abuela*'s cooking, and what's the good in *that*? So if you didn't get well acquainted with these recipes in *Daisy Cooks!,* you have a chance to make them part of your repertoire now. You'll also find new "keepers" like the Mushroom Broth on page 304. It is so easy to make (and inexpensive!) that you'll find yourself inventing recipes of your own to use it!

Homemade Chicken Broth

Growing up, I never ate chicken from a supermarket. *Mami* and *Abuela* always bought theirs from the poultry market. Their chicken broth was rich and flavorful, delicious enough to enjoy on its own, sipped from a teacup. I still shop at the poultry market for my chickens, and I continue to use the recipe for this healing broth that my mother and grandmother taught me way back when. You may not have a poultry market near you, but it has become much easier to find organic or naturally raised birds that do, in fact, make an enormous difference in flavor. If the price tag seems a little high, remember this: one chicken yields not only a potful of broth, but enough cooked chicken to feed 3 or 4 people in a dish like Chicken Enchiladas (page 277) or Chicken Braised in Peruvian Yellow Pepper Puree (page 273). Even if you must cut corners and use a store-bought broth, at least punch up the flavors by enriching that broth, as I do in a pinch—see "Paging Doctored Broth!" on page 305.

When I was a little girl, *Mami* would ladle out a little of her *caldito* into a cup to sip on before she used the rest of the broth for rice, *asopao* (page 148), or whatever else was on the menu. Each time she made broth, she gently poached the chicken liver right in the broth and then slipped it into *Papi*'s cup as a treat. *Papi* divided it into little pieces so each kid had a bite (except for my brother Joey, who hated liver!). Today I scoop out a cup of *caldo* for any of my children who are home and for Jerry. Jerry gets the liver . . . he gives me his heart in return.

MAKES 3 TO 3½ QUARTS • PREP TIME: 15 MINUTES • COOK TIME: 2 HOURS

One 5-pound chicken, cut into 10 pieces (see Notes)

2 pounds chicken necks, backs, wings, and giblets (any combination)

2 large Spanish onions (about 1½ pounds), unpeeled

1 large red bell pepper, cored, seeded, and cut into quarters

1 large head garlic

1 large bunch cilantro

2 teaspoons black peppercorns

2 bay leaves

1 ham hock (optional)

Kosher or fine sea salt

1. Put all the chicken, the onions, and bell pepper in a pot large enough to hold them comfortably. Rinse the garlic head in cold water, then peel off the outer papery skin. Break up the garlic head into individual cloves, but leave them unpeeled. Cut off the roots if the cilantro has any and rinse the leaves and stems. Cut a piece of cheesecloth the size of a kitchen towel. Put the garlic cloves, peppercorns, cilantro, and bay leaves on the cheesecloth and tie the whole thing into a neat bundle with kitchen twine. Whack the bundle a few times with a kitchen mallet or a small heavy saucepan and put it into the pot along with the ham hock, if you are using it.

2. Pour in cold water to cover everything by 3 inches. Bring to a boil over medium-high heat. When the water comes to a boil, adjust the heat so the broth cooks at a gentle boil and start skimming the foam from the top. Cook for 30 minutes.

3. Check to make sure the breasts are cooked through, and remove them from the pot. Cook the broth for about 15 minutes more. Check that the thighs and legs are done, and remove them. Leave the backs, necks, and gizzards in the pot. Set the chicken pieces aside to make another chicken dish and cook the broth for another hour. As soon as

the chicken pieces that you removed have cooled enough to handle, shred the meat and set aside; return the bones to the pot.

4. Line a sieve with a double thickness of cheesecloth and set over a large bowl. Ladle the broth through the cheesecloth. Season with salt to taste. The broth can be refrigerated for up to 4 days or frozen for up to 3 months.

NOTES

- The easiest way to get a chicken cut into 10 pieces—2 wings, 2 thighs, 2 drumsticks, and 4 breast pieces—is to ask a butcher to do it for you. Even supermarket meat counters are usually happy to oblige. Failing that, start with a chicken cut into 8 pieces, which is the way most cut-up chickens are sold in supermarkets. Then simply lay the 2 breasts bone side down on a cutting board and, with a sharp heavy knife, whack them in half crosswise.

- You can make the broth with 5 pounds of chicken backs, necks, wings, and giblets instead of using the whole chicken. There won't be any poached chicken for another meal or for soup, but it will taste mighty good.

Mushroom Broth

I first made this as part of the Egg, Refried Bean, and Mushroom Casserole on page 17, then went on to discover that it adds mushroomy wonderfulness to a whole bunch of dishes, from soups and sauces to a simple pot of beans or rice. And it couldn't be easier. Keep some in your freezer, right next to the Sofrito (page 305). I do.

MAKES ABOUT 4 CUPS • PREP TIME: 5 MINUTES • COOK TIME: 20 MINUTES

¾ pound portobello mushrooms (see Notes)

One 26-ounce container reduced-sodium beef broth (see Notes)

2 bay leaves

Trim the hard ends from the mushroom stems and cut the rest of the stems and the caps into ½-inch pieces. You will have about 6 cups. Pour the broth into a medium saucepan, add the mushrooms and bay leaves, and bring to a boil over high heat. Adjust the heat so the broth is simmering and cook, partially covered, for 20 minutes. Strain. Can be refrigerated for up to 5 days or frozen for up to 1 month.

NOTES

- Portobello mushrooms add a lot of earthy mushroom flavor for not a lot of money. However, if you have plain button mushrooms or creminis on hand, go ahead and use those. Even reserved mushroom stems make a good broth. If you have some stems left over from a recipe, like the Chorizo-Stuffed Mushrooms on page 192, for example, measure them and add as much portobello (or other) mushrooms as needed to make the 6 cups called for in the recipe.
- For supercharged mushroom flavor, add ¼ to ½ cup of dried mushrooms along with the fresh. Be sure to strain broth made with dried mushrooms through a very fine sieve (or, better yet, cheesecloth), as dried mushrooms can be rather gritty.
- Substitute chicken or vegetable broth for the beef broth if you like.
- Freeze the broth in small—about ½-cup—amounts. You might even want to freeze some of it in an ice cube tray. The individual cubes can be slipped into single servings of soup or pasta sauce for a little hit of mushroom flavor.

"Paging Doctored Broth!"

There is nothing that beats homemade broth for depth of flavor, color, and aroma. But let's face it, if my supply from Sunday (see page 127) runs out, I'm not going to do without until next Sunday. This 30-minute quick fix for doctoring store-bought chicken broth simmers away on any given weeknight while you get the rest of the meal together.

MAKES ABOUT 7 CUPS • PREP TIME: 5 MINUTES • COOK MINUTES • COOK TIME: 30 MINUTES

1 large Spanish onion

1 bunch cilantro

One 48-ounce can chicken broth

1 red bell pepper, cored, seeded, and cut into ½-inch dice

6 cloves garlic, unpeeled, lightly smashed

2 bay leaves

1. Trim the root end off the onion but leave the onion unpeeled and whole. Wash the cilantro and tie the bunch together firmly with a length of kitchen twine.

2. Bring all the ingredients to a boil in a 3-quart pot. Adjust the heat so the broth is simmering and cook 20 to 30 minutes. Scoop out the onion, cilantro, garlic and bay leaves, but leave the red pepper behind. The broth is ready to use or it may be refrigerated for up to 5 days or frozen for up to 2 months.

Sofrito

I wish I had a nickel for every time someone told me how making sofrito has changed their lives for the better! And that is not an exaggeration—sofrito is so easy to make, so adaptable to all sorts of cooking (I make my spaghetti sauce with it!), and so full of flavor that putting a batch in the freezer (see Sundays in the Kitchen with Daisy, page 127) means a week's worth of quick and flavorful meals ahead. Sofrito is the heart of the Latin kitchen, and a staple in mine.

MAKES ABOUT 4 CUPS • PREP TIME: 15 MINUTES

2 medium Spanish onions, cut into large chunks

3 to 4 cubanelle or Italian frying peppers

16 to 20 cloves garlic, peeled

1 large bunch of cilantro

7 to 10 ajices dulces (see Note)

4 leaves of culantro (see Note)

3 to 4 ripe plum tomatoes, cored and cut into chunks

1 large red bell pepper, cored seeded and cut into large chunks

Put the onions and peppers in the work bowl of a food processor and process until coarsely chopped. With the motor running, add the remaining ingre-

dients one at a time, processing until smooth. The sofrito will keep in the refrigerator for up to 3 days; it also freezes beautifully.

> **NOTE:** *Ajíes dulces*, sometimes called *ajicitos*, are tiny peppers similar in appearance to habaneros and Scotch bonnet peppers but at the other end of the heat scale. They are sweet with a bright green, herbal flavor. Culantro is a leafy herb that smells and tastes like cilantro on steroids. Both *ajíes dulces* and culantro are available in Latin markets. You can see them in the photo—right in front of the food processor. If you cannot find them, simply leave them out and use 1½ bunches of cilantro.

Spooning the sofrito into freezer bags.

Achiote Oil

While achiote is very popular in the Latin kitchens of the Caribbean and Central and South America, I love to use it in place of saffron when I cook the fabulous food of Spain. The taste is a bit more delicate than saffron, and it's easier on the pocketbook too!

MAKES ABOUT 1 CUP • COOK TIME: 3 TO 4 MINUTES

1 cup olive oil

2 tablespoons achiote seeds (see page 310)

Heat the oil and achiote seeds in a small skillet over medium heat just until the seeds give off a lively, steady sizzle. Don't overheat the mixture, or the seeds will turn black and the oil a nasty green. As soon as they're sizzling away, pull the pan from the heat and let stand until the sizzling stops. Strain the oil. (The oil can be stored for up to 5 days at room temperature in a jar with a tight-fitting lid.)

The Adobo Brothers

The word "adobo" comes from the Spanish verb *adobar*, which means "to season." You will come across adobo in any country that has had a strong Spanish influence—from the Caribbean and South America to Mexico and the Philippines. If you haven't met the adobo brothers, wet or dry, it's high time you did.

DRY ADOBO is a spice rub you can buy in supermarkets or put together, most likely, with ingredients that are already in your pantry, including salt, black pepper, onion powder, garlic powder, and oregano. From there it is up to you—enrich the flavors with ground cumin, ground achiote powder, or even citrus zest. It is a quick, economical way to enhance the flavors of meats, poultry, and fish. I even love a sprinkle when making scrambled eggs or popcorn! When I use adobo on chicken, meat, or fish, I usually combine it with an acid, like vinegar or citrus juice, which helps the flavors of the adobo permeate the meat. My recipe for dry adobo is a bare-bones basic (not necessarily a bad thing), and I encourage you to fiddle around with it until you find your magic combination!

WET ADOBO is a bit (but not much!) more complicated. It is a paste made of garlic, salt, black peppercorns, oregano, olive oil, and vinegar. A roast chicken rubbed inside and out with adobo before roasting is one of life's great simple pleasures. Or rub adobo over the surface of smaller cuts of meat, like pork chops, or spoon it into deep slits of a larger cut, as I do with the *pernil* on page 268. When the meat is roasted, the garlicky paste cooks along with it, and the end result is a fragrant, mouthwatering dish that will have you and everyone at your table reaching for seconds. Again, the recipe for wet adobo that I give here is just begging for personalization. Feel free to try additions like ground cumin, red pepper flakes or minced chiles (oooohhh, spicy!), ground cloves, citrus juice. . . . The possibilities are limited only by your imagination. Have fun!

Dry Adobo Rub

MAKES ABOUT 1 CUP • PREP TIME: 5 MINUTES

6 tablespoons kosher or fine sea salt

3 tablespoons freshly ground pepper

3 tablespoons onion powder

3 tablespoons garlic powder

1½ teaspoons ground oregano

Stir all the ingredients together in a small bowl until well blended. Store at room temperature in a tightly sealed jar for up to 1 month.

Wet Adobo Rub (*Adobo Mojado*)

MAKES ABOUT ½ CUP • PREP TIME: 10 MINUTES

12 cloves garlic

1½ tablespoons kosher or fine sea salt

1 tablespoon black peppercorns

2 tablespoons dried oregano

2 tablespoons olive oil

2 tablespoons white wine vinegar

Place the garlic cloves and salt in a mortar and pestle (the salt keeps the garlic from flying around) and pound them

Vinagre

2 ripe pineapples

½ large Spanish onion, thinly sliced

20 cloves garlic, smashed and peeled

6 habanero peppers or chile pepper of your choice (see page 314), stemmed and coarsely chopped

1 tablespoon cider vinegar, plus more as needed

1 tablespoon smashed fresh oregano leaves

1 teaspoon black peppercorns

½ teaspoon kosher or fine sea salt, plus more as needed

1. Trim and peel the pineapples as described in the recipe for Caribbean Breeze on page 32, reserving the rinds; discard the tops and reserve the peeled pineapple for another use. Put the rinds in a pot large enough to hold them comfortably, pour in enough cold water to cover them, and bring to a boil over high heat. Adjust the heat so the liquid is at a gentle boil and cook until the rinds are very tender, about 30 minutes. If the water dips below the rinds, top off as necessary to keep them submerged.

2. Meanwhile, put the onion, garlic, chiles, vinegar, oregano, peppercorns, and salt in a large jar with a tight-fitting lid.

3. Strain the pineapple liquid into a large measuring cup or a bowl. Pour the liquid into the jar of seasonings. If there is not enough liquid to cover the ingredients, cover the pineapple rinds with water again and boil for 20 minutes, then strain the liquid. Taste and add a little salt and/or a little vinegar if you think it needs it. You can use this as soon as it cools, but it will get better as it sits. Keeps for up to 2 months in the refrigerator.

to a paste. Add the peppercorns and oregano, pounding each into the mix before adding the next. Stir in the olive oil and vinegar. This is best used when freshly made.

> **NOTE:** To make wet adobo in a food processor, pulse the garlic and salt until the garlic is coarsely chopped. Add the remaining ingredients, substituting coarsely cracked peppercorns for the whole peppercorns (the processor won't crush them). Process until the garlic is finely chopped.

Spicy Pineapple Vinegar (*Vinagre*)

A bottle of this spicy condiment is found on every table of every *fonda* in Puerto Rico. It is, easily, more popular than ketchup. Its sweet-tart herby flavor and tongue-tickling heat go with everything from beans, rice, and scrambled eggs to grilled chicken, fish, and hamburgers.

MAKES ABOUT 4 CUPS • PREP TIME: 45 MINUTES

Spicy Ancho Chile *Mojo*

You will want to commit this recipe to memory. It is my new favorite go-to, all-purpose, get-me-out-of-a-jam recipe, right up there with *vinagre*. Brush this on pork chops or chicken a minute or two before taking them off the grill (not earlier—it will burn if left on the heat for too long). Spread a little on a tortilla, pile on the scrambled eggs, and roll it up for a fast breakfast. Or serve as a dipping sauce for fried shrimp, fish fillets, or the Stovetop "Wrinkled" Potatoes on page 150.

MAKES ABOUT: 1½ CUPS • PREP TIME: 10 MINUTES

¼ cup ancho chile paste (see Note)

6 cloves roasted garlic, homemade (see below) or store-bought

1 teaspoon smoked paprika

1 teaspoon ground cumin

½ teaspoon cayenne pepper

1 cup olive oil

¼ cup sherry vinegar

Kosher or fine sea salt and freshly ground pepper

Put the ancho paste, roasted garlic, paprika, cumin, and cayenne in a blender jar. With the blender running, add the olive oil, drop by drop at first to keep the mixture smooth and prevent the oil from separating. When you've added about half the oil, add the remaining oil in a very slow, steady stream. Add the sherry vinegar and blend until smooth. Season with salt and pepper to taste.

NOTE: Ancho chile paste is available online from Purcell Mountain Farms, through their Web site, www.purcellmountainfarms.com. Or if you prefer, you can make your own (though anytime someone is willing to do some of my prep work for me, I'm all over it!): For ¼ cup ancho paste, remove the stems from 6 dried ancho chiles and shake out the seeds. Put the chiles in a heatproof bowl and pour in enough boiling water to cover. Set aside to soften, 30 to 45 minutes. Drain the anchos and slit them up the sides to cut them in half. Scrape the pulp off the skin with the blade of a knife.

Roasted Garlic

Roasting garlic turns the cloves into soft, sweet, spreadable deliciousness. You can roast a single head of garlic, but while you're at it, you may as well do more—it keeps well and has a million uses. Preheat the oven to 350°F. Peel the outermost papery coating from however many heads of garlic you'd like to roast (the more the merrier!), but leave the heads intact. Cut off the top ½ inch of the pointy tops with a serrated knife. Make a double-layer square of aluminum foil large enough to hold all the garlic comfortably when sealed. Drizzle a light coating of olive oil over the garlic. Bring up the edges of the foil to meet over the garlic and crimp them together to completely enclose the garlic. If you've sealed the foil packet nice and tight, you won't need a baking sheet. Just bake the garlic right on the oven rack until the cloves are very tender when poked with a paring knife, about 1 hour.

Serve the roasted garlic warm as a side dish and let people squeeze the sweet pulp from the cloves. Or let cool, squeeze the pulp from the cloves, and scrape it into a bowl. Flatten out the top of the garlic and pour enough olive oil over the garlic to cover it. Sealed with olive oil like this and tightly covered, it will keep in the refrigerator for a week or more.

A STITCH IN TIME: Many supermarkets, especially more upscale ones, now feature olive bars that, in addition to olives, sell ingredients like capers, roasted peppers, and, if you're lucky, roasted garlic. While roasting garlic isn't difficult, it never hurts to pick up a little extra for an emergency.

INGREDIENTS

ACHIOTE SEEDS (see photo, opposite) are small, irregularly shaped seeds gathered from the pods of a tropical shrub. They are a deep rust color and tiny (about the size of a lentil). A small amount will color and flavor a fair amount of oil (see Achiote Oil, page 306), which can be used to season and color dishes like Basic Yellow Rice (page 158) and "Soupy Rice" with Pigeon Peas (page 148). In addition to the striking color, achiote seeds impart a subtle, nutty flavor. If you cannot find achiote seeds (also called annatto seeds) in your supermarket, try www.kalustyans.com.

ALCAPARRADO (see photo, opposite) is nothing more than a jarred condiment containing olives (pitted or unpitted, check the label), diced pimientos, and capers. It adds a briny richness to many dishes. If you cannot find alcaparrado, make your own by tossing small green olives with whole capers and finely diced canned pimientos.

ALMOND FLOUR, sometimes called almond meal, is very finely ground almonds. It is available in many supermarkets. If you can't find it, pulse sliced blanched almonds in the work bowl of a food processor until finely ground. Use quick on/off pulses—constant grinding will turn the almonds oily.

BITTER ORANGE MARINADE: (see photo, opposite) For a convenience food found in the Latin food aisle of many supermarkets, bitter orange marinade has a pretty fancy list of ingredients, including Seville (bitter) orange pulp and grapefruit extract. Combined with store-bought or homemade dry adobo (page 306), it makes an instant marinade for meat, fish, or poultry. Try it in place of the suggested marinades for Barbecued Beef Short Ribs (page 88) and Daisy's Grilled Chicken Express (page 92).

CHILE POWDER has, in many parts of the country, taken on a new meaning. Once upon a time, "chili powder" meant a spice blend made with who-knows-what that cooks used to season pots of chili. Now even moderately well stocked supermarkets may feature one or more "chile powders"—i.e., pure chile powders made by grinding one type of dried chile. The advantage of these single-chile powders is a cleaner flavor, without a lot of seasonings that you may not want in the dish. The most common single-chile powders found in supermarkets are chipotle, with a smoky, lingering heat, and ancho, with a medium, sweet, subtle heat; www.mexgrocer.com stocks single-chile powders made from Anaheim, cayenne, chipotle, ancho, and Santa Fe chiles.

CHIPOTLES IN ADOBO (see photo, opposite) are chipotles (smoked dried jalapeños) that have been cooked and plumped up in a tomato sauce before being canned. Both the chipotles themselves and the adobo sauce add heat, smoke, and depth of flavor to everything from salsas to stews. A very simple staple to keep on hand is chipotle-adobo puree, made by pureeing the entire contents of the can until smooth. It will keep, well covered in the refrigerator, for weeks. With the growing popularity of all things Latin and spicy and chipotle-related, chipotles in adobo are increasingly easy to find. Or order them online at www.mexgrocer.com.

Center, left to right: Marcona almonds, store-bought adobo powder, and canned chipotle peppers in adobo; clockwise around center, starting at top: bitter orange marinade, sweetened condensed milk, guava paste, smoked paprika, fresh tomatillos, achiote seeds, alcaparrado, bottled piquillo peppers, and Mexican chocolate

CHORIZO: From my point of view, there are three main types of *chorizo* in this book, although there are myriad varieties within these categories. *Mexican chorizo* is an uncooked sausage made from finely ground pork seasoned generously with achiote and other spices. It is sold in links or loose. *Spanish chorizo* is a dry-cured sausage made from coarsely ground pork seasoned with paprika and, in some cases, garlic and other spices. It is available hot or sweet, smoked or unsmoked. Spanish chorizo requires no cooking, although cooking (as in the Huevos a la Paloma on page 14) brings out its perfume. *Argentinean chorizo* resembles Italian sausage more than it does other types of chorizos. It is usually made from medium-grind pork with minimal seasonings—salt, pepper, and not much else. It must be cooked before serving.

COTIJA is a cow's-milk cheese with a discernible tang and a crumbly texture. It is moist and crumbly like feta when young, and dry and crumbly like a lightly aged Parmesan when aged (then it is called *añejado*). It is delicious crumbled into green salads or fruity salads (try it with the Mango and Black Bean Salad, page 160) or over soups, like the Grilled-Tomato-and-Onion Soup on page 45, or into a simple pot of beans.

CREMA MEXICANA is a mildly acidic dairy product with a consistency (and flavor) similar to thinned-down sour cream, which makes it perfect for drizzling over finished dishes. It is available in Latin markets and some supermarkets. If you cannot find it, substitute sour cream thinned with water.

GUAVA PASTE (see photo, page 311) is a very thick paste (think super-dense gumdrops) made by slow-cooking guava pulp and sugar. It is available commercially in large, flat, round cans or in bars. It is delicious cut into small squares and served with salty firm cheeses like queso blanco, or used in baked goods like the turnovers on page 168.

MARCONA ALMONDS (see photo, page 311) look like a squatter, flatter version of California almonds with distinct ridges that run along both sides. They are almost buttery—closer in texture, I think, to a macadamia than a California almond. Lightly toasted, they are one of the simplest tapas you can serve.

MEXICAN CHOCOLATE (see photo, page 311), or *chocolate para la mesa* (table chocolate), is available in large or small bars, but more often in hexagonal tablets, packed into distinctive-looking little cartons. Because it contains sugar crystals, which give it a gritty texture, it isn't usually eaten on its own, but is turned into hot chocolate (see page 12). It is flavored with cinnamon, a nice addition to any cup of hot chocolate.

PHYLLO: Once upon a time, phyllo came in large (about 13 × 18-inch) sheets. Now most often what I find is a 1-pound package containing 2 sleeves, each with about twenty 12 × 8-inch sheets. The best way to defrost phyllo dough is overnight in the refrigerator. Phyllo sheets are very thin and fragile, and a slow, steady defrosting keeps them intact and easy to work with. Once the sheets are completely defrosted, open them up and lay them out on your work surface. Cover the stack of phyllo with a sheet of plastic wrap and top it with a damp kitchen towel. Then lift the plastic wrap and towel, remove just the number of sheets you need, and quickly re-cover the phyllo. This will keep the sheets from drying out.

PIQUILLO PEPPERS (see photos, pages 245 and 311) are smallish—1½- to 3-inch—peppers that come (mostly) from northern Spain. The name means "little beak" and refers to the peppers' triangular shape. They are difficult to find fresh but, fortunately, the bottled type, which are roasted and peeled, have a wonderful deep, rich flavor that makes them delicious on their own as a tapa or as a vehicle for any number of stuffings. Bottled piquillo peppers are available in many well-stocked supermarkets; I have even seen them included in "olive bars" of some supermarkets. They are also available online at www.tienda.com. See page 246 for a few ideas and page 177 for a recipe.

QUESO FRESCO is a soft but crumbly cheese with a mild flavor. Although it is available in many supermarkets, smaller markets that specialize in Mexican ingredients may be a better bet. Some supermarket brands tend to be drier and less interesting flavorwise.

QUESO OAXACA, Oaxaca string cheese, is a mild cheese from the state of Oaxaca in Mexico. It is available in Latin markets and some supermarkets. It is delicious eaten as is. Shredded or pulled apart into coarser pieces, it makes a delicious topping for casseroles or other foods headed for the broiler. Whole-milk mozzarella is an ideal substitute.

SMOKED PAPRIKA (*pimentón;* see photo, page 311) is made from sweet to mildly hot peppers that have been dried slowly over wood fires, then ground to a powder. It is available in several forms, but there are two main types—sweet *(dulce)* and hot *(picante)*. The natural sweetness of the peppers—even the hotter varieties retain some sweetness—and the smoke make an irresistible combo that lends itself to virtually anything from a pot of chowder to a grilled burger.

SPANISH-STYLE TOMATO SAUCE, usually sold in convenient 8-ounce cans, is a staple in my pantry. It is available in a range of flavors, but I stick to the original; unlike flavored tomato sauces or sauces meant for pasta, Spanish-style tomato sauce is very lightly seasoned, more like a tomato puree. It adds tomato flavor without any unwanted seasonings to a dish.

Fresh Chiles

The type and amount of chile you add to any recipe calling for fresh chiles is up to you. Choose one like a serrano, Hungarian wax, or jalapeño and remove the seeds before mincing for a milder result. (The seeds and "ribs" inside the chile are responsible for a good amount of any chile's heat.) Pick a fiery chile like Scotch bonnet, Thai bird, habanero, or cayenne (the "mildest" of these four chiles) and leave the seeds in for a real jolt. But be warned: even mild chiles can kick up their heels every once in a while. The same market where you bought those very mild serranos last week could have a binful of fireballs this week.

Poblanos, which are relatively mild, are unusual in the world of chiles; they are rarely used to add heat and flavor to a dish. Most often they are roasted and peeled (see page 274) and then cut into strips called *rajas* (see page 77) or left whole and stuffed.

It is a very good idea to put on a pair of latex gloves when working with chiles of any type—and a very silly idea not to when working with really hot chiles like habaneros. The gloves are cheap (I buy them by the boxful at home improvement stores) and will keep the chiles' essential oils off your hands, where they can come back to burn you (literally!) even hours after you've worked with the chiles.

Clockwise from upper left: fiery orange habanero chiles (habaneros come in shades of green, yellow, red, and orange—color is no indication of heat); Hungarian wax; the trusty (and relatively mild) jalapeño; Thai bird chiles (fairly formidable); fresh cayenne peppers; serranos (from mild to fairly hot—luck of the draw!); and poblanos (mild kick and a beautiful flavor)

Plantains

In Latin America, plantains are abundant, inexpensive, and usable in any degree of ripeness. Green unripe plantains are starchy and suited for boiling and mashing (see page 193) or for slicing and frying for crisp *tostones* (see page 189). As they ripen, and the skin progresses from green to greenish-yellow to yellow to black (see photo), the plantain flesh changes too. More and more of the starch converts to sugar and the flesh softens, making the plantains sweeter and more tender. Riper plantains need less cooking.

Yellow plantains—halfway through the journey to ripeness—can be grilled or roasted right in their skins and served as a side dish or peeled and cut into 1-inch rounds and added to soups and stews. (Give them about 20 minutes of cooking time.) Ripe plantains *(maduros)*, with mostly or all-black

Plantains in varying degrees of ripeness, from starchy and green to dead ripe, sweet, and black.

skin, can be sliced and fried and served with savory dishes like stews or rice, for a quick side dish. Or try this favorite of mine: Roast a *maduro* in its skin, then make a slit through the shorter curved side of the skin and into the flesh of the plantain. Open up the plantain, leaving it in its skin, and spoon some well-seasoned picadillo (like the one used in the *pastelón* on page 255 or the filling for the tamales on page 24) into it. Serve just like that.

Peeling Green Plantains

Green plantains may look like green bananas, but they are tougher to peel. (The more plantains ripen, the easier they are to peel. When dead-ripe with a completely black skin, they are as easy to peel as a banana.) Cut off the stem of the plantain to expose a little of the flesh. Make a slit down the length of the outer, longer side of the plantain all the way through the skin but not into the flesh (if you can help it). Starting at one end of the slit, peel back the skin. This will get easier as you go along. Green plantains can be peeled up to 2 hours before cooking them if they are kept in a bowl of cold water. Drain and pat dry before cooking.

ACKNOWLEDGMENTS

When I wrote my first book, a notebook of family recipes in hand, I told my collaborator and brother from another mother, Chris Styler, "I have all the recipes . . . the hard work is done!" To which he replied with the wisest words regarding the writing of a cookbook: "Honey, a cookbook is a *lot* more than just recipes!" Truer words were never spoken. Chris, I couldn't have done it without you before, and I certainly couldn't have done it without you now. Thank you for being an incredible friend, colleague, and mentor, not to mention for giving me my first professional job in the culinary field!

This time around, the process was a bit different. *Abuela's, Mami's,* and Captain Ray's recipes didn't feature as prominently, although their influence is something I will always carry with me. I love the fact that nowadays *Mami* calls me for recipes and tips. These recipes aren't the ones I grew up making and eating, but they certainly became the recipes of my children's youth. I'd like to thank all my kids for being such good travel companions and for their natural inquisitiveness about food. Erik, Marc, David, and Angela, I thank you for teaching me something new every day, for helping me create these wonderful memories, and for allowing me the opportunity to preserve them for you in the form of recipes. It is my gift to you.

Well-deserved thanks to Suzanne Gluck and Jon Rosen, my agents at the WME Entertainment Agency, for their continued faith in me and for working so diligently to help me find this book a happy home at Atria Books. That said, I must thank Judith Curr, my sassy publisher; Johanna Castillo, my adorable, tireless editor; Jeanne Lee, my brilliant art director; and the rest of the team at Atria for their unceasing support, belief, and artistic vision.

A tip of my jaunty cap to the most unsung of my heroes, my attorney Jonathan Ehrlich, for helping me navigate uncharted waters and delivering me safely to the other side. I don't know what I would have done without his sage advice and rapier-sharp sense of humor through it all.

There is a special place saved in these acknowledgments for a person who has been with me since the *Daisy Cooks!* days. Carolina Peñafiel, my assistant, is a fabulous Chilena who doesn't know the meaning of "I don't do that!" Carolina is the girl who always finds a way to get things done with good cheer and grace. Anytime of the day or night, Carolina is there with a smile to lend a hand, solve a problem, test a recipe, or mix me a *michelada*! *Gracias,* Carolina, you are a gem!

Finally (again), to my husband, Jerry, who, no matter how full his plate is, always has room for me and my issues. Honey, thank you for your rabid loyalty, for your unconditional love, and for still making me laugh after thirty years.

¡Buen provecho!

INDEX